Diversified Secondary Education and Development

A World Bank Publication

Diversified Secondary Education and Development

Evidence from Colombia and Tanzania

George Psacharopoulos and William Loxley

PUBLISHED FOR THE WORLD BANK
The Johns Hopkins University Press
BALTIMORE AND LONDON

The Johns Hopkins University Press
Baltimore, Maryland 21211, U.S.A.

Library of Congress Cataloging-in-Publication Data

Psacharopoulos, George.
  Diversified secondary education and development.

  Includes bibliographical references and index.
  1. Education, Secondary—Colombia—Curricula—Case
studies. 2. Education, Secondary—Tanzania—Curricula—
Case studies. 3. Vocational education—Colombia—Case
studies. 4. Vocational education—Tanzania—Case studies.
I. Loxley, William A.   II. Title.
LB1629.5.C7P73 1985   373.19'09861   85-45103
ISBN 0-8018-3119-9

R00 514 560 88

Contents

Preface

DURING THE PAST DECADE many developing countries started to "diversify" their curricula at the secondary school level by introducing prevocational subjects in addition to traditional academic courses. The most frequently stated reason for this change was that prevocational subjects would widen students' choices of future careers and thus make the school system more relevant to the world of work.

Given the popularity of such educational innovation, it is surprising that no comprehensive studies or empirical evaluations have been made of its impact on national economic development. Policymaking has been based on an intuitive assumption that the inclusion of prevocational subjects in the secondary education curriculum offers a more solid basis for career choices than does traditional academic schooling alone.

The World Bank, which has lent extensively for curriculum diversification, therefore undertook an evaluation of secondary school systems in Colombia and Tanzania that had been diversified with Bank assistance. This book reports the results of that study. A random sample of over 10,000 students following either diversified or conventional (academic or vocational) curricula was taken just before graduation in order to obtain information on their socioeconomic background and educational characteristics. The same students were contacted one to three years later to find out what further education they had received and what their experience in the labor market had been.

Four major criteria were used to compare schools offering diversified curricula with those offering only academic or only vocational subjects. The principal considerations were:

- Access to the different types of school by students with different socioeconomic origins (equity)
- Cognitive learning of the students (internal efficiency)
- Labor market experience of the graduates (external efficiency)
- Cost-effectiveness (economic efficiency).

Although there were some differences between the two countries and particular courses of study, the results can be summarized as follows. Compared with schools offering only conventional curricula, the diversified schools recruit more students from low-income backgrounds and provide better cognitive skills to their graduates. However, it costs more to educate students in diversified schools than those in control (academic or vocational) schools. Moreover, despite their superior cognitive skills, graduates of diversified schools do not find jobs more easily and do not earn more than the graduates of control schools.

The explanation for this negative result may be the short horizon of the longitudinal tracer study. Hence, another survey of the same sample is contemplated in future years, when the graduates have become more settled in their careers.

AKLILU HABTE
Director
Education and Training Department
The World Bank

Acknowledgments

THIS STUDY of Diversified Secondary Education Curricula (better known under its DiSCuS acronym) was funded by the World Bank's Research Committee in July 1981 and conducted under the Education Department of the Operations Policy Staff. George Psacharopoulos served as principal investigator and project director. William Loxley was a consultant for the two-year duration of the study. Ana-Maria Arriagada served as research assistant to the project.

The research design of the two-country case study required a sampling framework, questionnaires, the collection and processing of base-year data, and a follow-up survey of the national cohorts of secondary school graduates. To this end, ministries, research organizations, and scholars in the host countries provided the skills and staff needed to make this project possible.

In Colombia, Eduardo B. Velez and Carlos C. Rojas of the Instituto SER de Investigación in collaboration with the Colombian Ministry of Education carried out the enormous task of surveying 8,000 students in public and private secondary schools nationwide and tracing them one year later. They also raised data retrospectively on 2,000 graduates of an older cohort.

In Tanzania, Issa M. Omari, in collaboration with staff at the Education Department of the University of Dar es Salaam, staff at the Institute of Education, and officials of the Ministries of Education and Manpower and the Examination Council carried out the complex tasks of surveying more than 4,000 secondary school students in 1981 and following up the cohort in 1982.

This book has benefited from the input of a number of consultants. Paul Hurst, Kevin Lillis, and Desmond Hogan reviewed the literature. Keith Hinchliffe provided the unit costing of the different types of schools and carried out the first cost-benefit calculations. Antonio Zabalza analyzed the returns of the 1978 Colombian cohort. Philip Foster made valuable comments on an early draft of the manuscript. Robin Horn revised several statistical tables in the second draft. John Smyth, Michael Crossley, and John Adams also read drafts of the manuscript and offered suggestions for improvement. Richard Kollodge organized and verified references and citations.

Several World Bank staff have been involved in this project from its inception to conclusion. Wadi Haddad, Jack Mass, Ralph Harbison, and Lawrence Wolff, among many others, have significantly contributed to various stages of this research. Liliana Longo has efficiently administered the various logistical aspects of the study.

Diversified Secondary Education and Development

1. Introduction

SECONDARY SCHOOLS that offer prevocational courses in conjunction with traditional ones have flourished over the past decade in many developing countries. In fact, interest in these "diversified" schools seems to be growing because more and more governments are seeking assistance to establish diversified curricula. Although the World Bank has been investing heavily in these educational programs, there have not been any studies on the impact of diversified education on economic development.

These innovative secondary schools are neither completely academically oriented nor are they simply vocational training institutions. Because the diversified curriculum concept weds academic with some degree of vocational education, students can develop not only vocational skills in the field of their choice, but also traditional cognitive skills in classes designed to prepare them for a university. The stated rationale for such schools—and the basis for their popularity—is to permit students a wider set of future career options than is offered by the usual technical or academic curricula.

The belief that this hybrid form of secondary schooling is also the best way to balance labor market needs with more equal access to education has led many governments to invest heavily in diversified schools. The World Bank has encouraged such innovation as a development strategy and as a means to make the rapid expansion of secondary education consistent with a better match between skills learned in school and those needed in the labor market.

Assumptions Underlying Diversification

As a strategy for revising the instructional content of secondary schools, curriculum diversification is based on a number of assumptions concerning the value of conventional secondary education, the need for educational innovation, and the kinds of employment opportunities available. In most cases, especially in developing countries, it is assumed that there exists a fundamental mismatch between the type of education and training offered in traditional academic schools and the skills and other characteristics required of graduates entering the labor market.

Variants of this argument have been discussed by a number of researchers, among them Ahmed and Coombs (1975), Dore (1975), Van Rensburg (1974), Court (1972), Orata (1972), Lourie (1978), Benoit (1974), Nyerere (1967), King (1977), Ruddell (1979), Weeks (1978), Schiefelbein (1979), Figueroa, Prieto, and Gutierrez (1974), and Unger (1980). A second assumption is that the content and methods of traditional secondary schooling unrealistically exaggerate the educational and occupational aspirations of graduates, creating excessive demand for university education and highly valued jobs. (See Klingelhofer 1967; Oxtoby 1977; Evans and Schimmel 1970; Silvey 1969; and Ruddell 1979.)

Diversification of secondary school curricula, it is argued, will ensure that more students, including those with less advantaged backgrounds, receive education and training better suited to their own social and economic conditions and the needs of their respective nations. Because such schooling is more closely attuned to the manpower requirements of industrialization and growth in the developing world, fewer graduates will select less-needed, middle-level jobs, and fewer will elect to continue their education. A combination of traditional academic education and prevocational training, it is contended, will give students more accurate information about the less prestigious jobs available and will arm them with more realistic attitudes and aspirations toward the world of work.

Little evidence exists to support or refute these hypotheses; to date, there has been no large-scale investigation of diversified secondary school experiences among developing nations. Given that lack of information, the World Bank embarked on a study of the subject in cooperation with government authorities. Approximately 20 percent of the costs of education projects financed by the Bank in the past twenty years can be directly or indirectly attributed to components for diversified education. All the Bank's secondary education projects have supported this kind of curriculum. The pattern is as much a result of World Bank policy as it is of the demand for such schools by national governments. After more than fifty such projects had been completed, it was felt that enough time had elapsed to warrant testing the comparative effectiveness of the diversified school model against the more traditional types of academic or vocational education.

An internal review of diversified education components in World Bank projects over the past two decades (Haddad 1979) identified several questions. The review indicated a lack of evidence that the new type of schools improved the quality of education, changed student attitudes toward the labor market, or had the desired effect of directing graduates to areas of employment where they allegedly were most needed. Diversified education projects assisted by the Bank have not contained enough tracer (follow-up) studies or other types of evaluation to show whether diversification has met its objectives.

Scope of the Study

The present study was intended to begin a comparison of the advantages accruing to students and graduates of diversified schools and those with more traditional types of formal training. Potential advantages of diversification can be measured in these ways:

- Wider access to secondary schooling by less privileged socioeconomic groups
- Cognitive attainment, as measured by test scores in both prevocational and academic subjects
- Occupational choice consistent with a student's interests
- Returns to national investments from workers who have a combination of academic and prevocational skills, rather than merely one or the other.

Specific hypotheses about the internal and external efficiency of diversified education need to be tested in order to obtain a clearer picture of its effect on economic development. Using nationally representative longitudinal samples of graduates who attended either academic or prevocational secondary schools, the study tests the following hypotheses to measure the relative effectiveness of diversification:

- Diversification favors the recruitment of students from lower-income families and thus provides more equitable access to schooling.
- Diversification enhances cognitive achievement in the field of vocational course work and later on the job.
- Diversification creates a desire for further training and instills occupational aspirations better suited to national economic needs.
- Diversification diminishes the private demand for postsecondary education, especially at the university level.
- Diversification increases the motivation to seek work at the end of secondary schooling.
- Diversification leads to employment in the field of vocational specialization at school.
- Diversification enables graduates to earn more than they would after other forms of schooling.
- Graduates of diversified schools have a shorter period of unemployment while seeking work after graduation than do graduates of other secondary schools.

• Investment in diversification has a higher social rate of return than that in either vocational or academic education alone.[1]

Colombia and Tanzania, the countries selected for the empirical investigation of diversification, met at least two criteria that would allow a sound evaluation of these postulates. First, their programs have been in place and well implemented for a relatively long time, and, second, diversification has been introduced on a scale large enough to permit a sufficient number of students to participate in a meaningful sample.

Secondary school diversification has proceeded furthest in Latin America and East Africa. Colombia was chosen to represent Latin America because it has implemented public diversified education extensively, along with purely vocational and academic secondary schools. Tanzania was selected in East Africa because diversification there is a well-established policy based on self-reliance and has spread throughout the educational system.[2]

A longitudinal tracer study methodology was adopted to assess the results of diversification. The methodological design required gathering data on schools and individual student characteristics from a cohort about to complete its secondary education. Data collected from students in their final year of studies represent base-year information. The base-year data set then was used to perform a cross-sectional analysis that compares students in diversified, vocational, and academic schools on their attitudes and cognitive skills.

In addition to base-year information collected during the first year of the study, tracer surveys were taken periodically to learn about the students' experience after leaving school—for example their employment experience and earnings—which could be used to conduct a cost-benefit analysis of different types of secondary education curricula. Finally, drawing on base-year data and the follow-up information, an assessment was made of the direct and indirect effects of key policy decisions, such as the type of curriculum followed, on what students learn and what happens to them later in the labor market. Such analyses can indicate whether students' cognitive achievements, attitudes, or graduate earnings differ (and by how much) by type of curriculum. It is also possible to assess the extent to which changes in curriculum are cost-effective.

The following chapter of this study provides a brief history of diversified

---

1. The social rate of return measures the economic payoff of an investment in human resources relative to its cost. For an elaboration of this concept, see Psacharopoulos (1981b).

2. The concept of education for self-reliance stems from the general movement in Africa in the 1960s that a country should develop on the basis of its own resources (see Nyerere 1967). It is thought that schools should teach students to behave collectively and that the curriculum should be geared toward practical subjects relating to work—mostly agricultural—the graduates will be doing later in life.

education worldwide and examines the role of the World Bank in this respect. Chapter 3 reviews evaluations of past World Bank projects and discusses problems of implementation. Chapter 4 describes the research design of the two case studies in Colombia and Tanzania and discusses sampling and survey instruments.

Chapters 5 and 6 present the results of the case studies of the two countries. Beginning with descriptions of their national education systems, the chapters include base-year analyses of the internal efficiency of diversified schools, followed by an evaluation of the tracer study and an examination of the external efficiency of diversified education based on the choice of further study or work, and the determinants of earnings. Also presented is a cost-benefit analysis of the alternative curricula.

The final chapter synthesizes the results of the study by assessing the contribution of diversification to economic and social development.

2. Historical Background

In RESPONSE to economic, social, and political pressures in developing countries, governments have introduced prevocational training into the traditional academic curriculum in secondary schools. These pressures continue to shape schooling policies and often lead to educational reform of the type evaluated in this study. (For a review of implementing educational innovations, see Lillis and Hogan 1983; and Heyneman 1984.)

The Diversification Debate

During the 1960s, after many nations had achieved independence from colonial rule, it was rightly thought that investment in education would significantly improve the prospects for economic and social development. Education systems rapidly expanded, but skyrocketing recurrent costs forced many governments to cut back the pace of expansion. Shortages of materials, equipment, and teachers widened the qualitative differences among schools, both private and public, rural and urban. The rapid expansion was blamed for the diminution of educational quality and high wastage rates within the education system.

The number of students graduating exceeded the positions available to them in the job market. In addition, graduates' skills often did not match the requirements for the jobs that were available. Clerical and sales positions were filled by academic school graduates, but technical jobs went begging. Traditional schools had not provided the necessary vocational training, while less formal, on-the-job apprenticeship programs were too poorly organized to meet the rapidly increasing demand for special skills.

In the midst of rising unemployment among both educated and uneducated, the governments of developing nations found it difficult to meet the need to expand education with the limited resources available. Many parents hoped that education would enable their children to escape poverty and better their lives through instruction in skills that would help them enter employment in the wage sector of the economy. Parents believed—and rightly so—that the chances of at least one child successfully completing schooling would rise with the numbers of children they had who attended school.

Given these considerations, there have been at least two major arguments for and against the introduction of a vocational emphasis in the traditional academic secondary curriculum. One is economic and the other is political.

Economic Efficiency

The economic argument for diversification is focused on a perceived need to orient the formal education system to the world of work. (See Cliffe 1973; Diyasena 1976; Figueroa, Prieto, and Gutierrez 1974; Lema 1978; Price 1973; Sato 1974; Tchen 1977; and Vulliamy 1980.) It is based on the assumption that traditional education, apprenticeship, and on-the-job training cannot train enough workers to meet current and future demands for skilled labor. Those arguing for an emphasis on vocational courses in secondary education cite evidence that a system of academically oriented education predisposes students to enter white-collar jobs and not ones that require manual labor and skills in short supply. It is often argued that schools should equip students with the knowledge, skills, and attitudes they need to enter specific vocational fields, such as commerce, agriculture, and technical trades, whether as employees or self-employed. Proponents of vocational education agree that if a formal education system is to be viable for developing nations in the 1980s and beyond, then more vocational schooling will be necessary.

Some opponents of diversification may accept this diagnosis, but they emphasize the costliness of the strategy and its inability to attract competent teachers and suitable equipment. They also warn that the overall quality of education may decline, so that graduates will be proficient in neither academic knowledge nor specialized vocational skills; as a result, they will be less able to acquire skills on the job (Foster 1965; Blaug 1979; Grubb 1979). At best, it is contended, students will acquire only a vague general introduction to vocational skills. Finally, there is a fear that a diversified education system may give rise to implicit and hidden tracking, locking students into career paths that convey lower status and create invidious distinctions between social groups. Opponents of diversified education also argue that curriculum reform is not the most efficient way to implement education for self-reliance. Of greater importance, especially in low-quality school systems, is upgrading the caliber of the teachers.

Another factor to be considered is the type of skills to be taught in the classroom. Usually, a hierarchy of skills can be agreed upon: academic education prepares graduates for numerous careers that require verbal and quantitative skills; professional or vocational education prepares the graduate for a more specific type of job in a single field; work-based training generally prepares the individual for only a single job. Consequently, a loosely defined lexicon of formal cognitive skills would include academic, prevocational, and vocational education, as well as apprenticeship training and work experience (Zymelman 1976).[1] A number of experts, however, believe that schools should not train students only for specifically defined jobs. The most schools should be expected to do, according to this view, is to provide a broad technical foundation that will be refined by further off- or on-the-job training. In short, so this argument goes, the problem of reconciling any mismatch between the world of work and the world of education cannot be solved merely by reforming the curriculum (Foster 1965; Blaug 1979; and Grubb 1979).

Sociopolitical Considerations

A second major argument for diversifying secondary education concerns considerations of equity. There are those who believe that an academically oriented system in a developing country will produce gross long-term inequalities between a small elite of educated and their uneducated counterparts.

The vast majority of citizens in developing nations are rural and uneducated. If governments wish to retain the support of their principal constituents, they must find means to satisfy the social demand for "free" education. They may do so by instituting a traditional education curriculum, or programs outside the formal education system, or schooling of such short duration that many students are given no incentive to go on to universities. Some governments have attempted to check the growth of academic enrollments by offering combined academic-vocational programs along with solely academic ones. But unless the two curricula are given equal recognition and support, this strategy is doomed to failure once parents and students realize the implied low status of and low economic returns to the vocational programs.

Opponents of secondary diversified education programs complain that because vocational secondary schooling is often more costly than academic secondary programs (because of the need for specialized equipment), introducing such a curriculum is a less cost-effective way of eliminating enrollment discrepancies between rich and poor and urban and rural students than is expanding access to traditional academic schooling.

Historically, formal schools in industrial nations have served social class interests. Because primary and secondary schooling is a prerequisite for

---

1. Lillis and Hogan (1983, p. 92) claim that technological development in most rural areas is still at a level where skill development and preparation for employment occur naturally on the job rather than in school.

university enrollment, the middle and upper classes have wanted schools to have a highly academic content. For working-class students, however, primary and secondary schooling has been viewed as the end of their educational careers; hence, the curriculum for these students has usually been oriented to trade and vocational subjects and rarely to the humanities and sciences. As a result, dual secondary education systems have evolved that restrict the choice of occupation for working-class students (Williamson 1979).

Generally, however, ethnic and social cleavages in developing nations have not been reinforced by the types of curricula offered to different groups. Far greater inequities have been perpetrated by the scarcity of school places than by explicit educational policies created "to provide different structures and types of schooling for distinct social strata" (Foster 1983, pp. 1–4).

Vocational Education Worldwide

A strong positive association has been well extablished between a country's level of economic development and the percentage of secondary students in vocational education. Yet over the past thirty years there has been a decline in the share of resources devoted to vocational education within almost all national systems. Whereas in 1950, 25 percent of all secondary students were in vocational programs, by 1975 the percentage had fallen to 17. That decline (documented by Benavot 1983) indicates a trend toward less differentiated and more comprehensive forms of secondary schooling of which diversified education is only a part.

Africa

Secondary education played an important role in Africa during the colonial period. The emphasis in educational policy had vacillated between training for specific skills and providing merely an overall vocational orientation. Just before independence there was a shift toward a more academic orientation, in response to the need to educate a competent cadre of civil servants, and away from a system of mass education designed to assist in the process of democratization (Lillis and Hogan 1983). At the time most countries were acquiring independence, it was already widely believed that the best preparation for work was to learn broad categories of skills that could be applied in a variety of work situations; that is, vocational and technical knowledge should prepare graduates for additional training on the job, while theoretical knowledge needed for more highly skilled or professional jobs is best learned in the classroom (Clignet and Foster 1966; Dodd 1969; Jolly and others 1973; Moris 1972; Omari 1984).

After independence, most African nations shifted from an emphasis on academic education toward programs that were intended to dampen the rising expectations of students for higher education and employment in the prestigious public sector. The dilemma in Africa over the past twenty years has essentially been to reconcile a growing social demand for all kinds of education, but especially academic education, with what were thought to be the demands of the labor market.

In Kenya, as elsewhere in Africa, the fine-tuning required to match vocational curricula with the actual needs of the labor market was never adequately achieved. Colonial trade schools, still in existence today, have found their graduates to be increasingly unacceptable to employers in the majority of Kenyan industry. Kenyan firms have preferred to recruit from lower down the educational ladder (King 1977), because younger and less educated employees could be paid lower wages while learning the necessary skills on the job. Furthermore, by continuously requiring additional theoretical knowledge, these schools narrowed the marketability of their graduates' skills. By contrast, Court (1972) and Kipkorir (1975) have noted the success of village polytechnical schools in Kenya that train young people for self-employment.

Efforts to diversify secondary education in the region stem largely from the nature of African economies. In these largely rural societies, farming, industrial, and commercial sectors are not sufficiently developed to utilize the advanced technology generally taught in schools; the modern sector (both public and private) is less and less able to create jobs; and there are weak links between school and work. As a result, prevocational courses have been added to traditional academic programs in an attempt to instill in students the concept of self-reliance.

Since many African nations have a large public sector and a strong tradition of manpower planning, they have opted for diversified education programs that dilute traditional academic course work with vocational subjects. These countries include Lesotho, Botswana, Ethiopia, Somalia, Uganda, Cameroon, Gabon, Nigeria, Swaziland, Tunisia, Morocco, and Tanzania.

Latin America

Unlike the situation in many African countries, formal education in Latin America is closely tied to market economies with large private and public industrial sectors. These conditions have made it easier to maintain a strong private academic system with links to universities while supporting vocational schools that feed directly into the job market. When governments needed to drastically expand the secondary education system, they did so by encouraging the formation of multi-track schools that would offer both vocational and academic programs under one roof.

Assisted by World Bank education projects, diversification has proceeded far in Colombia, the Dominican Republic, El Salvador, Jamaica, Guyana, Trinidad and Tobago, Brazil, and Peru. Similar in organization to the European comprehensive school, diversified education in Latin America has attempted to eradicate the highly rigid organizational structure of separate secondary vocational and academic schools that had existed. By introducing comprehensive schools, students were free to combine academic and vocational programs without foreclosing future training or career options.

National apprenticeship programs have been most characteristic of vocational training in Latin America. They include SENAI in Brazil, SENA in Colombia, IICA in Costa Rica, SENATI in Peru, and INCE in Venezuela.[2] These programs graduate small numbers of well-trained students who have worked in close association with employers who have paid for the training through a payroll tax deduction (Castro 1976). However, such programs traditionally have been outside the mainstream of the formal secondary school vocational programs prevalent in Latin America.

Asia and the Pacific

Diversification of the secondary school curriculum has also occurred in Asia and the Pacific. In Papua New Guinea a much publicized Secondary Schools Community Extension Project (SSCEP) was launched in 1978 in five provincial high schools. It planned to integrate academic and practical subjects to teach students the skills needed for self-employment in their home villages. This was to be done without allowing a decline in academic standards as measured in national examinations required for graduating from the tenth grade (Lillis and Hogan 1983; Vulliamy 1980; Weeks 1978). Standard syllabuses for the examination would be modified for those attending the SSCEP course (Crossley 1984a).

A comprehensive evaluation of the project was conducted by the educational research unit of the University of Papua New Guinea throughout the pilot phase. Its conclusion was that the SSCEP should be continued and expanded. Consequently, in 1984 a trial dissemination phase was inaugu-

2. Servicio Nacional de Aprendizaje Industrial (SENAI), Servicio Nacional de Aprendizaje (SENA), Instituto Interamericano de Capacitación Agropecuaria (IICA), Servicio Nacional de Adiestramiento en Trabajo Industrial (SENATI), and Instituto Nacional de Cooperación Educativa (INCE).

rated. Two new schools joined the project (with more expected during 1985), and a new university diploma course in educational studies was introduced to improve SSCEP in-service training and professional support services. There is a strong conviction that such diversified secondary education will contribute to the development of more appropriate skills and attitudes for graduates returning to village life. But whether such an intensively supported pilot project can be successfully replicated throughout the nation remains to be seen (Crossley 1984b).

Another diversification project has been undertaken by Thailand. With Canadian and World Bank assistance over the past twenty years, Thailand has moved to extensively reorganize and reshape secondary education. A Thai-Alberta Co-operative Assessment Project Report (Thailand Ministry of Education 1980), assessing thirty-two rural secondary schools, suggested that satisfactory progress had been made toward the objectives of a flexible diversified curriculum and adequate equipment, facilities, administration, teacher staffing, and training.

In Sri Lanka, a study by Wanasinghe (1982) reported that reform of the secondary school curriculum attempted to orient the teaching toward local opportunities for self-employment. Although no empirical evidence was presented, the author argued that the reform movement demanded too much of the available teachers and was poorly supported with training and materials.

In Indonesia, a tracer study by Clark (1983) looked at the performance of secondary school graduates in the labor market. Computing rates of return for graduates of academic and vocational programs, the author found academic tracks to be the better investment, but also that academic and vocational graduates had a substantial wage advantage over secondary school dropouts and primary school graduates.

Finally, Squire (1981) reported that in Korea, diversified curriculum programs have led to a better wedding of school skills and the requirements of the labor market.

United States

Interesting insights can be acquired by contrasting the experiences of industrialized nations with those of the developing countries. In the United States there has been a long debate over the best way to link education and work. Industrial trade schools flourished in the early 1900s when there was quickening demand for piecemeal machine work and when lengthy apprenticeships could not keep pace with demand. But that philosophy shifted during the depression era of the 1930s, when the costs of vocational education became more burdensome to a government that had to cope with substantial additional needs. Then, it was suggested that private industry pay for such training (Davis and Lewis 1975). During and after World War II, demand for skilled workers increased, again favoring a policy emphasis on formal training. For the past three decades, the United States has pursued a public school policy that has given fairly equal weight to academic and vocational subjects (Lecht 1979; Lewin-Epstein 1981).

Apparently, the emphasis and rationale for vocational schooling in the United States followed trends in the business cycle. In periods of peak demand for skilled workers, when apprenticeship programs were inadequate to meet the needs, formal vocational training programs sponsored by the government flourished and probably paid for themselves if for no other reason than that they helped alleviate bottlenecks in the skilled labor market. More recently, vocational training has been used as a means to create jobs for groups with special needs (such as the long-term unemployed or those with few marketable skills) rather than to train people for standard existing occupations.

Western Europe

By World War II most European countries had evolved a highly differentiated dual system of education based on social class (Foster 1983; Husen 1975; Boudon 1974; Lauglo 1983; Bellaby 1977; Ford 1969). Because of the strong class differentiation, students were subjected to a dual tracking system that destined them either to vocational or to academic pursuits. With postwar economic recovery, demand for a wide variety of skills created a need for a less rigidly differentiated educational system. By making secondary schools more comprehensive, students of all social classes could enroll in the curriculum of their choice if they had the aptitude, motivation, and, sometimes, the necessary financial means. Europe's comprehensive schools have served as a model for mixing curriculum programs under one roof, although some countries outside Europe have continued to impose rigid barriers between academic and vocational schooling (Husen 1975; Williamson 1979; McPherson, Gray, and Raffe 1983; Eggleston 1983).

Socialist Countries

Much as in Western Europe, the socialist nations responded to the needs of their industrial economies for a wide range of vocational and academic training with schooling that emphasized highly technical skills. As a result, Eastern bloc nations focused their efforts on vocational–technical education at the expense of a purely academic curriculum. Because the U.S.S.R. and its East European allies had repudiated the Western traditions relating social class to employment, young people were seldom stigmatized by following technical and trade, rather than academic, curricula. Many socialist governments in developing areas have followed the Soviet example and have emphasized a vocational orientation even more strongly in order to meet manpower requirements.

Socialist regimes have often turned to vocational education as a way of eradicating the differences between mental and physical labor—and hence class differences—that formal schooling was thought to have created. Perhaps China and Cuba have carried this distinction further than other nations (see Dumont 1974; Figueroa, Prieto, and Gutierrez 1974; Gray 1976; Leiner 1975; Lofstedt 1981; Price 1973; Roca 1977; Carnoy and Wharteim 1976, 1977). While work–study programs in those countries were intended to narrow the status differentials between occupations, the students' subsequent economic contributions have helped to offset the cost of their education, thereby allowing the educational system to accommodate greater numbers than would otherwise have been possible. Such financing of recurrent expenditures by students is rare in primary education systems.

In the U.S.S.R., the "factory schools" started in the 1920s have been a strong feature of Soviet education. Over the past forty years the U.S.S.R. has pursued a diversified education policy, with special emphasis on technical-vocational education (Blumenthal and Benson 1978). The reasons for the approach lie in the industrial needs of Russia's economic, scientific, and technological development plans since the revolution. The emphasis on science and technology and the consequent upgrading of vocational education have helped break the historical link between general academic school and higher education. Given the nature of Soviet society, social and occupational mobility—and hence class differentiation—are highly dependent on schooling. One result has been that students' expectations have become based on their individual educational records rather than on the specific courses they take.

The example of vocational education in the U.S.S.R. and China has influenced not only East European but also many developing countries, among them Ethiopia, Tanzania, Angola, Mozambique, Guinea Bissau, and Cuba.

Types of Diversified Education

For our purposes, diversified education refers to secondary schools that provide a wide range of courses which are typically found either in all-academic or in all-vocational schools. Furthermore, within the diversified curriculum, many areas of study such as agriculture, commerce, technical subjects, and home economics are offered under one roof. Students in such schools are encouraged to specialize in one of many vocational subjects and at the same time to continue academic courses. By encouraging flexibility, diversified schools allow students the options of pursuing either advanced technical training or continuing with university education.

The reasons for following a diversified education program have been varied, but the structure of educational institutions offering vocational curricula has remained fairly standard. Vocational and academic subjects have been taught in separate schools, or they have been placed together in a "comprehensive" school, with only little crossover permitted.

There are two common organizational structures for diversified secondary education. The first is a multitrack comprehensive school in which several vocational fields coexist with an academic course of study. This structure allows students to mix academic and vocational subjects, although students usually take vocational course work in only one field. Having several vocational options under one roof allows a large number of vocational students to gain exposure to academic courses as well. The main advantage of such a system is that it permits students to be exposed to academic courses while simultaneously pursuing a rigorous vocational program.

A less common diversified system is one that combines only one major vocational course (rather than two or more) with a high-quality academic curriculum, again under one roof. These double-stream schools were created by modifying the curriculum in previously all-academic schools. As in comprehensive schools, students pursue vocational course work in conjunction with academic subjects. Frequently, such schools require all their students to take some vocational courses.

Another way of looking at diversified education is to concentrate on the proportion of students' time devoted to academic or vocational subjects rather than on the type of institution in which the instruction is offered. Figure 2-1 portrays a time continuum, showing diversified schools as a midway response to the earlier segregated single-track academic or vocational institutions.

Diversification in Colombia and Tanzania

Colombia and Tanzania have experimented extensively with diversified secondary education over the past decade as part of an attempt to match schooling more closely with employment prospects.

Colombia's diversified secondary schools, called INEM (Institutos Nacionales de Educación Media), have a six-year program that combines academic with prevocational subjects. In addition to these schools, there remain private and public secondary schools offering an academic curriculum. It was hoped, however, that the diversified schools would attract many students away from inferior private academic schools and allow them to pursue vocational subjects of their choice while continuing a lighter load of academic course work. Colombia also has vocational schools confined to subject areas such as agriculture, technical trades, and commerce, that do not offer academic course work.

During their first two years in INEM schools, students study prevocational subjects to familiarize themselves with career options in the various trades. After two years of study, their work becomes more concentrated on a particular vocational field, such as agriculture or commerce, though students continue to take some additional academic courses. During their final two years, the students specialize. A student who has enrolled in the general industrial training program in the preceding two-year cycle may either focus on metalwork, construction, or perhaps electrical mechanics, or concentrate on an academic subject.

Graduates of INEM schools differ from those of other Colombian educational institutions. Because they have pursued both academic and vocational curricula, their range of future educational and occupational opportunities is presumed to be wider. Students who choose not to continue schooling after graduation still have obtained specialized skills and technical knowledge that allow them greater employment options. Nonetheless, it remains to be see what long-term advantages accrue to INEM graduates compared with those who have either conventional vocational or academic schooling in terms of skill in specific trades, academic knowledge, and capacity to benefit from further training or to find and succeed at jobs.

Tanzania's experience offers an interesting comparison with that of Colombia. Tanzania's economic system stresses public ownership and control of most major enterprises. The educational system has been designed to provide the trained manpower needed for the public sector to run

Figure 2-1. *Class Time Intensity Continuum by Type of Education*

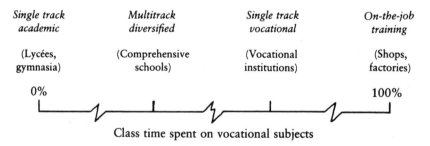

Single track academic	*Multitrack diversified*	*Single track vocational*	*On-the-job training*
(Lycées, gymnasia)	(Comprehensive schools)	(Vocational institutions)	(Shops, factories)

0%   100%

Class time spent on vocational subjects

efficiently. In contrast to Colombia, Tanzania has not introduced diversification merely as a means to match middle-level skills with manpower requirements. Rather, the main impetus for Tanzania's diversification efforts stems from a strong commitment to the ideals of work education similar to that found in the Chinese, Cuban, and Soviet vocational educational systems.

Because of Tanzania's philosophy of self-reliance and self-sufficiency in skilled manpower, students are required to gain experience in practical subjects in addition to academic pursuits by majoring in a vocational subject of their choice while in secondary school. Very few students continue their formal education after Form IV. (Secondary education in Tanzania consists of a four-year cycle—Forms I to IV—followed by a two-year cycle—Forms V and VI.) Combining practical work experience with formal academic training in the first four years of secondary school is intended to orient all secondary school students toward careers in such vocational subjects as commerce, agriculture, domestic sciences, and the technical fields. Those who are selected to continue their studies in upper secondary school and eventually at a university will henceforth be exposed to a purely academic curriculum, yet they will have acquired some vocational training in the lower secondary cycle.

During their four years in lower secondary school, students pursue one of four general vocational courses—in commerce, agriculture, or technical or domestic science—that supplement their regular academic course work. The amount of time they devote to all vocational and academic subjects is prescribed by the Ministry of Education. Anywhere from 25 to 40 percent of course-work periods per week is spent on the vocational course during the fourth year alone. On completion of the four-year program, students are considered sufficiently trained in their respective vocational area to seek on-the-job training, enter government-run training institutes, or seek employment in their area of specialization.

Tanzania has proceeded far in its effort to institutionalize vocational subjects along with the academic curriculum. The purpose of the diversified system is not to prepare students for a university, but neither is it intended to provide vocational skills divorced from a meaningful academic education.

One major issue regarding the evaluation of diversified schools is whether such schools should fully prepare students for jobs or whether they should simply teach prevocational skills. The terms "prevocational" and "vocational" have been used interchangeably in the literature to describe such schools, and they have therefore been used interchangeably in this study, although we prefer the term "prevocational." The rationale for full vocational preparation may be more debatable than the argument for prevocational education, however. For this reason, and because some of the evaluation criteria used in this study pertain to labor market considerations, we offer the following quotations to show that in the two case countries diversification was also meant to prepare students directly for work (emphasis added throughout).

G. Varner (1965), consultant to Unesco and the World Bank, made the following observations about Colombia's experience:

> Colombia has a large deficit in human resources . . . for its economic development . . . this deficit has been caused by inadequate educational programs . . . The number . . . of students is inadequate to satisfy . . . future needs for growth and development . . . (p. 53). Curricula should differ for different students according to . . . their *vocational* objectives (p. 58). Since *vocational goals* of students vary, it is convenient for secondary schools to make available different types of curricular experiences to prepare students for different *vocational objectives* . . . (p. 23).

The law instituting diversified schools is very explicit on their purpose:

> Instituto de Educación Media Diversificada is one which . . . offers several academic and *vocational* programs (Decree 1962, no. 20, 1969, art. 4).

> . . . education should respond to the *need for human resources* required for development of the country (Decree 1085, no. 195, June 8, 1971).

> Modalidad means a set of related subjects aiming at training pupils in aspects *specific to an economic sector* (Decree 1085, 1971).

> Secondary education will include two cycles . . . 1. Basic Cycle . . . and 2. *Vocational* Cycle (Decree 080, January 22, 1974, art 3).

> We believe in success of the INEM system because . . . thousands of *conventional high school* graduates multiply the number of applicants for college, unfortunately still a traditional one . . . which *does not contribute to* . . . *development* (INEM, "Principios Fundamentales de la Educación Media Diversificada en Colombia," [Medellín, April 1973]).

Similar quotations on the vocational intention of diversified schools can be found in Tanzanian government documents:

> The general aim of education in Tanzania is to . . . prepare the young people for *work* . . . Secondary education is *terminal* and aims at equipping the pupils with *skills* . . . To achieve this, secondary education is diversified and *vocationalized* into commercial, technical, agricultural and home economics biases. Biasing of schools aims at (a) putting emphasis on *manual work* that ties in with *economic* and social development of the country; (b) *preparing pupils for work* in the villages and towns. (Tanzania Ministry of National Education 1980, pp. 3, 4.)

The goal of the commercial bias is to provide skills that enable the Form IV school leavers to attain the Accountant Assistant, Grade II . . . The goal of the agricultural bias is to provide knowledge and skills equivalent to the level of Agricultural Assistant . . . The goal of the technical bias is to provide knowledge and skills equivalent to Trade Test, Grade III. (Tanzania Ministry of National Education 1979b, pp. 63–68.)

The biases can be considered vocational or pre-vocational. In the case of technical bias, students who do not get a place in form five, do trade test which upon success qualify them as craftsmen. For them *the bias is vocational* because they can be employed directly as craftsmen. The bias is pre-vocational for those who pursue Full Technician course. The Form IV examinations for those in Commercial bias are equivalent to National Business Examinations at stage two level and they can be employed directly. (Tanzania Ministry of National Education, letter to the Diversified Secondary Curriculum Study research team, January 25, 1984, p. 6.)

In fact, Tanzania went one step further regarding such curricula and in the process cleared up one of the semantic ambiguities regarding their vocational or prevocational character. According to a 1984 report of the Presidential Commission on Education, "Diversified secondary education will now be called 'Basic *Vocational* Education and Training' and *will continue* to be provided by emphasizing basic *vocational skills*" (Tanzania Ministry of National Education 1984, p. 23; emphasis added).

3. Previous Evaluations

LITTLE EVIDENCE EXISTS to show unequivocally that vocational schooling has either failed or succeeded in its intended goals. Consequently, it is difficult to know whether the social and economic benefits of vocational schooling in general, or diversified education in particular, exceed the benefits accruing to academic secondary education and how these benefits compare with the relative costs of such schools.

In evaluating the results of educational reform along vocational-diversified lines, four broad effects of diversified education might be examined:

- Access to schooling by various socioeconomic groups
- Degree of cognitive achievement in the subjects studied
- Differences in students' ambitions, motivations, attitudes, aspirations, and other noncognitive expectations concerning occupational careers and further education
- Post-school experiences in further training and employment of graduates.

While there is considerable speculation about the overall success or failure of diversified education, it is more likely that educational reforms succeed or fail in relation to the particular situation; hence, an assessment of each national experience should be evaluated on its own merits.

This chapter reviews past attempts to evaluate vocational education programs in the United States and European nations. Although these countries are highly industrialized, there are many parallels with developing nations regarding philosophy, design, implementation, and historical development of educational programs, as well as evaluation problems encountered in understanding vocational education. The chapter also addresses the scant evidence available from studies of developing nations and compares the two sets of experience. There follows a brief discussion of the relationship between vocational education and economic growth and development. Finally, there is a review of the World Bank's experience in financing diversified education in a number of countries.

Review of the Literature

Social Influences on Enrollment

Do working-class parents send their children primarily to vocational schools, while white-collar workers more often enroll their children in university-bound programs? That is, do the patterns of enrollment cause or reinforce the perpetuation of social class distinctions by an educational system that offers different curriculum programs for each group?

Loxley (1983), using data for Europe compiled by the International Association for the Evaluation of Educational Achievement (IEA), found that parents of students attending vocational schools differed in their level of educational attainment from those of students attending academic schools. Parents of vocational students tended to be engaged in manual occupations and have less-educated backgrounds than did parents of students attending academic programs. The secondary vocational school population drew from families headed by predominantly blue-collar workers and persons with less than a full secondary school education. In Italy, for example, fathers of fourteen- and eighteen-year-old students in the academic track had an average of one more year of schooling than fathers of students in nonacademic courses. Those findings are similar to profiles for students in the United States (Silberman 1978; Lecht 1979).

Vocational students are not a homogeneous group, however; some vocational curriculum programs are likely to attract a greater percentage of enrollees from families in which the father received more education than the typical father of a vocational school student. For example, in Italy, eighteen-year-old students enrolled in technical fields had a mean parental education two years higher than students in industrial fields, which implies that more of their fathers were foremen and craftsmen. Similarly in the Federal Republic of Germany, fathers of fourteen-year-old vocational students were generally in more highly skilled occupations than fathers of students in the academic track.

In assessing differences in the social background of both fourteen- and eighteen-year-old vocational and nonvocational students in eight industrialized nations, there appears to be a typical pattern: the educational systems are highly differentiated, separating students by social class characteristics fairly early in their school careers. (For documentation of the variability of social influences on educational access at different levels of economic development, see Anderson 1983.)

Formation of Expectations

As noted in the previous chapter, secondary education systems in Western Europe have been structurally differentiated by curriculum: one track is reserved mainly for middle-class and the other for working-class students. Given such conditions, it is unlikely that students trained for white-collar occupations and students trained for blue-collar employment will perceive their future in quite the same way (Boudon 1974; Passow and others 1976). If the dual system of secondary education were not rigid, then all students would probably perceive their future opportunities in much the same way.

High educational expectations among a large number of vocational students, however, would imply that perhaps "too many" plan to go on to college rather than terminate their formal education upon graduation from secondary vocational school, as envisaged in educational policy. It would also suggest that many vocational graduates would try to move out of the trades for which they had been trained. Among nonvocational students, high educational aspirations would suggest that these students are likely to continue their training within their chosen field of study.

In 1971, the IEA completed a large-scale study of many European educational systems covering vocational and academic track students (Comber and Keeves 1973). Using these data, Loxley (1983) reported significant differences in the educational and occupational aspirations of fourteen- and eighteen-year-old students in a number of European countries. Vocational students trained for specific blue-collar employment aspired to occupations of a lower status than the white-collar professional jobs sought by secondary academic students. In sum, in the 1970s Europe's dual system of education continued to be a powerful influence on shaping the expectations of its students in conformity with the intention of the curriculum.

Little is reported in the literature on developing countries about the attitudes instilled by vocational and nonvocational courses of study. (Evans and Schimmel 1970; Moris 1966). Pioneering work by Foster (1965) in Ghana and later in Cameroon (Clignet and Foster 1966) showed that all students uniformly aspired to higher education and occupations of high status. Similar work was carried out by Olson (1974) in Kenya over a period of several years. He, too, revealed that aspirations were consistently and often unrealistically high, considering that so many vocational as well as nonvocational students aspired to white-collar positions. However, because secondary school students in East and West Africa during the 1960s and early 1970s represented a very small proportion of their age group, they might not have been acting irrationally in expecting high occupational rewards. In the early 1970s acute shortages of upper- and middle-level manpower in the public sector were widespread, and students' expectations reflected this situation.

Gouveia (1972) examined preferences for types of secondary schooling by social class origin in São Paulo, Brazil. Because São Paulo was a dynamic industrial setting at the time of the study, the author found no difference in the choice of vocational subjects by either middle- or working-class youth; all showed a predilection for industrial courses. A principal cause of this was the structure of the São Paulo economy at the time: the wages paid to skilled labor were higher than those paid to clerical and sales employees.

Studies on Cuba (Bowles 1971) and Tanzania (Mbilinyi 1974a) have indicated that ideological indoctrination dampens personal ambitions in socialist systems. Little is known about how pursuing a vocational curriculum affects the aspirations of those destined to attend such institutions in lieu of going on to a university. But Zachariah and Hoffman (1984) report that the introduction of manual labor into schools failed in two very different societies: India under Gandhi and China under Mao.

Finally, there have been numerous qualitative assessments of the impact of innovations in vocational education worldwide. Such assessments do not offer data to support either failure or success but, rather, provide subjective conclusions reached by experts in the field. Wanasinghe's (1982) assessment of Sri Lanka's problems in implementing its experiment in a compulsory prevocational education curriculum is an example. After examining the relationship between the school curriculum and community work prospects, teachers' receptivity to the prevocational curriculum, and its costs, the author concluded that prevocational studies should be made optional rather than mandatory. This assessment was based not only on the slight prospects for successful implementation, given teachers' attitudes and the program's costs, but also on the fact that vocational education did not change student attitudes about work or further education.

Differences in Cognitive Achievement

Within the United States and Europe there are substantial differences in vocational and academic students' achievement, with nonacademic-track students performing less well than college preparatory students (Plowden 1967; Breneman and Nelson 1981; Husen 1975). These variations often are attributed to differences in ability rather than in social class. The consensus of educators is that offering either a vocational or an academic curriculum seems to produce gains for some students at the expense of others, but that these gains do not always occur for the same socioeconomic groups. (See Rosenbaum 1976 for a review.)

Few researchers have studied vocational test results because they have been more interested in knowing how well students perform on universally accepted standard tests of verbal and quantitative skills, rather than on narrower, vocationally oriented subjects. Thus, while it is known that vocational-track students perform less well in academic pursuits than do students in college preparatory courses (Woods and Haney 1981; Wiley and Harnischfeger 1980; McPherson, Gray, and Raffe 1983)—and this might be expected because the vocational curriculum is less tied to those pursuits than the academic curriculum—it is not known whether students in vocational programs could outscore academic students on tests of vocational content. Again, no studies have ever attempted to measure these differences because tests of commercial or industrial content are not given routinely to students studying mathematics, science, and the humanities.

Data extracted from a 1971 IEA multinational study of science achievement, made available to the Bank for analysis, offer some indication of the pattern found in industrial countries. Although no published accounts other than Loxley's use IEA data to compare the achievements of students in different curriculum tracks, data collected on large national samples of students in 1971 can be divided by curriculum placement into academic, vocational, and comprehensive tracks. While this distinction is not universal, essentially the tripartite system is intended to distinguish between (1) college-bound students; (2) those who are being trained in specific trades, whether highly technical, industrial, agricultural, or commercial; and (3) those following a "comprehensive" course that offers neither a specific vocational nor a purely academic curriculum (that is, students are offered fewer academic subjects than those in college preparatory schools but have a smattering of vocational course work).

In every European country studied (England, France, Sweden, Germany, Italy, Hungary, and Finland) fourteen-year-old students taking academic courses were well ahead of vocational-track students in academic performance. These differences in mean achievement scores are maintained even after a number of out-of-school factors influencing achievement (including sex, social class, and innate ability) are taken into account. In addition, mean differences in vocabulary scores measuring verbal facility favored academic-track students. If vocabulary scores are taken as a measure of aptitude acquired out of school (because verbal facility is acquired primarily in the home), the implication is that the tracking system in industrialized nations has clearly separated students by innate ability and socioeconomic origin at a fairly early age.

Similar results were obtained for Italy, Hungary, Sweden, France, and the United States, using the same international achievement survey in science but conducted for eighteen-year-olds rather than fourteen-year olds. By the time students reach age eighteen, their number has been reduced by the selection process. One might therefore expect to find no difference in achievement or verbal ability in the sciences across vocational and nonvocational tracks. Despite this greater selectivity, however, college preparatory students in all five countries had higher scores than did vocational students.

The conclusions reached from the IEA multicountry study of both fourteen- and eighteen-year-old groups strongly imply that significant differences in science and verbal achievement are based on the curriculum program a student pursues. Vocational students in both age groups do less well than their academic school counterparts on both types of tests. It is clear that industrial societies in the early 1970s tended to channel their less academically able students into trade programs. Why and how vocational programs came to include a substantial concentration of students of below-average academic ability (as measured by tests of verbal reasoning) in less important than the fact that cognitive differences exist across curriculum tracks at ages fourteen and eighteen.

First-generation achievement studies have recently been undertaken in many developing nations, but they have seldom been directed at determining differences between vocational and nonvocational education. What little evidence exists suggests that students in a vocational course do poorly in academic subjects, compared with students enrolled in academic programs (Comber and Keeves 1973 [Thailand, India, Iran, and Chile]; Fuller 1976 [India]). Again, however, the tests measured achievement in math or science, to which all students had had some exposure, rather than achievement in vocational subjects, with which the academic track students had little familiarity. Further, it is not known whether the lower test scores might be the result of students' taking courses for which they are not well suited, preselectivity based on ability grouping, or social class differences across curriculum programs.

Experiences after Schooling

Although vocational education in the United States served only about 12 percent of the students of secondary school age, recent debate has focused on increasing its relevance as a means of reducing the imbalances expected in the labor market. After years of falling economic productivity, rising unemployment, and decreasing occupational mobility, the idea of giving every high school graduate a marketable skill is appealing. Advocates of vocational schooling want to provide students with such skills, and they also want schools to simulate the work environment for future job satisfaction and higher productivity.

Those who have opposed the vocational school concept as a viable alternative or complement to an academic course have forcefully argued that vocational education reshapes curriculum and teaching philosophy to fit the socioeconomic background, ability, and aspirations of lower-class youths, thereby placing a stigma on vocational programs, separating manual from mental skills, and offering a false hope that vocational education will guarantee a specific job or enhance employment mobility. This argument is quite similar to the one mentioned in chapter 2 and is widely cited in developing countries.

Opponents of vocational education (among them Grubb 1979) argue that employers should be the judges of its effectiveness. Because most employers, according to these observers, do not prefer vocational over academic school graduates, and because most students seldom find jobs in areas for which they were specifically trained, the economic value of vocational education as a panacea for the ills of structural unemployment can be challenged.

Cost-benefit studies assessing the rate of return to vocational education in the United States have produced mixed evidence, although they seem to point to few or no differences in economic returns that would support vocational education. In general, private rates of return to U.S. secondary schools over time have ranged between 14 and 20 percent. Social rates of return have averaged between 10 and 12 percent (Weisberg 1983; Meyer 1980; Cohn 1979). Higher rates of return to secondary technical education (relative to general) have been reported for Colombia, but lower ones for the Philippines, Turkey, and Thailand (Psacharopoulos 1973). In Thailand, the social rate of return to secondary technical education is negative. Also Clark (1983) reports higher rates of return to secondary general relative to vocational education in Indonesia (26 and 14 percent, respectively).

Graduates of post–high school training programs would have to earn more than graduates of high school vocational programs if the investment in post–high school training is to be economically rational. Corazzini (1968) contrasted a four-year high school vocational program with a two-year post–high school vocational training program. After comparing benefits and costs for each program, he concluded that graduates of post–high school programs open only to high school graduates found better-paying jobs—usually in a slightly higher technical category—than high school graduates who went immediately to work. However, graduates of the post–high school vocational program represented a poor investment if, once trained, they chose to compete at the same skill level in trades open to vocational high school graduates with job experience only.

Hu and others (1971) compared private returns to both academic and vocational education in the United States and found very high rates of return for vocational schooling (more than 50 percent). But different findings reported by Corazzini (1968) and Taussig (1968) indicate much lower rates of return for vocational education (about 10 percent) and suggest that the extra costs of such education are generally not fully recovered by additional benefits.

Studies have also been conducted for postsecondary vocational education (Watson 1977; Carroll and Ihnen 1967), revealing that the discounted benefits exceed the costs. Freeman (1974) has examined returns to proprietary school training (such as in data processing, auto maintenance, cosmetology, and barbering). Because the length of training is relatively shorter, the total cost of proprietary schooling is similar to that of colleges and universities despite higher tuition. And the returns to the national economy appear to exceed those of higher education.

Rate of return studies for secondary schools in developing countries (Psacharopoulos 1981b) show that private returns average about 15 to 20 percent (the social rates are between 12 and 15 percent). Low returns to secondary education in middle-income countries, such as Israel and Greece, reflect specific socioeconomic conditions prevailing in those countries. For example, under Israel's highly egalitarian system, high school diplomas do not carry much greater weight in the labor market than do primary school certificates. For this reason, apprenticeship programs in Israel are more cost-effective than formal vocational education programs because, expenditures for formal education are also higher than those for apprenticeship programs (Cohn 1979, p. 127).

Large-scale tracer studies showing rates of return for vocational schooling and training programs are lacking for most developing countries. One reason for this is that the programs were started too recently to gain a clear picture of their graduates' earnings (Van Rensburg 1974; Perry 1981). Benefits resulting from vocational schooling have been reported by Schiefelbein (1979) in Chile and Colombia. Vocational education graduates in those countries obtain higher salaries than those from academic tracks with the same number of years of education. According to Schiefelbein, students are increasingly aware of the labor market payoff from opting to follow a particular curriculum. Puryear (1979) reports the same results in Colombia for those graduating from SENA programs when compared with academic students.

Two studies by Bukhari (1968a, 1968b) looked at short- and long-range benefits derived from specialized secondary vocational programs in Jordan and Tunisia. These studies concluded that (1) the more specific the vocational training, the less likely it was to be relevant to the actual needs of the job market; (2) vocational secondary schooling in Jordan cost ten times more per pupil than academic secondary schooling; and (3) the benefit-cost ratio for vocational graduates was 2:1, while for academic secondary graduates the ratio was 3:1. Bukhari concluded that vocational schools should be integrated into the general academic educational system to create comprehensive schools because few students were using their specialized skills in the industries in which they were later employed and the costs of educating vocational students exceeded those of general secondary students.

Other studies of vocational school programs—in Sri Lanka (Wijemanna and Welkala 1975), India (Fuller 1976), Barbados (Oxtoby 1977), and Swaziland (Sullivan 1981)—have pointed to similar conclusions. In general, (1) if they have a choice students attend an academic school; (2) teachers who possess both theoretical and practical ability in vocational education are difficult to find; (3) industry is reluctant to pay the salaries expected by vocational graduates; (4) there is a realization that maintaining up-to-date shop equipment similar to that used in modern industry is too costly for most school budgets; and (5) students often do not take jobs in the field for which they were trained.

In 1971 El Salvador implemented a diversified secondary school program that provided academic and commercial subjects as well as industrial arts, agriculture, pedagogy, health, navigation, fishery, and hotel administration. The objective of the program was to improve the employability of secondary school leavers and to prepare them for further specialized studies in secondary schools. McGinn and Balart (1980) report an evaluation of this program, carried out by ODEPOR (Oficina de Planificación y Desarollo Organizacional). The evaluation was a cross-sectional study of a weighted sample of 613 members of the first class (5 percent of those graduating in 1974), to determine their success in the labor market one year after graduation. The basic hypotheses tested referred to the relationships between employment and field of specialization, earnings and academic success, and secondary school stream and higher education career. The findings show no significant differences among graduates of different fields of study with respect to labor market success (in terms of employment opportunities or earnings), even though unit costs of different educational streams vary considerably. In terms of further education, no functional relationship was found between the course taken in secondary school and the field of specialization in higher education. The evaluation concluded that the diversification reform in El Salvador was a failure because (1) the results of target schools were no different from those of traditional academic secondary schools, and (2) diversified schools were on average more expensive than traditional secondary schools.

In Brazil, a 1970 law required all secondary schools to introduce vocational subjects in addition to academic curriculum, with the ultimate aim of imparting occupational skills to all high school graduates. According to Castro (1983, p. 9), this "country-wide school reform that was to offer practical content to all students turned out to be a failure."

A 1984 paper by Urevbu provides a critical appraisal of Nigerian vocational education. (The term "vocational education" is used explicitly in government documents to refer to the lower secondary school curriculum, which is terminal for those who do not have the aptitude for academic subjects.) The author concludes that it is uncertain whether vocational education in Nigeria promotes economic development any more than does traditional schooling.

A study of schools in Kenya, however, produced negative preliminary results. A tracer study of industrial school graduates did not reveal any employment advantage over a control group of academic secondary school graduates (Narman and others 1984, table 3). Moreover, the per student cost of industrial schools is about double that of control schools (Cumming 1984, para. 6.1.2). In a similar vein, a comparative study of the introduction of manual training schools in China and India gives a series of reasons for the reversal of such educational policy in both countries (Zachariah and Hoffman 1984).

Summarizing the attributes and drawbacks of secondary vocational education, one may conclude that, especially in the advanced countries, students have traditionally been guided into different curriculum streams in accordance with their fathers' educational levels and the students' own abilities; that academic students expect jobs with higher pay and more status and perform better in academic subjects than do vocational students; and that the evidence on the relative earnings of vocational and academic school graduates is very mixed. This study addresses the question whether that pattern is also typical of developing nations, which have drawn on Europe's experience in the past, or whether vocational schooling is too recent an innovation to have formed the basis for a stratified educational system in those countries. The empirical studies on Colombia and Tanzania throw some light on these questions.

Vocational Education and Economic Development

To determine the way in which the level or type of education influences a nation's economic output, one must first assume that an increase in economic productivity requires enhancement of the quantity or quality of resources or the efficiency with which they are used. Education can make its most direct contribution to economic growth by improving the quality of labor—that is, by making the work force more productive, more disciplined and reliable, healthier, and more mobile. In turn, higher quality labor may alter the amount of available physical capital by increasing the rates of savings and investment, and it may boost the efficiency with which resources are used. The two most important factors affecting the quality of labor in any economy are (1) formal education and training and (2) work experience (on-the-job learning), both of which improve labor productivity.

There is considerable evidence attesting to the contribution of education in general (that is, undifferentiated by level and type of schooling) to the economic growth of many countries. Psacharopoulos (1984) reviewed the existing data relating economic growth to advancements in education. Although no universal pattern was found, education's contribution to growth tended to be higher in Asia, Africa, and Latin America and lower in Europe and North America. The results of this survey lead to the conclusion that education has been one of the dominant contributors to developing nations' economic growth.

Biede (1970) has argued that investment in vocational education is a major factor in economic development. Walters and Rubinson (1981) estimated the effect of U.S. educational expansion on aggregate economic activity over the past century, after first controlling for the inputs of increased labor and capital in the production process. Looking at the period since the depression of the 1930s, and distinguishing educational levels (primary through the Ph.D. level), they found that advancements in secondary schooling had contributed more to the growth of output than had advancements in higher education. In addition, however, increases in the number of doctorates granted over this forty-year period had a significant positive effect on gross national product (GNP) per capita.

Meyer (1979), using data for more than 100 countries, reported that secondary school enrollment was a principal factor affecting economic development in 1950–75. Extending Meyer's analysis, Benavot (1983) related secondary enrollment rates to the GNP by distinguishing vocational from traditional academic secondary education. Benavot reasoned that if vocational education was the most productive form of schooling, there should be a relationship between a country's level of economic development and the vocational share of formal education at the secondary level. The author distinguished the economic effects of vocational education from those of general academic secondary education using data on more than 100 countries over three fifteen-year periods (1950–65, 1955–70, 1960–75). His hypothesis, that countries with relatively stronger vocational systems would achieve faster economic growth, was only partly substantiated. Apparently, while both vocational and general education contribute to economic growth, the positive impact of general secondary education is far more pronounced than is that of vocational schooling alone. How can these results be explained?

Formal vocational training is thought to fulfill its purpose when it provides needed skills for the economy that cannot be offered elsewhere more efficiently. In a country with a very limited industrial base, for example, on-the-job training will not supply all the skilled labor needed for growth. Moreover, beyond a certain level of sophistication trade skills demand a theoretical foundation in order to be understood and properly applied. The abstract knowledge that provides a sound basis for training in sophisticated labor skills is best imparted in the classroom. In developing countries, as long as the average level of education is very low, vocational schools must undertake a substantial amount of general education. This function overlaps with that of the general academic secondary school, and its economic effects are difficult to measure.

In a country where the literacy rate is sufficiently high, vocational educational institutions can begin to train students in highly specialized and technical skills requiring a strong theoretical base. Here, too, however, there is a danger of overspecializing to the point where it is difficult for graduates to use their expertise because there are not enough highly skilled jobs available. Very little more is known about training for employment in general than is known for employment in a particular field of work. Do certain kinds of curriculum and institutional arrangements promote the ability to learn from work experience? Blaug (1973, p. 38) states that "education is economically valuable not because of what students know but because of how they approach the problem of knowing."

In sum, there is considerable debate over and conflicting evidence about whether vocational education imparts knowledge and skills unlike those found in secondary academic settings. Because the consequences for employment and for national economic development are considerable, the questions should therefore be more fully examined.

World Bank Projects

One hundred seventeen secondary education projects assisted by the World Bank between 1963 and 1982 contained provisions for a diversified curriculum. (For the evolution of Bank policy on diversified schools, see Heyneman 1984.) Because of problems involved in distinguishing the costs of individual components, it is difficult to arrive at exact expenditures for diversification in these projects. A conservative estimate is that the Bank has devoted 20 percent of its education sector lending to diversified education components over the past twenty years, at a cost of about $800 million (1983 prices).

Except for the occasional use of tracer studies, the Bank's most common method of judging the success of diversified secondary curriculum projects has been to determine whether the original objectives stated in appraisal reports were being implemented. The five most commonly stated objectives for diversifying curricula are listed below (with the percentage of the 117 projects that had each item as an objective):

1. To meet qualitative manpower needs (57 percent)
2. To meet quantitative manpower needs by expanding secondary school enrollment (44 percent)
3. To offer broader curricula to rectify the bias toward academic education and to make the curricula more relevant to the needs of the economy (38 percent)
4. To upgrade overall secondary education (38 percent)
5. To improve the employment prospects of graduates (35 percent).

Some of the stated objectives are too broadly conceived to be measurable. Ten of fifteen projects that cited enrollment expansion as a goal met their target. But of these ten, four faced severe problems in placing their graduates (because of slower than anticipated workforce growth or more rapid than planned expansion of secondary school enrollments).

With respect to the fourth goal, improving the quality of education, reasons for failing to meet this stated objective included shortages of qualified staff, teachers' reluctance to grapple with new orientations, and inadequate provision of essential instructional material. The lack of these resources perpetuated conventional teaching practices. Failure to implement curriculum reform was due most often to lack of materials as well as lack of teacher commitment and support.

"Hardware" items—buildings, laboratories, workshops, machinery, and furniture—are the major cost items in most education projects, and diversified education programs are no exception. Nonetheless, to ensure the success of diversified education programs once buildings, laboratories, workshops, and machinery are in place, it is essential to prepare teachers and school principals for the new curriculum and to provide them with instructional materials. The World Bank's early loans provided too little funding for such "software" relative to hardware, since the Bank expected borrowers to finance this task. For example, funding for the preparation of teaching materials was included in only 30 percent of the 117 projects, and the training of school principals to implement diversification was funded in only 25 percent of the projects. Eighty-five percent of all projects included proposals for some form of curriculum development such as the preparation of syllabi for prevocational subjects. Yet no evaluation scheme was devised to rate the quality or appropriateness of these teacher guides. Bank analysis revealed further that the major problem with diversified curriculum development arose during implementation: in 75 percent of projects including software funding, implementation of curriculum changes needed to meet the needs of the new programs was marginal. This was due either to a lack of instructional materials or to shortages of qualified teachers.

Another consideration in the discussion of curriculum development concerns whether the examination system should be revamped to accommodate changes in the increasing variations in fields of study. In examinations to qualify for promotion to the next schooling cycles the persistent dominance of academic subjects tends to foster an attitude on the part of both teachers and students that these subjects are most essential. The result in many cases is that the time and interests of teachers and students are diverted from practical academic subjects.

These observations point to the conclusion that specialized teachers are needed for diversified secondary education. Teachers trained in standard lecture procedures for academic subjects are not appropriate for the more manual material taught in shops and laboratories. Eighty-five percent of Bank-supported projects providing for teacher training as part of curriculum diversification registered a chronic lack of competent teachers, particularly in science and practical subjects. Because of these shortages, it is not surprising that most of the teachers continued to provide conventional lecturing and exposition. Some projects did report an improvement in the educational environment at the project schools, with teachers using new teaching methods extensively.

No evaluation has previously been made of the overall efficiency of diversified curricula relative to traditional academic or vocational schooling, as measured by unit costs and rates of repetition of grades among students. In fact, because of three major limitations, it was not possible to make a full scientific assessment of whether the completed projects achieved their stated or implied objectives or of the effectiveness of diversification as an educational model. First, the Bank completion reports are written as soon as a project has been implemented and therefore are not able to provide any inferential data about the effects of diversification on students' training, expectations, or employment experience. Second, very few projects have been in operation long enough to permit the examination of their effects on general economic efficiency. Third, the efficacy of a system or model cannot be evaluated fairly if the prerequisites—buildings and workshops ("hardware") or teaching materials ("software")—are not all in place.

This situation has now been partially remedied. In Colombia and Tanzania diversification took place long ago and has been reasonably well implemented. It has therefore been possible for the World Bank, in cooperation of the governments of the two countries, to undertake detailed case studies of their experience with diversified education.

4. Research Design and Methodology

THE PRINCIPAL POLICY ISSUE addressed in the study of Colombia's and Tanzania's school systems is whether the outcomes of diversified education differ substantially from those of conventional academic and purely vocational secondary schooling. The findings are based on two main dependent variables: what is learned in school, and what graduates accomplish in the world of work.

This study also investigates the question whether selection into various curriculum streams affects students' postsecondary school opportunities. The construction of student profiles can show how students differ across streams, both intellectually and socially, and the way their career patterns are affected by exposure to different curricula. This in turn can provide the basis for an assessment of the impact of students' home and school resources on their learning and earning capacity. The extent to which the schools studied nullify or reinforce social stratification processes also can be documented.

As mentioned previously, whether a diversified educational system has significant advantages over a nondiversified one is a hotly debated issue. Intuition suggests that teaching specialized knowledge in schools would be beneficial for an expanding modernizing economy, but there exists no definitive evidence to support this position. Opponents of diversified education have argued that vocational knowledge provides more restricted employment and earnings opportunities than does general academic knowledge (Blaug 1979; Conroy 1979; Dore 1975; Evans and Schimmel 1970; Godfrey 1977). If that is true, perhaps school systems should leave highly differentiated training to firms in the private sector and specialized vocational training organizations, and instead concentrate on teaching students to use established knowledge and to use analytical methods for problem solving.

Future earnings and employment prospects are not the only measures of the value associated with a given course of study. One can also look at the economic returns to public and private investment. Differences between the achievements of graduates of different curriculum programs reflect the particular skills taught in each program. In the case of competitive labor

36

markets, it is assumed that the value of these skills will be reflected in the going wage rate for a particular job (Lewin-Epstein 1981). Comparing the returns to investment in specialized training with those accruing from general academic education can point to situations in which investments pay off and thereby can indirectly suggest education strategies for enhancing national economic development. The findings could be used to offer policy advice regarding priorities in educational investment for the various types of schools.

In this chapter, we discuss the methodology adopted for testing differences in characteristics of students and graduates participating in alternative curriculum programs. We also describe the way in which information on schools, students, and graduates was obtained and list the main variables.

Research Design

Chapter 1 gave a short list of hypotheses used to test whether diversification leads students to pursue careers that are different from what might be expected if they followed traditional academic or purely vocational courses. For example, do prevocational secondary school students obtain higher test scores in their specialization subject than nonvocational students? Do prevocational graduates have lower expectations of attending university than students in an academic setting? Does diversification lead to differences in postsecondary activities? How do the benefits of diversification compare with the costs?

Ideally, the benefits to the economy of a diversified curriculum program could be isolated by using an aggregate production function such as $X = f(D, Z)$, where, in summary form, X is a measure of outcome, such as productivity; D is a set of variables denoting the number of graduates who followed academic, vocational, or diversified curricula; and Z is a vector of standardizing factors, such as family characteristics and school inputs.[1] In fact, this method was ruled out because diversified schools have so far produced only a small number of graduates; hence, the impact of diversified education is unlikely to be adequately revealed in such an aggregate, macro production function.

We therefore designed our research to concentrate on three possible effects of a diversified curriculum on students and graduates: (1) changes in cognitive achievement in school, (2) changes in student attitudes about

---

1. That is, the methodology would be similar to the one used to examine the effect of education on farmer productivity (Jamison and Lau 1982).

future career opportunities, and (3) changes in occupational attainment and employment prospects after students leave school.

These effects can best be described by using the example of graduates of a diversified school who have specialized in agriculture. In the case of cognitive achievement (1), the question is whether, other things being equal, these students have a greater knowledge of agricultural practices and less knowledge in other fields than do students who followed nonagricultural curricula. With regard to attitudes (2), we need to determine whether agricultural graduates, regardless of their background, express a preference for work in rural areas. To show the effect on employment (3), we must know whether agricultural graduates work in the farming sector of the economy immediately after leaving school. If there are negative results in knowledge (1) and attitude (2), there is a strong presumption against economic benefits (3) from the diversified programs. However, positive results in (1) and (2) do not establish that there are benefits to the economy, although they do indicate it is worthwhile to pursue the issue.

Testing Points

We have defined three points in time for assessing the possible effects of diversified curricula: while the student is still in school; about one year after graduation, when the graduate might be in his first employment or continuing his education; and several years after graduation. A longitudinal tracer study framework was adopted. Cognitive and attitudinal tests were given to students in their last year of secondary school, and a questionnaire asked about their backgrounds and family characteristics at the same time. A second questionnaire was administered to the same students one year after leaving school.

A third assessment, several years later, is not part of this study because of cost and timing, and because the project was designed to stimulate local research. The foundations have been laid for tracing the graduates further, however, so that the governments and local research institutions participating in this study may collect more information in the future.

Longitudinal Information

It was decided not to collect retrospective data on the graduates' past school and occupational records, but to undertake a longitudinal study of current students so as to avoid issues of selectivity bias, which might have made it difficult to test our hypotheses (Psacharopoulos 1981a).[2]

2. Data were retrospectively collected on a "pseudo-panel" cohort of 1978 graduates in Colombia to permit an assessment of some of the longer-term effects of diversification,

The starting point in the Colombia and Tanzania case studies was the schools in a district where diversified curricula have been taught for a number of years, along with nondiversified schools. To test whether diversification leads to different educational and employment experiences, research included several components:

- First, nationwide random sampling was used to obtain a representative group of high school students in proportion to their enrollment in the different curricula.
- Second, a survey administered to high school seniors just prior to graduation was used to collect base-line information for comparing diversified, vocational, and academic students.
- Third, a follow-up survey was administered to the same cohort one year after graduation to assess students' experiences immediately after they left school.

In this study, the subjects (high school seniors) were not assigned to conditions (the various curricula); instead, observations were made of students who were already enrolled in the different tracks. Because of the nonexperimental design, selection bias may well have occurred if some parents had placed their children in a certain program because they expected it to lead to better economic rewards than another. Schools themselves may have restricted entry into their programs on the basis of the students' past school performances. These choices involve ability screening or possession of prior information and represent the two most likely sources of bias in a study of this kind. The effects of these biases can usually be adjusted for by taking into account the student's background and some measure of previous school performance or natural ability. Thus, the longitudinal character of the study makes it superior to a cross-sectional study of graduates because of the implicit standardization for attributes that are not easily observed.

In a sense, the design of the study was formulated retroactively, because there are no pre-test observations on the same or equivalent scales as the post-test observations. However, a tradition has developed in the social sciences of seeking out pre-test measures which correlate with the post-test results within experimental groups, even though they are not measured on the same scales as the post-test. More easily retrieved measures, such as the respondent's age, sex, social background, mental ability, and place of residence, can often be obtained from school records or from respondents themselves and substituted for the lack of pre-test observations.

---

although the limitations of this technique were recognized (see Psacharopoulos and Hinchliffe 1983).

To assess the performance of students from diversified schools (the target group), the research design had to include an adequate number of observations of students who did *not* attend such schools (the control group). Thus, the testing of hypotheses depends on the statistical significance of differences between the mean performance of the target and control groups on a set of indicators, standardized for a set of factors outside the school setting.

For example, in Tanzania where each school has its own special field of study, the control and target group comparisons would be across the vector shown in table 4-1. In Colombia, where several subjects are offered under one roof or in a separate institution, the comparison is more complicated, corresponding to the matrix shown in table 4-2. Both vertical and horizontal comparisons are possible, to address such questions as where a given subject is best taught (horizontal) or what kind of subject is more conducive to further employment prospects (vertical).

In addition to determining the direct and indirect effects of home and school variables on students' cognitive and noncognitive achievements, it is also possible to use longitudinal data to examine the influence of home and school on post–secondary school outcomes, such as students' first jobs and earnings. For example, if the curriculum can be shown to affect earnings, it may be concluded that a particular educational program contributes more to individual or social gain, and hence to the economic development of the nation, than do others. The magnitude of this contribution will suggest where rates of investment might be increased or reduced.

No data on earnings are available for the many secondary school graduates in the sample who were pursuing further education and training. One can, however, analyze these students' academic career paths and note their decisions to continue training in their field of specialization.

To predict discrete events such as the probability of working, not working, studying, or not studying, logit analysis has been applied. Because the dependent variable in this case is dichotomous, an ordinary least

Table 4-1. *Target-Control Group Comparisons in a Single-Stream Diversified School System (Tanzania)*

Curriculum		School type
Academic	$[X_1]$	Nondiversified
Commercial	X_2	Diversified
Technical	X_3	Diversified
Agricultural	X_4	Diversified
Home economics	X_5	Diversified

Note: Brackets denote the control group.

squares (OLS) regression would skew the results (Hanushek and Jackson 1977; Rumberger 1983). The effects of independent variables from logit estimates can be interpreted in the same way as estimates obtained from ordinary regression techniques: The sign of the coefficient indicates a positive or negative effect of the corresponding independent variable, and the asymptotic *t*-values indicate whether the effect is significant. The major difference between logit and ordinary regression techniques lies in the fact that because the logit model is nonlinear, the magnitude of each effect depends on the value of the other independent variables.

Finally, rates of return are calculated to determine the social profitability of various school curricula.

Hypothesis Testing

OLS regression or logit analysis has been used to search for significant effects that particular curricula have on students' attitudes or graduates' performance. The regressions are of the general type: $Y = f$ (curriculum, family characteristics, individual student characteristics, school characteristics, regional characteristics), where Y could be any of the outcomes discussed earlier.

The first test is whether the coefficient referring to curriculum is significantly different from zero and, if that is the case, whether it has the expected sign.

Assuming that the coefficient is significant and has the expected sign, the next question is: how does its size compare with the cost of obtaining this effect? For example, studying subject X may raise a graduate's earnings somewhat more than studying subject Z, but if it costs considerably more to teach subject X, then subject Z is more cost-effective and hence should be promoted.

Table 4-2. *Target-Control Group Comparisons in a Multi-Track Diversified School System (Colombia)*

	School type	
	Diversified, multi-stream (target group)	*Nondiversified, single stream (control group)*
Curriculum		
Academic (control)	$[X_{11}]$	$[X_{12}]$
Commercial	X_{21}	X_{22}
Industrial	X_{31}	X_{32}
Agricultural	X_{41}	X_{42}
Social services	X_{51}	X_{52}

Note: Brackets denote possible control groups.

Beyond single equation regression analysis one may fit recursive path models of the type illustrated in figure 4-1, in which five major variables are interrelated in an initial-to-eventual-outcome time sequence. The variables include:

1. Family background, one measurement of which is father's occupation (OCCFATH)
2. Student's ability, as measured by an aptitude test (ABILITY)
3. School type or curriculum the student actually followed (BIAS)
4. Measure of cognitive achievement on subject matter taught in school (COGN)
5. Eventual labor market performance measured, for example, by labor earnings (Y).

The recursive model would be

(1) ABILITY $= \beta_1$ OCCFATH
(2) BIAS $= \beta_2$ OCCFATH $+ \beta_3$ ABILITY

Figure 4-1.   *Path Model for Assessing the Effect of School Type on Cognitive Achievement and Graduate Performance*

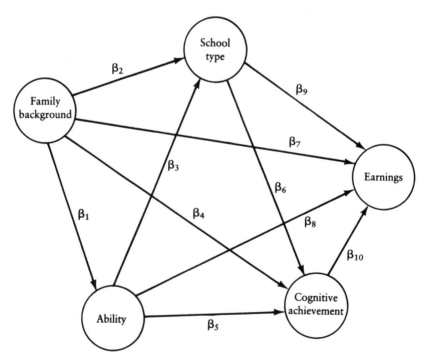

(3) COGN = β_4 OCCFATH + β_5 ABILITY + [β_6] BIAS

(4) Y = β_7 OCCFATH + β_8 ABILITY + [β_9] BIAS + [β_{10}] COGN

The β-coefficients in the above equations are standardized betas, and those of greatest interest to this study are β_6, β_9, and β_{10}. That is, having standardized for antecedent factors, we want to find out the extent to which the diversified curriculum affects students' cognitive skills and eventual labor market outcomes. In other words, one of the main objectives of the inquiry is to quantify the triangle shown in figure 4-2.

The central hypothesis to be tested is that there exist both direct (positive) effects (arrow A) and indirect effects (arrows B and C) of curriculum type. To put it differently, the *total* effect of curriculum on eventual labor market outcome (and, by extension, the contributions of school type to economic development) is measured by the sum of direct and indirect effects.

Total effects of diversified curriculum = β_9 + (β_6) (β_{10}).

Survey Instruments

Three sets of questionnaires have been used in the Colombia and Tanzania studies to obtain the information necessary to test the hypothesis:

Figure 4-2. *Direct versus Indirect Effect of Curriculum Type on Student Attitudes and Graduate Performance*

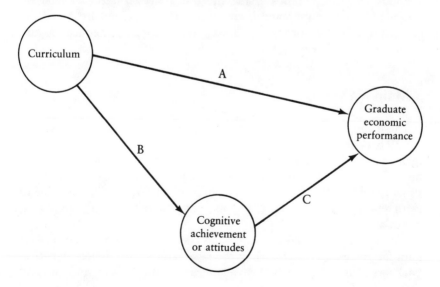

- School questionnaires filled in by the headmasters of the schools in the survey
- Individual questionnaires administered to secondary students still in the last year of target and control schools
- Follow-up questionnaires administered to the same students one year after graduating.

Data were obtained from several sources, including students, school principals, Ministry of Education officials, and graduates. Questionnaires administered to students were filled out in school during the last quarter of the final year of secondary school. They provided information on students' attitudes and behavior, social background, ability, future career plans, and aspirations. In addition, achievement tests in the various academic and vocational subjects were administered to all students irrespective of the curriculum stream they were enrolled in. (For the questionnaires and tests, see Psacharopoulos and Loxley 1984.)

Questionnaires given to school principals yielded a wealth of information on school expenditures, resources such as textbooks and equipment, the amount of class time devoted to the curriculum, and teacher characteristics such as work experience and degrees held. Data on school size and class time were obtained from Ministry of Education officials. From outside bodies (such as the Examination Council in Tanzania and the Instituto Colombiano para el Fomento de la Educación Superior [ICFES 1979, 1980] in Colombia), student scores were obtained on a battery of other tests.

Follow-up information on students was collected one year later by means of a mail survey and home visits. The questionnaire asked the graduates what decisions they had made regarding further education and employment after leaving secondary school.

Main Variables

These surveys made it possible to categorize each student by sex, age, social background, curriculum program studied, and type of school (general, prevocational, public, private). Information was obtained on the number of times a student repeated a year (whether in high school or primary school) or changed curriculum programs. It was also possible to learn about secondary school students' educationally related aspirations, plans, and attitudes.

The information from all sources has been merged into a single master data file for each country, using the SPSS and SAS computer statistical packages. The data, which are available at the World Bank and the local country research institutions, contain a wealth of information that can be used to analyze questions beyond the immediate scope of this study. It is hoped that the data base will continue to be analyzed and interpreted for many years to come.

What follows is a description of the main types of information obtained about the students and the schools they attended.

Social Background Indicators

Questions to the students asked about parental education, occupation, and income level, as well as about possessions such as the number of books in the house. These measures are believed to be a proxy of the social well-being or status of a family and to reflect the degree to which the home environment is able to support students in their school endeavors. In both industrialized and developing societies, parents with more education, higher incomes, and higher occupational ranking are thought to provide a better learning environment for their offspring than less privileged families. Although education in years and income in the local currency are relatively straightforward measures of family resources, the rankings of particular jobs in different societies are more arbitrary.

Future Plans and Aspirations

In addition to data on the objective variables such as age, sex, mental ability, and socioeconomic status, information was also obtained about students' educational and occupational expectations. These more subjective measures can serve as either independent or intermediate variables to isolate the different effects of curriculum programs. Because the occupational choices listed in the student questionnaire can be grouped into categories corresponding to the curricula offered (for example, technical, agricultural, or commercial), it was possible to ascertain whether students chose to follow occupations inside or outside their field of study.

In addition, students were asked to state how much they expected to earn on their first job. These predictions can serve not only to measure expectations and aspirations but also to assess how realistically students view the conditions in the labor market.

Exposure to Curricula

To determine their amount of exposure to given fields of study, students were asked to list the courses they took and the number of class periods attended in each subject per week. Information was also obtained from the headmaster on the class time allotted to each subject. In both countries the data allowed us to construct an index of class time devoted to academic and to individual vocational subjects. As a result, it was possible to group individuals by degree of exposure to learning and test for the impact of exposure time on achievement in the various curricula.

School Quality

In both Tanzania and Colombia, questionnaires given to principals and headmasters of each secondary school in the sample were designed to elicit quantitative information that would suggest the overall quality of each school's learning environment. Such data are helpful in obtaining an average measure of school quality against which to rank individual schools. The information also makes it possible to control for the effects on learning of variable school resources and to gauge how strongly the quality of the school affects students' achievement in various programs.

For example, if the educational attainment of teachers and the number of textbooks in a school are measured in their respective units and regressed on the achievement of the school's commerce students, the resulting standardized partial regression coefficient would indicate the extent to which the two factors influence student achievement. These coefficients provide the necessary weights for determining the benefits associated with the two measures of school quality. The results of the regression approach could also be supplemented with cost accounting to determine the monetary value of each indicator of quality, provided that the monetary value of a unit of achievement (output) can be estimated. If there are accurate measures of the incremental income of graduates strictly attributable to each curriculum program, that estimate can be made.

Cognitive Achievement Tests

Special tests were administered to each student in the various core curriculum subjects (such as commerce, agriculture, technical, and academic). Scores obtained for each student made it possible to compare strengths and weaknesses in knowledge across all curriculum subjects, regardless of the stream in which the student was enrolled.[3]

---

3. One could argue that paper and pencil tests do not tap the vocational skills learned in school simply because such tests do not measure manual dexterity or evaluate procedures and products. Because of the logistical complexity of measuring individual performance, however, a test of manual skills would have been difficult to administer, especially since we wished to test all students in the sample. Agriculture schools would not necessarily have had typewriters, for example, and commercial schools would undoubtedly not have had plowing equipment. There would also have been difficulties in rating welding, cabinet making, or physics experiments.   (continued)

The tests were constructed by the local research teams and were based on examinations that had previously been given in the various curriculum programs. The tests are therefore likely to be a valid measure of the knowledge instilled by the various curricula. For example, an item designed to test commercial knowledge reads, "When a variation of over 1% in the quantity demanded results from a variation of 1% in price, demand is said to be: (A) completely inelastic, (B) completely elastic, (C) of unitary elasticity, (D) relatively inelastic, (E) relatively elastic." Presumably those exposed to economics in the commercial stream should find this question easier to answer than those without such exposure. In the same way, test items in each subject area measured factual knowledge, although higher levels of reasoning (such as synthesis and evaluation) were required to answer some of the items.

General Ability Tests

In addition to measuring cognitive achievement in specific curriculum subjects, we recorded information about students' general abilities. General ability or aptitude tests measure innate mental proficiency and hence predict how well students may learn in whatever field they pursue. In contrast, achievement tests (both academic and vocational) measure the effect of formal instruction on a student's level of knowledge in a specific area and contain more questions on knowledge and mental skills taught in the school than do aptitude tests (both verbal and nonverbal). As measured by achievement tests, performance in the academic and more abstract subjects, such as math and science, is likely to be more closely correlated with general ability than is performance in subjects that require special abilities (such as shorthand and manual skills). Differences in the degree to which the results of general ability tests can be correlated with the results of achievement tests arise because some subjects require more ability in abstraction and deduction than others.

We supplemented the achievement test data with measures of students' general ability for at least two reasons. First, we needed to control for innate ability in case some students had been selected to follow a given curriculum stream on the basis of their perceived ability to learn. Second, because we did not conduct a pre- and post-test experiment, testing and retesting students to see whether their scores improved, it is difficult to

---

Although it is not feasible to test manual dexterity in a study of this kind, one can assume that paper and pencil tests at least measure how well students learn what is taught in the classroom. Because our paper and pencil tests were based on curriculum content, they measure cognitive learning and provide at least an indirect measure of the vocational skills acquired.

determine whether those who scored highly in curriculum tests of achievement did so because of what they had learned in school or because they were more clever than other students to begin with. Distinguishing the influence of students' innate ability to learn from the influence of what is taught in school allows one to obtain a "purer" measure of the effect of school-related factors on cognitive learning.

A good measure of general ability would be a student's test scores on leaving primary school because such a test would indicate what a pupil knew before entering secondary school. In Tanzania and Colombia, however, these early attainment scores could not be secured for various logistical reasons. Consequently, in Colombia individual scores on the 1981 ICFES aptitude test administered to students in secondary school were used as measures of ability or proxies for intelligence. (Each student's identifying code in the sample was matched with the ICFES code.) These tests were found to be highly reliable and were designed to elicit information on general aptitude rather than achievement in a specific subject. In Tanzania both verbal and quantitative tests of general ability were constructed by the local research team and administered to students in the sample when the base-year data were being collected. The reliability of these tests was acceptably high.

In both Colombia and Tanzania achievement tests were strongly directed toward subjects in the schools' curricula, while the aptitude measures were not; hence the aptitude-achievement distinction is preserved in this study.

Noncognitive Outcomes (Modernity)

It is thought that in the absence of a milieu conducive to change, risk-taking, and innovative speculation, traditional patterns and values will persist and thereby hinder social change and economic development. McClelland (1961) has reasoned that if schools can make students less traditional in their beliefs and attitudes, they will serve as agents of social change and ultimately influence economic development. In both Colombia and Tanzania, therefore, noncognitive tests of the degree of students' psychological "modernity" were constructed and administered to test the hypothesis that students acquire different attitudes according to the curriculum in which they are enrolled. Students with more traditional attitudes were expected to be less inclined to enter a university, for example, and more likely to go directly into the labor market than others.

Presumably, the more education one has, the more modern are one's ideas. But it remains uncertain why students enrolled in agriculture, for example, might be more or less bound by tradition than those enrolled in a commercial program. What aspects of secondary school in general and of particular curriculum programs can be expected to modernize the attitudes of students? Presumably, traditional customs and attitudes cannot be significantly altered until a large segment of the community is exposed at a fairly young age to new ideas and ways of doing things. If this is true, then primary schools are the obvious place to begin inculcating modern values because formal education at an early age plays a key role in modern society (Inkeles 1983).

Tests of modernity seek to measure differences in student perceptions along a hypothesized traditional-modern axis of personality traits. Movement from the traditional to the modern end of the spectrum is called modernization. Inkeles and Smith (1974) worldwide, Kahl (1968) in Mexico, Schnaiberg (1971) in Turkey, Armer and Youtz (1971) in Nigeria, and Holsinger (1973) in Brazil are among those pursuing this traditional-modern concept. Holsinger showed that primary school students in Brazil acquired more modern values each year they remained in school. Although Holsinger never was able to isolate specific factors in the school setting that contributed directly to modernity, he argued that students pick up modern values from the social structure, patterns of interpersonal relations, organizational arrangements, and the hidden network of institutionalized rules in the classroom. Learning to respect the dignity of others may be only incidental to the business of formal instruction, but it may be powerfully instilled by daily interaction among pupils and between pupils and teachers. In vocational programs with different degrees of emphasis on learning and instruction, the extent to which students acquire a more modern outlook may vary with the curriculum.

Inkeles and Smith have identified a number of characteristics that can be used to measure degree of modernity. They include commitment to women's rights, recognition of the value of time, optimism with regard to national development, use of mass media, identification with nationalism, active public participation, few kinship obligations, and the ability to plan ahead. Some of these dimensions are tapped in this study with the use of items taken from the Inkeles scale. In the Colombian case study, for example, a typical question asked of respondents was, "How often do you read a newspaper? (never, seldom, a few days a week, or every day)." Another question asked was, "Do you think that a person can be good without having any religious belief? (yes, no)." In the first example, the "modern" person is more likely to be literate and read outside sources of news and information than is the traditional student. In the second instance, the traditionalist would view the criterion of morality as tied almost exclusively to religion, while the "modern" student would be more open to other interpretations.

The modernity test used in Tanzania was based on analyses prepared by Inkeles and Smith (1974), Dodd (1969), and Grant (1964). Although the

Tanzanian modernity scale uses many of the Inkeles dimensions of tradi-
tion-modernity, the format calls for agree-disagree responses, not as "yes"
or "no," but in terms of degree (agree strongly, agree, disagree, disagree
strongly). The scale is based on previous studies of modernity that address
dimensions such as openness to change, orientation to the future, concern
with planning, individual competitiveness, and achievement orientation.
The scale can be validated by relating the modernity scores obtained to
indices such as education that are assumed to have some connection with
modernity. The reliability coefficient on the twenty-one-item scale used in
Tanzania is 0.76, which suggests a fairly accurate measure of modern
attitudes.

Further Training and Employment

The follow-up survey solicited information on what the members of the
base-year cohort were actually doing one year after graduation. For those
who were in training or continuing their education, the type of institution
and field of study were recorded. For those in employment, we surveyed
graduates' sector of economic activity, occupation, earnings, hours of
work, and how long they had to wait before getting a job. For those still
seeking employment, information was obtained on their interim financial
resources. Job changes within the one-year span were noted as well.

Test Reliability

In psychometrics, it is essential that measurements be reliable. The
devices used for measurement, such as achievement tests, must be applied
consistently to ensure that the results are repeatable and that error is kept
to a minimum

When a well-anchored rifle is fired, if the shots are widely scattered
about the target the rifle is said to be unreliable. If the shots are closely
concentrated around the target the rifle is considered reliable. Similarly,
when achievement tests are unreliable, it becomes difficult to draw firm
conclusions because the variance among subjects becomes too large.
Highly reliable test instruments display little random error and hence more
consistency. Usually, as random error increases, reliability is reduced until
the point is reached at which all observed variance is random and reliability is zero.

Statistical methods have been devised to indicate the reliability of a test
by evaluating the relationship among its components (usually items or
questions). One common procedure is to look at all possible correlations
of test items and compute an average intercorrelation between them by

correlating all parts of the measure with the total score. When the average correlation among test items is low, so is the reliability coefficient. In general, as the number of items and the average correlation among them increase, reliability takes on a larger vaue as well. Reliability values can range between 0 and 0.99. Usually 0.60 is the minimum level at which a test is judged to be reliable.

Reliability coefficients for the various tests administered in Colombia and Tanzania range above the minimum (from 0.61 to 0.69). The acceptable minimum coefficient, however, depends on what the tests are to be used for. If students are to be selected for curriculum programs on the basis of their examination results, for example, reliabilities from 0.85 to 0.89 would be mandatory because a person's future career should not be determined by a test that was only moderately reliable. But, if the objective is to detect differences among groups, then acceptable reliabilities can be considerably lower than the level obtained in this study.

Psychometric measurements must also be valid in the sense that they in fact measure what they purport to measure. The validity of tests developed for this study can be established only by judgment. Do the tests, according to expert opinion, appear to measure vocational, agricultural, or commercial knowledge? Because all items were extracted from former vocational achievement tests by teachers familiar with the subject areas in the respective countries, it is reasonable to assume that the final tests adequately represent the curriculum of the given vocational field.

List of Variables

The following list summarizes the clusters of the main dependent and independent variables for which information was collected in this study.

DEPENDENT VARIABLES

For those still in school

Continuous cognitive measures of performance in achievement tests developed by the local research teams

Attitude measures (such as willingness to enter jobs or to work in rural areas)

Plans for continuing further education (whether the graduate plans to seek entry to another educational institution)

Student expectations about future employment with regard to the sector of economic activity, occupation, earnings, and length of time before obtaining the first job

For those in first employment

Length of time unemployed since leaving school

Dummy 0–1 variable, the 1 indicating employment in an economic sector j (for example, in agriculture)

Earnings in first employment

For those who graduated several years previously

Continuous variable measuring the total time unemployed since graduation

Economic sector of first employment (information obtained retrospectively)

Sector of current occupation

First employment earnings (information obtained retrospectively)

Current earnings

First occupation (information obtained retrospectively)

Current occupation

Dummy 0–1 variable denoting the graduate's opinion on specific questions ("Do you feel you use the skills you were taught?")

INDEPENDENT VARIABLES

Student background

Set of 0–1 dummy variables indicating the student's or graduate's origin (such as farm or nonfarm)

Father's occupation

Father's income

Year of birth

Score on aptitude test

School characteristics

(Common values for all students and graduates of the same school)

Dummy 0–1 variable, the 1 indicating a diversified school (the target group) and the 0 indicating a school in the control group (private, technical, or nondiversified)

Dummy variable indicating the specialized field of study (subject bias) of a particular school

Student-teacher ratio of the particular school or class

School expenditure per pupil

Composite index of school quality, such as the percentage of teaching personnel having certain qualifications

Regional characteristics

Labor force participation rate of the region

Regional GNP per capita

Region in which the school is located

5. The Colombia Case Study

Dᴜʀɪɴɢ ᴛʜᴇ 1970s, Colombia, like many other industrializing nations, faced the policy dilemma of how to match education and training to changing economic needs in a way that would expand secondary education opportunities on an egalitarian basis. Policymakers concluded that teaching prevocational courses in secondary schools would help create a labor force more capable of using advanced agricultural, commercial, and industrial-manufacturing technology. Thus, a practical bias was introduced into the formal secondary educational curriculum, so as to channel students' attention toward employment in those sectors.

The Institutos Nacionales de Educación Media (ɪɴᴇᴍs) introduced in Colombia for that purpose, are similar to Europe's comprehensive schools (for a description, see chapter 2). Provision was also made for less formal training in centers that were closely linked to work within the local community. Called Centros Auxiliares de Servicios Docentes (ᴄᴀsᴅ), these schools pull students out of their formal schools for two or three days each week to give them special "hands-on" training in vocational skills locally in demand. With the spread of this system, it was expected that the content of secondary school training would increasingly reflect the prevailing availability of local jobs. Structural reforms were also undertaken to decentralize educational administration. (For a more comprehensive exposition of the Colombia study, see Psacharopoulos, Velez, and Zabalza 1985.)

The question addressed in this study is whether ɪɴᴇᴍ schools provide what the policymakers intended. In comparing the effectiveness of ɪɴᴇᴍ with non-ɪɴᴇᴍ (control) schools, five broad categories of questions were asked:

1. Do ɪɴᴇᴍ and control schools recruit students equally from all social backgrounds?
2. Are there significant differences in students' cognitive and noncognitive achievement between ɪɴᴇᴍ and non-ɪɴᴇᴍ schools across the various curriculum tracks?
3. If there are differences, how can they be accounted for?
4. How strongly do these differences affect postschool outcomes?
5. How cost-effective are the new schools?

Included in the second question are differences in graduates' specific achievements, occupational expectations, earning expectations, and sector of employment. Included in the third are effects of home environment and school quality on educational achievement. The fourth area seeks to determine how strongly the type of school or the curriculum content influences students' postschool prospects for more education, training, and access to the labor market.

In this chapter, we first discuss economic conditions in Colombia and review the Colombian educational system. After describing the characteristics of the student sample, we report the major differences among the outcomes of the various secondary school and alternative curricula, based on the 1981–82 longitudinal data set. The conclusions are checked against a longer time span in a tracer study of the 1978 cohort.

Background of the Study

With a US$1,400 gross national product (GNP) per capita and a 6 percent average annual growth rate during the 1970s (1.1 percent for 1979–83), Colombia has become a middle-income developing country. Manufacturing and industry, accounting for 47 percent of gross domestic product (GDP) and employing 23 percent of the labor force, grew at an average rate of 7 percent a year during the 1970s. Agriculture, supplying 31 percent of GDP and employing 30 percent of the labor force, increased by an annual rate of 5 percent during the same period. The service sector, accounting for 22 percent of GDP and 47 percent of the labor force, grew at an annual rate of 7 percent.

One-tenth of Colombia's economic growth during the 1970s has been attributed to improvements in the skill and educational level of the labor force (McCarthy, Hanson, and Kwon 1983). Employment growth has been concentrated in the middle-level skilled occupations and in industries in which education, training, and job experience are important. Labor productivity has markedly increased in agriculture, whose share of GDP dropped from 34 to 31 percent in the twenty-year period 1960–80, while the sector's share of the total labor force dropped from 52 to 30 percent. Over the same period the share of industry in GDP fell slightly, from 49 to 47 percent, while industrial employment as a share of the total labor force rose from 19 to 23 percent. The largest growth in employment occurred in the service sector, which grew from 29 to 47 percent of the labor force. Output from the service sector as a share of GDP, however, increased only from 17 to 22 percent.

Educational System

The Colombian educational system comprises a five-year primary school cycle followed by a six-year program of secondary education (see figure 5-1). While most children of primary school age were enrolled in schools in the mid-1980s, only half of the thirteen-year-olds were in secondary school (see figure 5-2). Of the latter, approximately half graduate from secondary school.

Until the early 1970s, most secondary schools in Colombia were privately run and academically oriented. Most graduates of secondary schools came from an academic stream that prepared them for university enrollment but little else. These graduates were judged ill-prepared for most jobs, other than clerical and sales, without further education. Their orientation, demographic pressures, and a strong social demand for uni-

Figure 5-1. *Flow Chart of the Colombian Educational System*

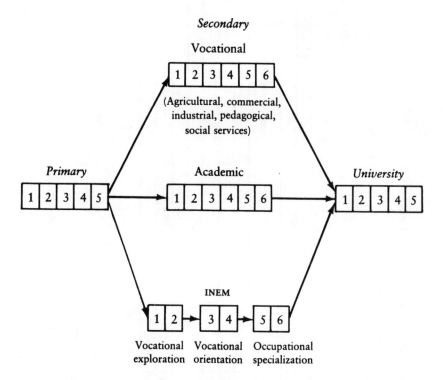

Secondary

Vocational

1 | 2 | 3 | 4 | 5 | 6

(Agricultural, commercial,
industrial, pedagogical,
social services)

Primary   Academic   University

1 | 2 | 3 | 4 | 5   1 | 2 | 3 | 4 | 5 | 6   1 | 2 | 3 | 4 | 5

INEM

1 | 2   3 | 4   5 | 6

Vocational   Vocational   Occupational
exploration   orientation   specialization

Figure 5-2. *Educational Pyramid, Colombia, 1968*

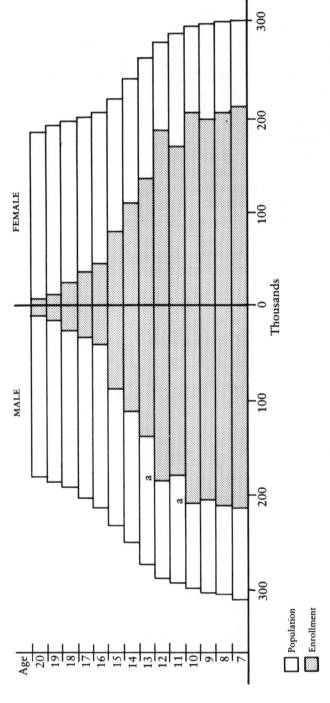

a. Portion of pyramid that reflects previous change of minimum age from eight to seven years and related intensive programs to re-enroll dropouts.

versity education resulted in (1) a proliferation of low quality over-crowded higher education institutions, (2) a surplus of university-trained graduates (such as engineers) in an economy already experiencing unem-ployment in excess of 10 percent at all levels of education, and (3) a high dropout rate among university enrollees (Haddad 1979).

These inefficiencies, combined with perceived changes in the manpower needs of an expanding economy, prompted the government to diversify secondary education in public schools. Aligning instruction in secondary schools with the more vocational-technical skills needed in the labor market was viewed as an urgent need (Varner 1965; Low-Maus 1971).

In 1973, 20 percent of the cohort of relevant age was enrolled in secondary schools. Of these, 70 percent followed the academic course of study, 9 percent studied to become primary school teachers, and 21 percent attended separate vocational programs in agriculture, commerce, technical, and industrial trades. Under the new program of diversified education, nineteen special secondary schools (INEMs) were built to sup-plement the purely vocational and academic schools. It was projected that, as a result of diversification, by 1980 roughly 48 percent of secondary school students would be enrolled in vocational-technical programs, and of these students, 15 percent would be following a diversified curriculum. However, because of the doubling of the secondary school enrollment base (from 20 to 40 percent of the secondary-school-age population in less than ten years), academic schools have maintained their share of enrolled students, so that INEM students represent only 3 percent of the entire secondary school cohort (DANE 1976).

The secondary education system in Colombia comprises three types of schools. First, public and private general academic schools (*colegios* and *liceos*), which teach essentially humanities and science, represent the bulk of secondary education and prepare students for university entrance. In 1981, close to 1.3 million students (72 percent of secondary enrollment) were in these schools. Second, trade and teacher training colleges, or single-track trade schools (*univocacionales*), represent another 25 percent of the secondary school population; these specialize in agriculture, com-merce, industrial-technical subjects, or teacher training. Although their students take core academic subjects, the schools emphasize vocational subjects throughout all six years. The third type of school is the INEM, which corresponds to the comprehensive multi-track secondary schools found in industrialized countries, offering academic and vocational cur-ricula under one roof. While accounting for only a small percentage of secondary school enrollment, these schools are thought to represent the "wave of the future" since it is hoped that they would ultimately be able to attract students away from academic programs in the liceos and colegios and into trade courses.

Figure 5-3. *Structure of the Six-Year INEM Program, Colombia*

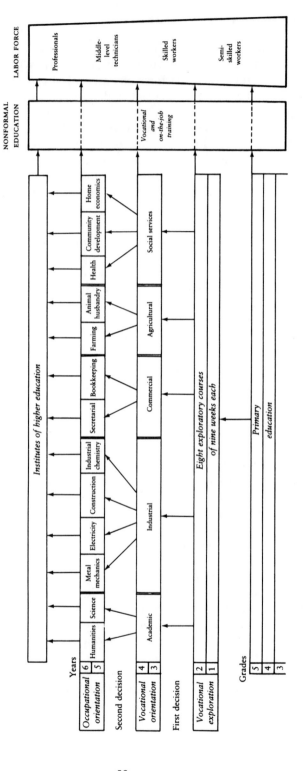

The INEMS offer a six-year program, as shown in figure 5-3. During the first two-year cycle, students are exposed to prevocational subjects to acquaint them with knowledge and career options in the various trades. Vocational learning occurs side-by-side with regular academic course work, with an emphasis on core academic subjects. The second two-year cycle is oriented to vocational subjects, such as agriculture or commerce, along with continuing academic study. Those who leave school at this stage are regarded as prepared for further training, for example in Servicio Nacional de Aprendizaje (SENA, national apprenticeship service) or in on-the-job apprenticeships. During the last two-year cycle, further specialization takes place. For example, a student enrolled in the industrial training program in the preceding cycle might now focus on metalwork, construction, or electrical mechanics, although more than half the time is still devoted to traditional academic course work.

Regardless of track or school placement, all students spend two-thirds of class time on academic work and one-third on vocational subjects in the first two years of the six-year secondary school cycle. Specifically, students take mostly mathematics, languages, social studies, and courses in natural sciences. In the last four years of the cycle, students enrolled in vocational programs specialize increasingly in the vocational subjects of their choice. By the last year of secondary school, agriculture students, for example, spend on the average sixteen of thirty-eight hours each week on such agricultural topics as crop production, cattle raising, and cooperative management. This represents 42 percent of their class time. In certain other tracks, the ratio is closer to 50 percent. Hence, in examining the effectiveness of this education, it becomes imperative to assess separately exposure to course work variables, both academic and vocational, in order to control for differences in learning outcomes by subject knowledge.

After completing the six-year course, students are issued diplomas, which give them the option of attending a university or some other form of higher education, such as a technical institute, provided the holder also passes the requisite entrance exams. Other graduates of the course seek employment in highly specialized trades.

A number of observations can be made concerning the quality and content of Colombia's secondary schools. The *academic secondary schools* vary greatly in quality of existing facilities, staff, and equipment. Some of the private schools were not originally built for educational use and therefore lack many features required for teaching modern science and mathematics. Traditional teaching methods with an emphasis on lecturing and rote learning are still the rule. But a recent shift away from the humanities and languages to mathematics and science has begun to broaden the range of teaching styles. Examination practices are geared closely to university selection.

Industrial education is mostly public, and the retention rate is similar to that found in the general academic schools. Five- to six-year courses lead to positions as skilled craftsmen in industry (for example, metal mechanics, electrical mechanics, construction, foundry work, and auto repair). Standards of training vary widely, but most graduates have been able to find employment in large manufacturing and other industries.

Commercial education is mostly private and mainly attracts females. Completion of a four-year program yields a certificate in typing, secretarial services, and bookkeeping; those who attend the full six-year course usually become accountants and data clerks.

Agricultural schools are 20 percent private and 80 percent public. Many lack facilities and equipment for proper teaching of agricultural technology. Of all single-track vocational schools, agricultural schools are perhaps most criticized for being too costly and inefficient—either teaching unduly specialized skills at too early an age or not meeting the demands for skilled farmers or middle-level agricultural technicians.

Curriculum schedules for the various tracks in all types of secondary schools, both public and private, are established by the Ministry of Education. Some variation occurs within schools because some lack the resources for teaching certain subjects.

Sampling Procedures

Sampling proceeded in two stages. In the first stage, twenty-seven cities (four large and twenty-three medium-size) were identified as having both INEM and control vocational schools (see figure 5-4). Sixteen INEM schools were selected. Within each INEM school, the population was established for all final (sixth) year students enrolled in each of the five curriculum programs. Then students from each curriculum program were randomly selected in proportion to their number in the INEM population. Sixty-seven percent of the students in INEM schools were included in the sample. The sample size was established to ensure enough observations in each curriculum program cell for a statistically significant test of differences among curriculum programs, with allowance for a possible 40 percent loss of respondents during the follow-up survey.

In the second stage of sampling, students in control schools (academic or straight vocational) were matched to those in the INEM schools already selected. The control schools were selected on the basis of their geographic proximity to the INEM schools and their similarity to the INEM schools in the curriculum programs offered. Five percent of Colombia's students in non-INEM schools were sampled.

To select academic control schools, the following procedure was used. Because these schools are either private or public and are located in either medium-size or large cities, a determination was first made of the number of academic schools necessary to represent each substratum (for example, government schools in large cities, private schools in medium-size cities). The goal was to include at least one control academic school in each of the twenty-three medium-size cities, and two or three control academic schools in each of the four large cities. The schools were then selected on a completely random basis. The same procedure was used to select single-track vocational schools teaching pedagogy, industrial trades, and commercial subjects.

The INEM and non-INEM subsamples cover roughly the same proportion

Figure 5-4. *Location of the INEM and Control Schools Surveyed, Colombia*

of the student population in each curriculum program—for example, 27 percent of commerce students in INEM schools and 30 percent of commerce students in non-INEM schools. Nearly twice as many students following academic programs were selected from control schools as from INEM schools (1,471 compared with 871) in order to take account of the heterogeneity of academic schools and to achieve a proportionate representation of public and private schools.

In the small substrata, such as private schools teaching industrial subjects, all schools and students were necessarily selected. For social services and agriculture, in which enrollments are very small, the selection embraced all schools and students graduating in the cities chosen for the sample and in nearby towns. The overall sample comprised a total of 8,051 students. (table 5-1).

Because of the limited time horizon of the follow-up of the 1981 cohort, the Colombian case study also included a retrospective survey of nearly 2,000 students who left INEM and control schools in 1978. The findings based on this component of the study are presented later in this chapter, following the analysis of the 1981 cohort.

In summary, there were two stages of sampling. First, sixteen INEM schools were selected and students sampled by curriculum modalities in such a way that 67 percent of all students in these schools were included in the samples. In a second stage, control schools were sampled in such a way they could be matched with INEMs already chosen, based on geographic proximity to the INEM schools. More important, all schools had to have similarity in course of instruction (that is, commerce with commerce, agriculture with agriculture, and so forth). Students in the control sample constitute 5 percent of Colombia's non-INEM students. (Descriptive statistics for the 1978 and 1981 cohorts are given in tables 5-64 through 5-67.)

Table 5-1. *Sample Distribution by School Type and Subject, Colombia, 1981 Cohort*

Subject	INEM	Control		Total
Academic	871	1,471	(35)[a]	2,342
Agricultural	174	370	(11)	544
Commercial	957	973	(24)	1,930
Industrial	869	945	(17)	1,814
Pedagogical	—[b]	767	(22)	767
Social services	380	274	(4)	654
Total	3,251(16)	4,800	(113)	8,051 (129)

a. Figures in parentheses are the number of schools.
b. INEM schools offer all subjects except the teacher training specialization.

Socioeconomic Profile of 1981 Cohort

Students entering secondary education often have a preferred school and course of study in mind. A student's choice of secondary school may be influenced by how well he or she has done in primary school and by certain family attributes, herein referred to collectively as socioeconomic status. Such characteristics as parents' income, occupation, education, and ownership of property indicate the family's resources for assisting children in further education. A student's age, sex, and innate ability are also thought to influence the choice of secondary school program.

Table 5-2 compares population and sample distributions by father's occupation and educational level. As the literature would lead one to expect, the graduating secondary school cohort comes disproportionately from families whose household heads are in professional-managerial occupations or have secondary or tertiary education. Professional classes are three times overrepresented in the secondary school sample relative to their number in the overall population. Students from blue-collar families are slightly overrepresented as well, reflecting the large number of our

Table 5-2. *Sample Representativeness by Father's Sector of Occupation and Educational Level, Colombia, 1981 Cohort*
(percent)

Father's background	Colombian population[a]	Base-year sample (1981)	Representation index[b]
Economic sector of occupation			
Agriculture	35	19	54
Commercial	18	19	105
Industrial (construction, manufacturing, trades)	28	39	140
Professional, technical	6	17	283
Services	13	8	62
Educational level			
No education	25	3	12
Primary education	55	62	113
Secondary education	16	28	175
University education	2	6	300

a. Based on census data, DANE (1976, p. 26).

b. The base-year sample as a percentage of the Colombian population. A value below 100 indicates underrepresentation of the particular socioeconomic group in the sample. A value over 100 denotes overrepresentation.

sample in vocational schools and curriculum programs. Farmers are underrepresented proportionate to their number in the population.

This comparison of the characteristics of the sample with those of the Colombian population as a whole gives an idea of the sample's selectivity. Comparing fathers' occupations with students' curriculum programs (table 5-3) shows that proportionately more INEM students come from blue-collar worker families than do control group students. INEMs were built in the poorest areas of the cities and were intended to provide educational opportunities to students from poorer socioeconomic backgrounds. Presumably, some of these students might not have attended high school if INEMs had not been introduced.

Table 5-3. *Father's Occupation by Students' School Type and Curriculum, Colombia, 1981 Cohort*
(percent)

Curriculum and father's occupation	INEM	Control
Academic		
Nonmanual employee	40	37
Business owner	10	12
Blue-collar worker	41	29
Agricultural worker	9	15
Agricultural		
Nonmanual employee	34	16
Business owner	7	6
Blue-collar worker	59	36
Agricultural worker	21	60
Commercial		
Nonmanual employee	37	38
Business owner	11	15
Blue-collar worker	42	37
Agricultural worker	8	9
Industrial		
Nonmanual employee	35	39
Business owner	8	12
Blue-collar worker	51	46
Agricultural worker	7	9
Social services		
Nonmanual employee	37	36
Business owner	12	13
Blue-collar worker	56	39
Agricultural worker	11	23

Note: For each group, column percentages do not necessarily add up to 100 because of overlapping classifications.

There are significant differences in family characteristics among students following different curriculum programs (table 5-4). Essentially, more affluent families prefer academic and commercial subjects for their children and prefer control to INEM schools. Regardless of the type of school, they deem agriculture least attractive for study, followed closely by industrial training. Thus, the social demand for secondary education among wealthier students favors non-INEM schools and academic and commercial subjects.

Internal Efficiency of Schools

Because students in all curriculum programs and types of secondary schools had been exposed to some academic course work, it seemed reasonable to test their academic achievement. The questions used ad-

Table 5-4. *Students' Family Characteristics by School Type and Curriculum, Colombia, 1981 Cohort*

Curriculum and family characteristic	INEM	Control
Academic		
Family income (thousands of monthly pesos)	24.60	37.56
Father's education (years)	6.9	7.8
Number of books at home	79	91
Agricultural		
Family income (thousands of monthly pesos)	17.23	19.34
Father's education (years)	5.4	4.7
Number of books at home	60	57
Commercial		
Family income (thousands of monthly pesos)	22.86	31.08
Father's education (years)	5.6	6.6
Number of books at home	71	82
Industrial		
Family income (thousands of monthly pesos)	21.37	25.52
Father's education (years)	5.6	6.3
Number of books at home	67	84
Social services		
Family income (thousands of monthly pesos)	19.59	29.56
Father's education (years)	5.5	7.4
Number of books at home	76	84
Overall		
Family income (thousands of monthly pesos)	22.22	30.28
Father's education (years)	5.9	6.8
Number of books at home	66	73

dressed problems frequently found in biology, chemistry, math, and social science classes, where achievement scores could be aggregated or used separately. Vocational achievement tests were based on the nationally recognized curriculum content in various vocational subjects. The tests were developed by the local research team and exhibit coefficients of reliability above 0.60 (Velez and Rojas 1983).

Cognitive Achievement

Differences in achievement scores by curriculum program and school type also were studied (table 5-5). To help in the comparison of students in different programs and schools, the tests were standardized to a mean of 50 and a standard deviation of 10 (see figure 5-5). On the academic test, students in the INEM academic program scored highest (54), and students of agriculture in control schools scored 45, or about one full standard deviation, below the top group. (A ten-point difference in this context is equivalent to the test score differences often found between minority and other students in the United States.)

The mean scores of students following different programs in INEM and control schools, shown in table 5-5 (not yet adjusted for out-of-school factors), reveal that those who specialized in a particular subject scored higher than others in the respective test. Figure 5-6 also shows that INEM schools often outperform control schools in other subjects, including academic knowledge. For example, agriculture students in INEM schools scored three points, or one-third standard deviation, above agriculture

Figure 5-5. *Relationship between Standard Deviation Units and the Percentage of Students Scoring above the Mean in a Normal Distribution*

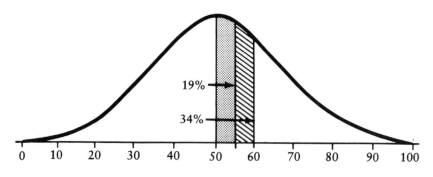

Mean = 50
Standard deviation = 10

students in control schools. In tests of knowledge of academic subjects, INEM students often perform better than their control counterparts. This may be explained by the fact that in INEM schools commercial, agricultural, and industrial students are taught academic subjects alongside INEM academic students. Furthermore, the INEM vocational programs usually require an additional rigorous program of applied math and science courses aimed at reinforcing the vocational specialization. The results just described suggest that INEM schools have their intended effect of exposing all their students to a quality academic program.

Mean achievement scores by selected characteristics of the entire sample also were considered in the study (table 5-6). One notable feature is that students with a farming background score substantially higher than the rest in the agricultural test.

Because the comparison of mean differences in INEM and control test scores described so far has not taken account of out-of-school influences, such as sex, age, innate ability, and social origins, it is uncertain whether the differences result from what is learned in school. For example, students in control schools might be initially better prepared when entering secondary school than are INEM students. To try to distinguish the effects of these influences, we first looked at students' scores in general aptitude tests. General aptitude tests can be used to control for reasoning power, or personal ability to think, that might influence one's score in tests of specialized knowledge. Scores were taken from school records based on the national examination administered by the Instituto Colombiano para el Fomento de la Educación Superior (ICFES 1979, 1980) to students in secondary school. These tests, similar to the American Scholastic Aptitude Tests (verbal and quantitative), tapped reasoning power and were not related to particular subjects taught in school.

Regression analysis was then employed to control for the influence of general reasoning power and other out-of-school factors on students' scores in tests on the curricula they had followed. Students of pedagogy were treated as the reference group (omitted dummy variable) because that subject is not taught in INEM schools. Eleven variables were included as proxies for out-of-school influences on learning. From table 5-7 it is clear that verbal aptitude is a prime out-of-school determinant of the general academic achievement measures. For the total achievement score of INEM students following an academic curriculum, the regression coefficient is 4.603, with a t-value of 9.30. This is interpreted as follows. The size of the coefficient denotes that in the academic achievement test, INEM academic students scored an average of 4.6 points above the reference group of students following pedagogy programs. Since the t-value is higher than two, students attending academic programs in INEM schools score much higher than the reference group.

Table 5-5. *Mean Scores by School Type and Curriculum, Colombia, 1981 Cohort*

School type and curriculum	Achievement score					
	Academic	Agricultural	Commercial	Industrial	Pedagogical	Social services
INEM						
Academic	**54**	51	49	51	51	54
Agricultural	50	**61**	47	51	50	49
Commercial	48	51	**60**	49	49	49
Industrial	50	51	48	**58**	50	49
Social services	47	51	47	49	53	**56**
Overall	50.5	51.4	51.4	51.6	50.2	51.0
Control						
Academic	**50**	49	49	49	49	50
Agricultural	45	**58**	46	49	49	46
Commercial	50	48	**57**	48	47	49
Industrial	51	48	46	**53**	48	48
Pedagogical	49		45	47	**58**	50
Social services	49	51	47	47	49	**54**
Overall	49.5	48.6	48.6	48.4	49.8	49.0

Note: Raw scores (x) on all tests are standardized (normalized) to a mean of 50 and a standard deviation of 10, according to the formula
$T = [10 (x - \bar{x})/S_x] + 50$.
Scores in boldface refer to those taking the test in the area of their curriculum specialization.

Figure 5-6. *Academic and Vocational Achievement by School Type, Colombia, 1981 Cohort*

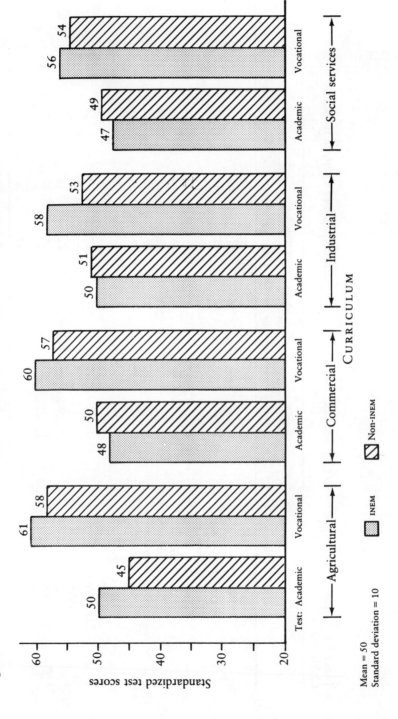

Table 5-6. *Mean Achievement Scores by Selected Student Characteristics, INEM and Control Schools, Colombia, 1981 Cohort*

Student characteristics	Achievement score					
	Academic	*Agricultural*	*Commercial*	*Industrial*	*Pedagogical*	*Social services*
Sex						
Male	51	51	48	51	49	49
Female	49	49	52	48	51	51
Father's occupation						
Farmer	48	52	48	49	49	49
Blue-collar	49	49	50	50	49	49
Nonmanual employee	51	50	50	50	50	50
Business owner	51	50	51	49	50	51
Self-employed	50	49	50	50	50	50
Type of school						
Public	51	51	50	50	49	48
Private	48	47	49	47	50	51
Other						
Urban born	50	50	50	50	50	50
Rural born	48	50	49	49	49	48
Repeater in primary school	49	50	50	50	49	50
Did not repeat	50	50	50	49	50	50

Of the ten dummy variables that were used to denote school placement and curriculum program followed, INEM-academic has the strongest effect on total academic score. Judging from the signs and magnitudes of the regression coefficients, INEM schools on balance seem to teach academic skills better than do the control schools.

The results of regressing achievement scores in industrial, commercial, agriculture, and social services tests on variables for school type and out-of-school influences are shown in table 5-8. Here, unlike in the previous table, we tried to isolate the effect of INEM versus control schools on vocational achievement. For example, the industrial achievement of industrial students enrolled in INEM and in control schools is compared. (The reference group in this case consists of all students, whether INEM or control, who take no industrial course work whatsoever.) With the exception of agriculture, the results for the vocational tests show that INEM students significantly outperform those in control schools in these tests, even after allowance for the effects of a series of out-of-school variables.

Influence of School Resources

Students' achievement may be influenced by specific school resources. Table 5-9 shows several quality indicators by school type and curriculum program. For the various INEM programs, total expenditure per student is very similar and averages 1,615 pesos a month. In non-INEM schools, academic and commercial curricula cost less per student (44 percent and 31 percent, respectively) than the average cost per student across all programs, while the agricultural and industrial specializations cost substantially more than the average. According to these figures, INEM schools are not much more costly to operate than the smaller public and private single-track schools. (These figures do not cover the capital costs of equipment or buildings and do not separate public from private control schools, a distinction that will be made later.)

Pupil-teacher ratios are similar among INEM tracks, and classes in INEMs are on average smaller than those in control schools. INEM schools have larger enrollments than control schools and have done remarkably well not only in adequately staffing their programs but also in attracting qualified teachers. INEM students clearly spend more of their class time on vocational subjects, and they also have better access to laboratories for practical work (see table 5-9).

Do the variables that affect school quality also influence cognitive achievement scores in academic and vocational subjects and, if so, are there differences between INEM and control schools? To test for such influences, one can again apply a multiple regression procedure, but with an expanded set of control variables.

The influence of in-school and out-of-school variables on two achieve-

Table 5-7. *Academic Achievement as a Function of School Type and Out-of-School Influences, Colombia, 1981 Cohort*

Independent variable	Total academic achievement		Verbal achievement		Mathematical achievement	
	Coefficient	t-value	Coefficient	t-value	Coefficient	t-value
Out-of-school factors						
Male	0.264	0.87	2.254[a]	9.20	−1.047	3.52
Age	−0.090	1.20	−0.554[a]	9.13	0.109	1.49
Family owns business[b]	−0.0951[a]	2.68	0.275	0.95	0.105	0.30
Household books	0.010[a]	4.07	0.004[a]	2.09	−0.010[a]	4.29
Father's education	0.087[a]	2.36	0.034	1.14	−0.115[a]	3.17
Log of family income	0.268[a]	3.27	0.244[a]	3.68	0.059	0.72
Father is employer[b]	0.802	1.85	0.456	1.29	0.146	0.34
Father blue-collar	−0.441	1.15	0.325	1.04	0.297	0.79
Father nonmanual employee	−0.419	1.49	0.320	1.40	−0.058	0.21
Verbal aptitude	0.416[a]	28.24	0.416[a]	34.86	0.051[a]	3.50
Math aptitude	0.067[a]	4.79	0.250[a]	22.06	−0.013	0.97

School type and curriculum

INEM

Academic	4.603[a]	9.30	1.274[a]	3.17	−3,976[a]	8.17
Agricultural	1.191	1.27	1.359	1.78	5.519[a]	5.97
Commercial	0.329	0.67	0.193	0.49	5.823[a]	12.13
Industrial	2.626[a]	4.89	2.040[a]	4.68	−7.685	14.53
Social services	−0.168	0.26	−0.816	1.58	−6.832[a]	10.92
Control						
Academic	0.732	1.58	−0.329	0.87	−3.916[a]	8.58
Agricultural	−0.474	0.71	−0.456	0.85	4.343[a]	6.65
Commercial	0.277	0.56	1.720[a]	4.27	2.646[a]	5.42
Industrial	1.541[a]	2.88	2.505	5.77	−5.345[a]	10.15
Social services	−0.567	0.60	−0.325	0.43	−0.055[a]	0.06
Constant	22.062[a]	10.90	27.753[a]	16.91	49.009[a]	24.63
R^2	0.22		0.43		0.23	
Sample size	5,838		5,838		5,838	

Note: Omitted occupational categories are farmer and self-employed; omitted school subject is pedagogy.

a. Statistically significant at the 5 percent level or better.

b. Despite the apparent similarity between "Family owns business" and "Father is employer," these variables behave quite differently from one another statistically.

Table 5-8. *Vocational Achievement Scores as a Function of School Type and Out-of-School Characteristics, Colombia, 1981 Cohort*

Independent variable	Agricultural achievement		Commercial achievement		Industrial achievement		Social services achievement	
	Coefficient	t-value	Coefficient	t-value	Coefficient	t-value	Coefficient	t-value
Out-of-school factors								
Male	0.950[a]	3.66	−0.804[a]	3.20	2.337[a]	8.07	−1.495	5.72
Age	0.141	1.81	0.153[a]	2.10	0.023	0.30	0.069	0.89
Family owns business	−0.497	1.34	−0.497	1.43	−0.551	1.48	−0.310	0.85
Household books	0.007[a]	2.59	0.003	1.38	0.009[a]	3.31	0.011[a]	4.24
Father's education	0.006	0.15	0.089[a]	2.50	0.026	0.69	0.153[a]	4.06
Log of family income	0.120	1.40	0.255[a]	3.18	0.125	1.45	0.351[a]	4.15
Father is employer	−0.593	1.30	0.346	0.81	−0.635	1.40	0.005	0.01
Father blue-collar	−1.427[a]	3.55	0.012	0.03	−0.972[a]	2.42	−0.280	0.71
Father nonmanual employee	−0.803[a]	2.73	0.041	0.15	−0.531	1.81	−0.701[a]	2.42
Verbal aptitude	0.233[a]	15.20	0.132[a]	9.17	0.112[a]	7.27	0.356[a]	23.50
Math aptitude	0.001	0.05	0.051[a]	3.74	0.029	1.96	0.001	0.04
Curriculum								
INEM specialty	10.970[a]	12.12	12.921[a]	35.86	6.385[a]	14.98	5.855[a]	10.20
Control specialty	11.500[a]	19.53	8.851[a]	23.13	1.070[a]	2.53	1.084	1.17
Constant	33.235[a]	15.95	32.249[a]	16.42	38.231[a]	18.30	25.996[a]	12.64
R^2	0.13		0.25		0.09		0.15	
Sample size	5,838		5,838		5,838		5,838	

Note: Each dependent variable is the score on the particular test in that column. The INEM specialty dummy refers to students enrolled in the INEM track corresponding to the particular test in that column. The control specialty variable represents students in the non-INEM specialty track. Regression coefficients are to be interpreted with reference to the omitted category—that is, all students not following that particular subject.

a. Statistically significant at the 5 percent level or better.

74

ment scores—one in the academic and one in the commercial curriculum program—has been studied (table 5-10). The results indicate that school quality has a considerable impact on both scores. Per pupil expenditure, a major proxy of school quality, significantly influences academic, but not commercial, achievement.

Another way to assess the impact of the INEM curriculum is depicted in table 5-11. For this table, the entire sample is divided into five groups on the basis of curriculum. For example, the first group under consideration consists of all students following an academic curriculum (1,545). Of these, roughly half (730) were in INEM schools and the remainder were in control schools. After statistically controlling for the influences of background and ability factors listed in table 5-10, as well as for teachers' mean salary, in a multiple regression equation, it is possible to determine the effect of curriculum on students' test scores. In the first example, INEM program students earned 3.28 points more on average than control students in the academic achievement test, after adjustments for differences in background, ability, and teachers' mean salary. Students in INEM indus-

Table 5-9. *Mean Indicators of School Quality by School Type and Curriculum, Colombia, 1981 Cohort*

School type and curriculum	Per pupil school expenditure[a]	Teacher's qualifications[b]	Vocational intensity[c]	Practical labs[d]	Pupil/ teacher ratio
INEM					
Academic	1,609	37	28	50	30
Agricultural	1,653	50	42	74	36
Commercial	1,612	47	50	47	28
Industrial	1,619	45	53	45	30
Social services	1,609	63	49	36	32
Average	1,615	46	46	47	30
Control[e]					
Academic	1,029	24	15	27	28
Agricultural	2,465	44	40	15	30
Commercial	1,270	55	20	50	36
Industrial	2,621	25	36	12	20
Pedagogical	1,062	70	30	45	36
Social services	1,783	38	30	31	18
Average	1,845	43	25	40	34

a. Monthly recurrent per pupil expenditure (in pesos).

b. Percentage of teachers with in-service training.

c. Percentage of time spent on vocational subjects.

d. Percentage of schools with science laboratories rated as having an "above average" supply of equipment and materials for biology, physics, and chemistry courses.

e. Control category includes private schools.

Table 5-10. *Academic and Commercial Achievement Scores as a Function of Out-of-School and School Characteristics, Colombia, 1981 Cohort*

Independent variable	Academic achievement		Commercial achievement	
	Coefficient	t-value	Coefficient	t-value
Intercept	23.748[a]	10.46	30.910[a]	13.62
Out-of-school factors				
Male	0.531	1.56	−0.598	1.75
Age	−0.070	0.82	0.484	0.57
Family owns business	−1.229[a]	3.07	−0.711[a]	1.78
Books owned by household	0.012[a]	4.25	0.003	1.06
Father's education	0.106[a]	2.49	0.345	0.81
Log of family income	0.118	1.31	0.235[a]	2.63
Father blue-collar	−0.880[a]	2.10	−0.390	0.93
Father nonmanual employee	−0.448	1.42	0.236	0.75
Father is employer	1.119[a]	2.27	1.071[a]	2.17
Verbal aptitude	0.387[a]	23.38	0.135[a]	8.17
Math aptitude	0.064[a]	4.08	0.062[a]	3.97
School type and curriculum				
INEM				
Academic	4.325[a]	7.71	3.832[a]	6.83
Agricultural	0.123	0.13	1.862[a]	1.97
Commercial	−0.007	0.01	15.289[a]	28.12
Industrial	1.833[a]	3.10	3.478[a]	5.88
Social services	0.291	0.43	2.551[a]	3.80
Control				
Academic	0.261	0.48	4.154[a]	7.58
Agricultural	−1.636[a]	2.24	1.554[a]	2.12
Commercial	0.763	1.43	11,043[a]	20.75
Industrial	0.372	0.53	0.412	0.58
Social services	−1.573	1.36	1.956	1.70
Other school characteristics				
Private school	−4.057[a]	9.59	−1.418[a]	3.36
Mean teacher salary	−0.62E7[a]	15.96	−0.32E7[a]	10.08
Per student expenditure	0.002[a]	18.91	0.001[a]	9.70
R^2	0.30		0.31	
Sample size	4,233		4,233	

Note: Curriculum categories are evaluated in relation to pedagogy (the omitted category).
a. Statistically significant at the 5 percent level or better.

Table 5-11. *Gains in Achievement Test Scores Associated with the INEM Program, Colombia, 1981 Cohort*

Curriculum	Achievement test	Score gain	Number of students
Academic	Academic	3.28	1,545
Agricultural	Agriculture	—[a]	394
	Academic	—[a]	
Commercial	Commercial	5.20	1,271
	Academic	0.43	
Industrial	Industrial	15.71	297
	Academic	8.01	
Social services	Social services	4.47	377
	Academic	—[a]	

Note: Background and ability factors are controlled for as in table 5-10. All score gains are statistically significant at the 5 percent level or better.

a. No significant difference.

trial programs performed substantially better (by 15.71 points) than control students in the industrial achievement test and in the academic achievement test (by 8.01 points). This implies that to do well in industrial subjects by national standards, INEM students did not have to compromise their achievement in academic subjects. The same is true of commercial and social services students as well, though the advantage of the INEM program is less marked. There were no significant differences between the adjusted means of INEM and non-INEM agricultural students.

One may conclude that from a policy standpoint, the INEM vocational program is clearly superior to non-INEM programs in imparting vocational knowledge.

Effect of Course Time on Achievement

One would suppose that greater exposure to vocational curricula would enhance students' vocational knowledge. INEM schools have offered more hours of vocational course work per vocational student than have the control schools. But within either the control or the INEM group, what little variation could be found in number of hours spent on vocational subjects seldom proved of much consequence for test performance in the subdiscipline. Differences between control and INEM schools are far larger than these differences within groups. As an example, the percentage of course hours industrial arts students spent on their specialization in INEM and non-INEM schools is tabulated in table 5-12.

In summary, the substantial differences between INEM and control students in the proportion of course hours spent on vocational subjects contributed heavily to differences in achievement scores on those subjects. Within INEM or control schools, however, variation in course hours by itself did not contribute significantly to variations in students' performance.

Modernity Attitudes

The influence of schooling on the psychological disposition to adopt modern attitudes has been examined by Inkeles and Smith (1974), Holsinger (1973), and others. If schooling effectively modernizes values and roles, then it can aid in developing entrepreneurship and other talents considered to be prerequisites for economic growth and development. It is thought that investment in human capital can help to overcome many characteristics of the labor force that impede greater productivity, such as poor health, illiteracy, resistance to new knowledge, fear of change, and immobility. It is through education that a society allows individuals to fulfill their capacities and change their values, thus allowing them to participate productively in the economic process. For example, Lewis (1966, p. 109) remarked that "a developing economy needs to have at least 50 percent of its children in primary school if traditional customs and attitudes are to be changed significantly. The idea is simply that until a large proportion of the community at a fairly young age is exposed to new ideas and ways of doing things, few old ideas will be challenged, and economic development will be retarded." Secondary schooling should certainly enhance this process. Does diversification of secondary education influence the acquisition of modern attitudes?

In the Colombian base-year survey, a series of questions taken from Inkeles and Smith (1974) asked students to identify their attitudes and

Table 5-12. *Time Spent on Industrial Courses and Achievement, Colombia, 1981 Cohort*

Course hours spent on industrial arts	Mean industrial test score	
	Control	INEM
Less than 35 percent	52.4	—
35 to 40 percent	53.6	—
41 to 50 percent	—	56.6
More than 50 percent	—	58.8

— Not applicable.

values. With reference to hypothetical cases, students were asked how they viewed various problems endemic to economic development. When we compare response frequencies by item across INEM and non-INEM schools, we find little difference across nine items hypothesized to capture dispositions to modernity (table 5-13). However, when these nine items are coded from low to high, based on orientation to modernity, and when the responses are added to form a composite scale, we find a small but significant difference in favor of the INEM group mean. This suggests that INEM students are slightly more disposed to adopt modern attitudes than are control students.

As was done for the previous achievement functions, the authors regressed psychological modernity scores on dummy variables representing curriculum programs, school type, family background, age, sex, and natural ability. The objective in this case was to observe which programs within INEM and control schools and which characteristics of students' backgrounds were associated with more modern attitudes. Again, pedagogy students were the omitted category and served as the base-line comparator.

Inspection of table 5-14 shows several out-of-school characteristics to

Table 5-13. *Responses to Selected Questions
on Modernity Attitudes, Colombia, 1981 Cohort*

	Percentage responding affirmatively	
Item	INEM	*Control*
Education prepares one for work	51	51
Lack of social organization responsible for a country's underdevelopment	87	88
Reads newspaper regularly	20	22
Personal economic situation will be much better in five years	26	27
Hard work of Colombian people necessary for nation's future success	79	77
Degree or specialization more important asset for job performance than personal contacts	66	65
Persons can be morally good without having religious beliefs	81	76
More interested in international news than in local sports news	31	33
Agrees with looking for alternatives to traditional production methods	86	86

be associated with a modern outlook. Younger students, those with higher verbal facility, females, those coming from homes with many books, those with highly educated mothers, those with relatively higher family incomes, and those whose families owned a business are more likely to be modern in outlook.

When we observe the curriculum programs of students attending INEM and control schools, only two tracks appear positively and significantly to predict modernity scores—the commercial INEM track and the agricultural

Table 5-14. *Modernity as a Function of Background and School-Related Characteristics, Colombia, 1981 Cohort*

Independent variable	Coefficient	t-value
Intercept	17.86	
Out-of-school factors		
Male	-0.465^a	9.68
Age	-0.061^a	4.35
Number of siblings	0.005	0.71
Attended private primary school	-0.022	0.39
Father's log income	0.178^a	2.09
Family owns business	0.191^a	3.67
Dictionary in home	0.195^a	3.25
Father's education in years	0.007	0.88
Mother's education in years	0.026^a	3.25
Father clerical	-0.057	1.10
Father professional	0.037	0.58
Books in home	0.198^a	8.25
Verbal aptitude	0.035^a	17.50
Math aptitude	0.003	1.50
School type and curriculum		
INEM		
Academic	-0.063	0.83
Agricultural	-0.109	0.74
Commercial	0.235^a	3.13
Industrial	-0.163	1.40
Social services	0.103	0.95
Control		
Academic	-0.103	1.58
Agricultural	0.040	0.52
Commercial	0.291^a	2.64
Industrial	0.025	0.20
Social services	0.141	1.09
R^2	0.075	
Sample size	7,813	

a. Statistically significant at the 5 percent level or better.

control track. The former group constitutes close to 10 percent of the sample and explains why INEM students appear overall to be more modern than control students. Although one might expect modernity to correspond somewhat with entrepreneurial skills, which are produced by both commercial and agricultural curricula, it is not clear why all students in these curricula, regardless of school type, do not score equally well. Given the above results and the fact that the internal reliability for the modernity scale was low (of the order of 0.40), we cannot reach a firm conclusion that diversification of the curriculum affects modernity attitudes one way or another.

School Experience and Expectations

Students were asked about their experiences in school—for example, how many times they repeated a grade in primary and secondary school, whether they had completed all their secondary schooling at one institution, or whether they were satisfied with their current curriculum placement (see table 5-15).

When we compare students attending INEM and control schools, we find that those who have repeated primary school are just as likely to be found in either type of school, more INEM students than control students had graduated from a public primary school, and students from the two types of school were equally satisfied with their course of study. Students who had attended more than one secondary school were more likely to be found in non-INEM schools, where some 48 percent of students had switched schools at least once. Few INEM students had attended another secondary school prior to enrolling in their current INEM school. (There is a no-transfer policy in INEM schools.)

To measure their ambitions on completing secondary school, students were asked to indicate the economic sector they expected to work in and whether they expected to undertake further studies or training. Seventy percent expect to study and work part-time; very few intend to be working

Table 5-15. *Selected Student Characteristics by Type of School, Colombia, 1981 Cohort*
(percent)

Characteristic	INEM	Control
Attended a private primary school	11	25
Repeated a grade in primary school	28	25
Repeated a grade in secondary school	28	33
Satisfied with present course of study	86	86

full-time; while 24 percent of students hope to be enrolled full-time in university study (table 5-16). This suggests that the social demand for some form of continued schooling is extremely high. While INEM students perceive themselves as significantly less likely to undertake full-time higher education, three-fourths of them expect to be taking some course work while working part-time.

More INEM than non-INEM students see themselves as likely to work full-time than part-time immediately after graduating. This trend probably reflects the INEM students' less privileged socioeconomic backgrounds, which may lead to family pressure to earn outside income before or during their postsecondary studies. Although small in absolute terms, the difference between school types in this respect is statistically significant.

Students clearly expected to be engaged in the sector for which they had been trained in secondary school (table 5-17). Social services students were an exception; only one-fifth of them expected to be working in the public and personal service sector. Overall, 15 percent of the students were undecided. INEM commercial students are the most likely to continue in their sector of study, and INEM social services and agricultural students are the least likely to do so.

Table 5-16 indicated that 94 percent of all students wanted to continue their education beyond secondary school. When asked what kind of further studies they wished to pursue, 93 percent stated that they wished to continue to the university, with no overall difference between INEM and control schools (table 5-18). Those studying social services in control

Table 5-16. *Expected Student Destination by School Type and Subject, Colombia, 1981 Cohort*
(percent)

Curriculum	Work full-time		Study full-time		Study and work		Other	
	INEM	Control	INEM	Control	INEM	Control	INEM	Control
Academic	2	2	35	44	62	53	1	1
Agricultural	9	10	20	16	70	74	1	0
Commercial	5	4	8	30	86	65	1	1
Industrial	5	4	19	25	74	70	2	1
Pedagogical	—	3	—	11	—	85	—	1
Social services	8	7	15	27	77	66	0	0
Overall	5	4	20	29	74	66	1	1

— Not applicable; INEM schools do not offer teacher training.

Table 5-17. *Students Planning to Seek Employment Inside or Outside Their Curriculum Specialization, by Type of School, Colombia, 1981 Cohort*
(percent)

Curriculum	Work inside field		Work outside field		Undecided	
	INEM	Control	INEM	Control	INEM	Control
Academic	61	60	14	15	25	25
Agricultural	48	52	31	24	21	24
Commercial	87	82	5	8	8	10
Industrial	67	63	25	24	8	13
Pedagogical	—	91	—	5	—	4
Social services	20	24	49	46	31	30
Average[a]	57	56	25	24	18	20

— Not applicable.
a. Average excludes pedagogy.

schools, however, were the least inclined to go to university.

Students were also asked to indicate which benefits they most wanted from an occupation they might engage in. The most commonly cited were social prestige and possibilities for further training and job advancement. Most students, regardless of school or curriculum program, sought jobs that offered the chance to obtain further general or specific training.

A question in the base-year survey asked respondents to indicate what

Table 5-18. *Percentage of Students Planning to Enter University by School Type and Curriculum, Colombia, 1981 Cohort*
(percent)

Curriculum	INEM	Control	Total sample
Academic	95	94	95
Agricultural	93	90	91
Commercial	90	94	92
Industrial	92	94	93
Social services	92	79	87
Pedagogical	—	94	94
Overall	93	93	93

— Not applicable.
Note: Percentages refer to those who planned to continue their education beyond secondary school.

earnings they expected to receive upon graduating from secondary school. The response, a hypothetical statistic, reflects a student's perception of the labor market conditions. Students were also asked what they thought they would earn if they did not have a secondary school diploma. This hypothetical statistic has been used in many studies to measure the self-assessed opportunity cost of studying; the difference between the two estimates represents the perceived monetary value of a secondary school diploma.

Comparisons by school type and curriculum program (table 5-19) show that, in almost all instances, control students expect to earn much more than their INEM counterparts. Generally, students in vocational subjects expect to earn more than those pursuing an academic course. With no secondary school diploma, all students expect to earn less, but again, INEM students expect to earn even less relative to the control group. Across curriculum program and school type, the perceived difference in earnings attributable to a secondary school diploma averages 28 percent, with INEM commercial and control industrial students perceiving the largest difference (36 and 35 percent, respectively) and control commercial students perceiving the smallest (21 percent).

When anticipated earnings five years after graduation are examined,

Table 5-19. *Expected Earnings by School Type and Subject, Colombia, 1981 Cohort*
(monthly pesos)

Type of school and curriculum	Expected earnings with secondary diploma	Expected earnings, no diploma	Expected earnings in five years	Difference in earnings with diploma	
				Amount	Percent
INEM					
Academic	10,235	7,990	34,939	2,245	28
Agricultural	10,275	7,924	32,204	2,351	30
Commercial	10,686	7,868	34,114	2,818	36
Industrial	10,941	8,439	38,019	2,502	25
Social services	9,161	7,362	30,531	1,799	24
Average	10,440	7,974	34,666	2,466	31
Control					
Academic	10,718	8,652	42,080	2,066	24
Agricultural	11,587	9,147	32,530	2,440	27
Commercial	10,681	8,830	36,953	1,851	21
Industrial	11,846	8,779	39,900	3,067	35
Pedagogical	9,546	7,616	31,706	1,930	25
Social services	10,972	8,164	36,592	2,808	34
Average	10,877	8,645	38,337	2,232	26
Overall average	10,700	8,374	36,854	2,326	28

general academic students expected earnings slightly above the group average, while agricultural, commercial, and social services students continued to view their earnings as considerably below the average figure. Industrial trade students expected to earn 5 percent above the average figure.

Comparing Costs with Outcomes

To make any judgments concerning the relationship between differences in cognitive achievements and the costs of producing them, one must first look at the costs of the different curriculum programs (academic, industrial, commercial, social services, and agricultural) offered by INEMs and then compare these with the costs of the equivalent programs offered by non-INEM schools. The data sources and assumptions for the cost calculations are briefly described below. More details are to be found in Hinchliffe (1983).

Unit Costs by Curriculum

The cost of schooling can be looked at from three viewpoints—costs to society as a whole, to government, and to the individual (or household). The cost components that may be relevant to one or more of the three are (1) forgone output or earnings; (2) capital costs of buildings, furniture, and equipment; and (3) direct recurrent costs. For calculations of social costs, it is immaterial how (2) and (3) are financed. Costs to the government or individual, however, obviously depend on who pays for these expenditures.

Opportunity costs, as measured by the earnings of workers with primary education, were based on a study by Psacharopoulos (1983) that used earnings data from a 1975 urban labor market survey in Colombia. Earnings of a worker aged twenty-two with a primary education were calculated to be 5,813 pesos a month at 1981 prices. Analysis of per-pupil capital costs have been based on World Bank appraisal reports for the INEM and other secondary education projects in Colombia. Recurrent expenditures financed by households are available in some detail from the student questionnaire. Data on school expenditures—for salaries, maintenance, utilities, materials, and equipment—were based on the school questionnaire and used to compare the costs of INEM and non-INEM schools and curriculum programs.

Each INEM school offers five curriculum programs, and in many non-INEM schools there are at least two. The costs per student for each curriculum had to be estimated because INEM schools did not keep a

Table 5-20. *Annual Cost per Student by School Type and Curriculum, Colombia, 1981 Cohort*
(pesos)

School type and cost component	Curriculum					
	Academic	Agricultural	Commercial	Industrial	Social services	Overall average
INEM						
Recurrent cost borne by						
Household	3,300	3,300	2,800	2,800	2,600	2,900
Rest of society	19,300	19,800	19,300	19,400	19,300	19,400
Total direct cost[a]	25,700	26,200	25,200	25,300	25,000	25,400
Total social cost[b]	95,400	95,900	94,900	95,000	94,700	95,100
Control[c]						
Recurrent cost borne by						
Household	4,300	4,000	3,800	4,400	3,600	4,300
Rest of society	15,100	25,200	16,600	23,000	21,400	22,900
Total direct cost[a]	22,200	33,700	23,200	31,900	27,800	30,600
Total social cost[b]	91,900	103,400	92,900	101,600	97,500	100,300

a. Including capital costs and recurrent costs.
b. Including forgone earnings.
c. Public schools only.

separate account for each program. To do this, each student in the sample was hypothetically assigned to a curriculum program and given the average per-student cost of the school he was enrolled in. Then the average of these costs for all students within each program was calculated. The rationale for using this method was that any variations in average cost among schools resulted from different combinations of curriculum programs within schools. For example, if one school had a higher proportion of commercial students and a lower proportion of agricultural students than another school and its average expenditure per pupil was lower, the sole reason for the difference was assumed to be that expenditures for commerce were less than those for agriculture.

This method led to an underestimation of the costs in agricultural and industrial curricula and an overestimation of the costs in the other curricula, especially within the INEM group. This is demonstrated by differentiating costs in the control schools, which teach fewer subjects than do INEM schools and hence separate expense accounts can be distinguished. The unit cost data appear in table 5-20, while selected cost items are converted into indices by using the INEM overall average cost as the base in table 5-21.

The conclusions reached by examining recurrent costs were:

- Variations in costs between curriculum programs in INEMs are very small.
- INEM academic and commercial programs are about 20 percent and 14 percent more expensive, respectively, than the control counterparts.
- INEM agricultural and industrial programs are significantly less expensive than their control counterparts (28 percent and 25 percent, respectively); the same is true for the social services specialty, but to a lesser extent (11 percent).

When capital and recurrent costs are taken together, variations among INEMs are very slight. There are, however, wide differences between the INEM average cost and costs of single- and multi-track control schools, with the latters' agricultural and industrial specialties being one-third and one-quarter more expensive, respectively, than the average INEM cost.

The total social costs of students in all programs in both types of school (INEM and non-INEM) are dominated by earnings forgone, which are assumed to be equal for all students. Differences in total costs lie within a range of only 12 percentage points.

Differences in total social costs between school types and between academic and prevocational programs are small. For capital and recurrent costs alone, however, there are significant differences among non-INEM programs and between these and similar programs in INEM schools.

Table 5-21. *Unit Cost Index by School Type and Curriculum, Colombia, 1981 Cohort*
(INEM average = 100)

Cost component	Academic	Agricultural	Commercial	Industrial	Social services	Overall
INEM						
Capital and recurrent costs	100	103	99	100	98	100
Social cost (including forgone earnings)	100	101	100	100	99	100
Control						
Capital and recurrent costs	87	133	91	126	109	120
Social cost (including forgone earnings)	97	109	98	105	102	105

Cost-Effectiveness of Cognitive Achievement

To relate costs to achievement performance, three pieces of information were examined: annual unit costs (capital and recurrent) of keeping a student in secondary school, group test-score means in academic achievement, and the test-score mean in each vocational specialization (table 5-22). Scores were adjusted for innate ability and out-of-school characteristics.

There are two relevant sets of cost and achievement comparisons. The first compares students studying the same subject but attending different types of school; the second compares the academic control group with students who have taken prevocational subjects.

First, when the costs of academic programs are compared, INEM schools require expenditures of 25,700 pesos per student year, while control schools require only 22,200 pesos per student year. The difference of 3,500 pesos (16 percent) can be interpreted as the average amount of additional expenditure per student year required to raise the academic achievement score five points, or 0.3 of one standard deviation, for INEM academic students. This five-point difference, applied to the percentage of INEM students who outscore control students on academic tests of achievement, is 12 percent. (Note that because test scores are standardized to a mean of 50 and a standard deviation of 10, a ten-point difference would encompass approximately one-third of the students in a particular group; see figure 5-5.) In short, 12 percent more INEM students than non-INEM students score above the mean, but 16 percent more resources are required per student.

Second, the net cost and achievement differences between INEM and control schools for the various curriculum programs are shown in table 5-23. The INEM industrial program costs 21 percent less per student year than its control group counterpart; yet INEM students score about 1.5 standard deviations, or 43 percent, above control students in industrial tests. On academic tests, INEM students score 0.8 standard deviations, or 29 percent, higher than non-INEM students. Thus, although it costs less, INEM industrial education raises both academic and vocational achievement levels above those in industrial education in control schools. Likewise, INEM agricultural students cost 22 percent less per year to educate, yet 19 percent of them score higher than control agricultural students in the agricultural tests. Only 14 percent, however, score higher than the mean on academic testing.

Social service education costs 10 percent less in INEM than in non-INEM schools, while 16 percent more INEM students than non-INEM students have higher than average scores the mean on the social service specializa-

Table 5-22. *Annual Cost per Student and Achievement by School Type and Curriculum, Colombia, 1981 Cohort*

School type and curriculum	Unit cost^a (pesos)	Adjusted academic achievement^b	Adjusted vocational achievement			
			Agricultural	Commercial	Industrial	Social services
Academic INEM	25,700	53	—	—	—	—
Academic control	22,200	50	—	—	—	—
Agricultural INEM	26,200	49	62	—	—	—
Agricultural control	33,700	48	58	—	—	—
Commercial INEM	25,200	49	—	61	—	—
Commercial control	23,200	49	—	56	—	—
Industrial INEM	25,300	55	—	—	62	—
Industrial control	31,900	47	—	—	46	—
Social services INEM	25,000	48	—	—	—	57
Social services control	27,800	48	—	—	—	53

— Not applicable.

a. Cost refers to public schools only and includes school-related expenses by students, government-financed recurrent costs, and annualized capital costs. It excludes forgone earnings.

b. Achievement scores are adjusted for out-of-school characteristics and ability (see table 5-10).

tion test. Social service students in INEM do not, however, score better on academic tests than social service students in control schools. The pattern is similar for the INEM commercial program. It costs 9 percent more pesos per year to educate INEM students, and for that amount 19 percent more INEM students than control students score above the mean on the commercial specialization test.

In summary, INEM students come from slightly less favored socioeconomic backgrounds and score lower than other students on tests of general ability, but once corrections for out-of-school factors have been made, their vocational test achievement scores are higher on average than those of the non-INEM control group. Moreover, INEM students in academic, industrial, and agricultural programs also score higher on academic tests than control school students.

Summary of Base-Year Results

Having searched for both cognitive and noncognitive school-related differences across types of school and curriculum programs, we have come to a guarded conclusion about which schools are doing better than others.

In academic achievement, INEM academic, industrial, and agricultural students do better than their control counterparts. In their vocational achievement scores, students in a given specialization, regardless of the type of school they attend, always dramatically outperform students not in that specialization.

INEM schools have more modern equipment than non-INEM schools. They appear to be achieving their goal of raising the level of students' vocational ability, while slightly increasing the level of their academic knowledge relative to non-INEM students in most curriculum streams.

Table 5-23. *Differences between* INEM *and Control Group in Cost and Achievement, Colombia, 1981 Cohort*

	INEM incremental cost (percent)	INEM incremental achievement (test score points)	
Curriculum		Academic	Vocational
Academic	+ 16	+ 3	—
Agricultural	− 22	+ 1	+ 4
Commercial	+ 9	0	+ 5
Industrial	− 21	+ 8	+ 16
Social services	− 10	0	+ 4

— Not applicable.
Source: Based on table 5-22.

Thus, INEM schools have the perhaps unintended, but welcome, effect of fostering academic knowledge more than their academic counterparts.

With regard to socioeconomic background and noncognitive outcomes, the average INEM student comes from a home where the father has less education and earns less than the fathers of students attending control schools. INEM students are, on the average, older than their counterparts, less likely to have attended a private primary school, more likely to have repeated a grade in primary school, and less likely to want to study full-time after secondary school, although they may wish to attend a university just as much as the non-INEM students. The INEM student is as satisfied with his or her course of secondary instruction as his fellow students from other schools. But INEM students anticipate earning less than their counterparts in every field. This appears to be true even after differences in ability and socioeconomic background have been taken into account through statistical controls.

Based on comparisons of costs and achievement gains in academic and vocational knowledge between INEM and control schools, INEM industrial, social service, and agricultural streams are substantially less expensive than their control counterparts. Combined with the fact that these programs substantially boost achievement scores, they are unquestionably successful. And although the INEM academic and commercial programs cost more than their control counterparts, they also substantially boost achievement.

Given the above findings, we conclude that INEM schools are certainly no less effective than non-INEM schools in imparting desired academic and vocational skills. The fact that INEM schools seem to teach vocational skills more effectively than academic skills is certainly consistent with their supposed function and mandate. Several questions remain, however, a major one being how INEM graduates fare in the labor market. We now turn our attention to the results of the follow-up survey in order to answer that question.

The Class of 1981 One Year Later

In 1982, approximately one year after receiving their diploma, the 1981 graduating class was again surveyed. The questionnaire elicited information on the graduates' current status; that is, whether they were studying full-time, working full-time, studying and working part-time, or other. Information was also obtained on postsecondary school experiences in the labor market, further schooling, training, and job search. Sector of employment, hours worked, and earnings were obtained from among those working. Those searching for a job were asked the minimum salary they would accept, while those in full-time education were asked what kind of curriculum they were pursuing. The follow-up survey aimed to assess whether postschool outcomes were different for students coming from the various curriculum programs pursued in INEM or control schools.

Before charting the entry and flow of students through postsecondary school activities, it is necessary to note the proportion of the original sample of 8,051 students who responded to the later questionnaire. The results reported below are based on a 62 percent response rate—slightly above the 60 percent minimum required by the sample design to yield school type curriculum cells containing enough observations for differences in outcomes to be statistically significant. (Efforts were continuing in 1983 to trace additional graduates of the original cohort; any responses from them will eventually be merged with the existing data base.) As shown in table 5-24, the respondents closely reflect the proportions of students by school type and curriculum track appearing in the base-year sample.

Graduate Destinations

Of those students who responded, 37 percent were studying full-time, 30 percent were working full-time, 11 percent were both studying and

Table 5-24. *Response to Activity Survey One Year after Graduation by School Type and Curriculum, Colombia, 1981 Cohort*

School type and curriculum	1981 base year		1982 follow-up		Response rate (percent)
	Number surveyed	Percent	Number surveyed	Percent	
INEM					
Academic	871	10.8	514	10.3	59
Agricultural	174	2.2	78	1.6	45
Commercial	957	11.9	588	11.8	61
Industrial	869	10.8	474	9.5	55
Social services	380	4.7	225	4.5	59
Control					
Academic	1,471	18.3	934	18.7	60
Agricultural	370	4.6	243	4.9	65
Commercial	973	12.1	557	11.2	59
Industrial	945	11.7	695	13.9	74
Pedagogical	767	9.5	559	11.2	72
Social services	274	3.4	124	2.5	56
Overall	8,051	100.0	4,991	100.0	62

working part-time, and 22 percent were in other activities (including nonparticipants staying at home or searching for a job or an opportunity for further training). The latter group includes many women and graduates who had entered the military. Table 5-25 gives the main activity destinations by school type and curriculum program. Thus, one year later, more than one-third of the graduates were in school, just under one-third were working full-time, and aside from 11 percent who were studying and working part-time simultaneously, about one-quarter of the sample was neither studying nor working.

There appear to be no major differences in postschool activity between the groups of INEM and non-INEM respondents, meaning that the type of school attended does not alter the initial decision of graduates concerning their academic or vocational pursuits (figure 5-7).

Table 5-26 compares students' expectations for postschool activities before leaving school in 1981 with their actual destination one year later. There was an increase of 14 percentage points in those who actually attended school full-time; this increase was greatest among INEM students (19 points compared with 11 points for control students). The number of graduates in full-time employment is higher by 26 percentage points than

Table 5-25. *1982 Destination by School Type and Curriculum, Colombia, 1981 Cohort*
(percent)

School type and curriculum, 1981	Postschool activity, 1982			
	Study	Work	Study and work	Other
INEM				
Academic	34	30	9	27
Agricultural	29	27	15	29
Commercial	39	29	10	22
Industrial	36	31	8	25
Social services	43	26	9	23
Average	37	29	10	24
Control				
Academic	38	29	13	20
Agricultural	34	36	11	19
Commercial	36	32	9	23
Industrial	34	32	11	23
Pedagogical	41	29	10	20
Social services	46	26	12	16
Average	37	30	11	22
Overall	37	30	11	22

Figure 5-7. *Distribution of Respondents by 1982 Activity, Colombia, 1981 Cohort*

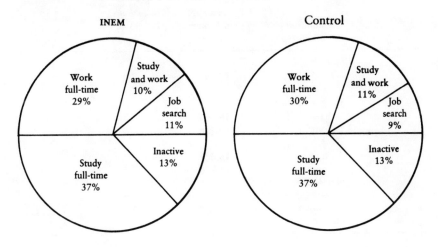

the number who one year earlier had envisaged themselves as working. On this latter statistic, no significant difference between INEM and non-INEM graduates is apparent. Thus, although when polled in 1981 INEM students had felt less likely than others to continue with full-time education, in practice they continued in roughly the same proportion as non-INEM respondents.

To what extent does socioeconomic background relate to postsecondary school activities? As table 5-27 shows, graduates who study full-time come from families with significantly higher incomes than do graduates staying at home, studying part-time, or working full-time. This suggests that the family's well-being determines in part whether a student will study

Table 5-26. *Planned (1981) versus Actual (1982) Destinations of Graduates, Colombia, 1981 Cohort*
(percent)

	INEM			Control			Overall		
Activity	Plan 1981	Actual 1982	Differ- ence	Plan 1981	Actual 1982	Differ- ence	Plan 1981	Actual 1982	Differ- ence
Study	18.0	37.0	+19.0	26.0	37.0	+11.0	23.0	37.0	+14.0
Study and work	77.0	10.0	−67.0	70.0	11.0	−59.0	73.0	11.0	−62.0
Work	4.5	29.0	+24.5	3.5	31.0	+28.0	3.7	30.0	+26.3
Other	0.5	24.0	+23.5	0.5	20.5	+20.0	0.3	22.0	+21.4

Table 5-27. *Father's Mean Income and Educational Level by 1982 Destination and School Type, Colombia, 1981 Cohort*

Destination and school type	Father's monthly income (pesos)	Father's educational level (Years)
Study		
INEM	23,198	7.0
Control	23,526	7.7
Study and work		
INEM	18,745	7.2
Control	20,738	7.8
Work		
INEM	18,226	7.0
Control	18,778	7.4
None of the above		
INEM	18,242	6.8
Control	17,957	7.4
Overall	20,346	7.4

full-time. In the following section we divide the 1982 respondents according to their postschool destinations in order to assess possible differences in experience by type of school or curriculum program.

Full-Time Students

One-third of the sample (1,665 respondents) were studying full-time in 1982. In the 1981 base-year survey, more than 90 percent of the secondary school students planning to continue their education wished to take university courses. In 1982, however, only 58 percent of those who were enrolled full-time actually were taking university-accredited courses. Table 5-28 gives a breakdown of the type of institution attended in 1982 by type of secondary school attended and type of curriculum (academic or vocational) followed in 1981. When all INEM graduates are combined, regardless of subject studied, no difference between control and INEM university attendance rates can be discerned. Of the INEM graduates enrolled in university courses, however, more had followed an academic than a vocational program.

A number of questions asked graduates' opinions regarding their current studies. Seventy-five percent of the INEM graduates reported they were satisfied, compared with 77 percent of the control group. From both types of schools, 62 percent of the respondents believed their secondary school course of study was extremely helpful in their present field of study, and only 18 percent claimed to be dissatisfied with their preparatory studies.

Table 5-28. *Type of Postsecondary Institution Attended by Those Studying in 1982, Colombia, 1981 Cohort*
(percent)

School type and curriculum, 1981	Postsecondary institution, 1982		
	University	Nonuniversity	Nonaccredited
INEM			
Academic	67	13	20
Vocational	49	23	28
Average	55	20	25
Control			
Academic	61	19	20
Vocational	59	21	20
Average	60	20	20
Overall average	58	20	22

On this subject, there were no significant differences in the opinions of the INEM and control groups.

Postsecondary training programs then were grouped into humanities-related subjects, commercial and technical areas, and a residual category. The distribution of graduates by school curriculum program across these postsecondary training programs is shown in table 5-29. Commercial courses dominate postsecondary training, and the proportion of agriculture graduates switching to commercial and technical courses is surprisingly high.

Graduates were asked what they could expect to earn if they were currently employed rather than studying, and what they hoped to earn upon completing their present education. The difference between the two values gives an indication of the perceived value of postsecondary school studies, based on revised expectations. The results for INEM and control groups in academic and vocational studies are presented in table 5-30. The self-assessed forgone earnings are generally consistent with students' expectations one year earlier (see table 5-19). Both INEM and other secondary graduates expect to more than triple their monthly earnings by undertaking further study. INEM graduates expect a slightly smaller gain than do control-school graduates.

One-fourth of the follow-up respondents were currently attending or had previously been in some sort of training program; there were no major differences in this respect between the INEM and control groups. Of those who opted for some type of training, 67 percent had taken at least one training course lasting an average of twenty-one weeks. Forty-three percent of these training courses were in business administration, which

Table 5-29. *Distribution of Students in 1982 Training Course, Colombia, 1981 Cohort*
(percent)

1981 School type and curriculum	1982 training course			
	Humanities	Commercial	Technical	Other
INEM				
Academic	37	37	16	10
Agricultural	26	32	32	10
Commercial	28	39	18	15
Industrial	25	41	21	13
Social services	31	39	15	15
Control				
Academic	26	42	18	14
Agricultural	17	34	28	21
Commercial	18	39	20	23
Industrial	27	46	12	15
Pedagogical	31	30	21	18
Social services	25	40	20	15
Overall	27	40	18	15

attracted INEM and non-INEM graduates equally. Fifty percent of all training occurred in technical institutes, another 25 percent in Servicio Nacional de Aprendizaje (SENA, the national apprenticeship service), 10 percent in firms, and only 5 percent in a university-sponsored environment. Again, equal proportions of INEM and control-group respondents were engaged in these kinds of training.

One-quarter of control graduates and 20 percent of INEM graduates fit into the general academic training category that combines arts, humanities, social sciences, and science education. The greater percentage of control-group graduates training in academic pursuits is the only significant difference found between INEM and non-INEM respondents who received training after secondary school graduation.

Full-Time Workers

The 1982 follow-up survey recorded 30 percent of the 1981 cohort (1,397 respondents) as working full-time. Do these graduates differ in their attitudes, experiences, and socioeconomic characteristics according to the type of secondary school they attended?

As shown in table 5-31, the profile for INEM and control respondents is very similar in two respects: their fathers' employment status and the proportion who cited poor academic records as the reason for not con-

Table 5-30. *Expected Earnings With and Without Postsecondary Studies, 1982 Follow-up Response, Colombia, 1981 Cohort*

| School type and curriculum | Pesos per month | | Increment due to post-secondary study (percent) |
	With secondary diploma	With postsecondary study	
INEM			
Academic	10,282	35,814	248
Agricultural	11,916	29,475	147
Commercial	10,505	31,014	195
Industrial	10,934	33,971	211
Social services	11,754	32,594	211
Average	10,760	33,198	213
Control			
Academic	10,950	37,697	244
Agricultural	10,065	32,653	244
Commercial	10,322	38,454	272
Industrial	11,043	35,203	219
Pedagogical	10,790	35,033	247
Social services	12,965	35,195	171
Average	10,841	36,303	241
Overall average	10,818	35,106	245

tinuing education. Those in full-time employment cited lack of financial resources as the reason for not continuing education more often than did students staying at home or those working and studying part-time.

One question asked students how they acquired their first job. One out of four found their job through independent means, such as a newspaper or the employment exchange. But the majority (75 percent) obtained their

Table 5-31. *Selected Characteristics of Full-Time Workers in the 1982 Follow-up, Colombia, 1981 Cohort*
(percent)

Characteristic	INEM	Control
Father is employer	28	29
Found job through friends, acquaintances	69	82
Working in the private sector	86	88
Financial reasons for not continuing study	37	23
Poor exams reason for not continuing study	26	23
Secondary school study very useful for current job	53	55
Should have studied more mathematics	15	20
Dissatisfied with current work	30	32

current jobs through relatives, friends, and personal acquaintances, which suggests that gainful employment in Colombia is still heavily influenced by family connections. Because more non-INEM than INEM graduates obtained employment in this fashion, it is possible that higher socioeconomic status and private school links help graduates land a job.

Table 5-32 indicates the probability of students' being employed one year after graduation. Those coming from control vocational schools are the most likely to be working one year later. Another way of identifying employment differences among students is to consider sectors of employment, as shown in table 5-33. Again, there are no major differences between types of school and curriculum, but INEM graduates are more likely to work in services.

The wide range of occupations entered into by graduates has been narrowed into six groupings. The distribution of students by school type and academic or vocational program across these groupings is shown in table 5-34. More than 60 percent of those with a full-time job in 1982 were engaged as secretaries, cashiers, bookkeepers, and salespersons. Interestingly, graduates who had followed an academic curriculum, regardless of INEM or non-INEM distinction, were just as likely to be employed in these categories as were those trained in vocational programs.

Table 5-35 gives the mean earnings of INEM and control graduates working full-time. Although differences in earnings are very modest, academic graduates from both types of schools earn more than the others. With the exception of INEM academic graduates, actual earnings are clearly less than what graduates were hoping to earn before entering the labor market (see, for example, tables 5-19 and 5-30).

Do those coming from INEM or vocational curricula experience have a shorter period of unemployment before landing a job? The data show, if anything, that those who have followed vocational courses in either INEM or control schools have significantly longer periods of unemployment

Table 5-32. *Percentage Working One Year after Graduation, by School Type and 1981 Program, Colombia, 1981 Cohort*
(percent)

School type	Academic	Vocational
INEM		
Full-time work	29.6	28.1
Work and study	39.1	39.3
Control		
Full-time work	28.7	33.7
Work and study	42.2	43.9

Table 5-33. *Employment of Secondary School Graduates by Economic Sector, Colombia, 1981 Cohort*
(percent)

| 1982 economic sector | INEM | | Non-INEM | | |
	Academic	Vocational	Academic	Vocational	Overall
Agricultural	2.6	2.3	1.5	2.1	2.0
Commercial[b]	40.5	40.8	41.8	46.0	43.0
Industrial[a]	19.8	17.6	18.6	15.9	17.0
Public utilities[c]	8.6	11.1	16.0	13.4	13.0
Services[d]	28.4	28.1	22.2	22.6	25.0
Total	100.0	100.0	100.0	100.0	100.0

a. The industrial sector includes construction, mining, and manufacturing.
b. The commercial sector includes finance.
c. The public utilities sector includes transportation.
d. Services include teaching.

(twenty-six weeks, as opposed to about twenty-one weeks for academic graduates of both types of school).

Part-Time Students and Workers

Ten percent of the 1982 respondents (500 individuals) identified themselves as working and studying at the time of the survey. Table 5-36 shows selected characteristics of those students who work and attend school simultaneously. No significant differences in the factors surveyed are visible between graduates from different types of school or curriculum. Essentially, average current earnings (8,655 pesos) and hours per week

Table 5-34. *Occupational Distribution of Graduates by School Type and Program, 1982 Follow-up, Colombia, 1981 Cohort*
(percent)

| 1982 occupation | INEM | | Non-INEM | |
	Academic	Vocational	Academic	Vocational
Agricultural	4.8	4.8	7.5	3.7
Blue-collar	23.8	23.0	24.7	20.3
Sales	17.1	23.0	25.8	21.8
Secretarial	15.2	11.0	10.8	18.9
Teaching	18.1	18.2	8.1	12.7
Other white-collar	21.0	20.0	23.1	22.6
Total	100.0	100.0	100.0	100.0

Table 5-35. *Monthly Earnings by School Type and Curriculum, 1982 Follow-up, Colombia, 1981 Cohort*
(pesos)

	1982 earnings		
Curriculum	INEM	Control	Sample
Academic	10,639	10,070	10,207
Agricultural	9,520	9,596	9,556
Commercial	9,664	9,322	9,493
Industrial	9,408	10,291	9,902
Pedagogical	—	10,426[a]	10,426[a]
Social services	9,556	9,577	9,568
Average	9,854	9,980	9,887

— Not applicable.
a. Not included in the average.

worked (thirty-six) indicate these graduates work close to full-time. Forty-eight percent on average had some training (23 percent in SENA, 60 percent with technical institutes, and 7 percent with firms). Almost one-fourth were looking for another type of work.

Graduates Looking for Work

Thirty-one percent of all graduates reported in the 1982 follow-up that they were currently looking for work. They included 23 percent of those studying, 26 percent of those working, 18 percent of those studying and working, and 58 percent of those neither studying nor working.

Clearly, those in full- or part-time study or employment cannot be classified as unemployed. Twenty-six percent of those already employed full-time were looking for other employment, and of those neither studying nor working 58 percent were actively seeking work and the rest were not participants in the labor force. Looking at the schools from which the graduates come, we note that 30 percent of the control graduates and 34 percent of INEM graduates were looking for work. The percentage difference in this case is statistically significant ($P = 0.001$) and suggests that INEM graduates are more likely to be actively looking for work than their control-school counterparts.

Of those graduates seeking jobs, 85 percent were still financially dependent on their parents or relatives, with no difference between INEM and non-INEM affiliation. On average, the job-seekers had been looking unsuccessfully for work for the previous twenty-two weeks, and had a reservation wage (minimum acceptable salary) of 12,000 pesos per month, much higher than the wages of those already employed (table 5-37).

Table 5-36. *Selected Characteristics of Part-Time Students and Workers in 1982, Colombia, 1981 Cohort*

School type and curriculum	Current earnings (pesos)	Hours worked per week	Weeks to find job	With post-secondary training (percent)	Looking for other work (percent)
INEM					
Academic	9,355	34	6	39	15
Agricultural	9,488	44	4	40	20
Commercial	8,350	39	6	46	19
Industrial	8,338	39	5	55	22
Social services	8,144	30	5	56	33
Control					
Academic	9,503	37	6	43	21
Agricultural	6,595	32	7	40	5
Commercial	8,398	36	6	56	22
Industrial	8,164	35	5	62	30
Social services	9,425	39	2	27	27
Overall	8,655	36	5.4	48	23

The kinds of jobs the respondents sought varied substantially, but the top five occupations are shown in table 5-38, further broken down by type of school and program. Major differences in job preferences of INEM and non-INEM job-seekers arise in secretarial, sales, and other office occupations. More control-group graduates than INEM graduates are looking for secretarial work, and these job-seekers come just as often from agricultural and industrial programs as from commercial ones. Those seeking jobs in sales are more likely to be INEM graduates (64 percent versus 36 percent) coming mostly from vocational programs.

In summary, while the proportions of INEM and control graduates looking for work are much the same, and while both groups expect to earn similar salaries once a job is found, a few differences can be discerned regarding the kind of employment sought by individuals from the two groups. Non-INEM job-seekers are relatively more interested in secretarial employment, while INEM graduates tend to gravitate toward sales and office management positions.

Summary of Findings

Descriptive profiles for full-time students, workers, job-seekers, and those enrolled in training programs reveal few major differences between INEM and control-school graduates.

Table 5-37. *Incidence and Duration of Job Search and Reservation Wage among Job-Seekers in 1982, Colombia, 1981 Cohort*

School type and curriculum	Percentage searching		Duration of search (weeks)		Reservation wage[c] (pesos a month)	
	Including part-time workers and students[a]	Exclud-ing workers and students[b]	Including part-time workers and students	Exclud-ing workers and students	Including part-time workers and students	Exclud-ing workers and students
INEM						
Academic	31	13	21.0	25.0	12,343	11,683
Agricultural	41	16	20.1	23.0	11,552	9,932
Commercial	33	10	18.8	25.1	11,691	10,936
Industrial	34	12	20.1	24.1	12,358	11,414
Social services	32	9	22.5	32.4	12,197	11,647
Average	32	11	20.0	25.2	12,121	11,308
Control						
Academic	28	9	19.7	24.2	12,370	11,735
Agricultural	30	9	18.6	29.1	12,170	10,790
Commercial	30	7	19.1	28.4	11,998	12,502
Industrial	31	10	18.7	23.0	12,725	11,226
Pedagogical	30	9	16.2	24.0	13,243	12,572
Social services	27	9	17.0	28.1	11,759	12,800
Average	29	9	19.3	25.0	12,517	11,791
Overall	30	10	19.7	25.1	12,331	11,575

a. $\dfrac{\text{(Number of graduates answering "Looking now")}}{\text{(Total number in 1982 cell for school type and curriculum)}} \times 100.$

b. Same as above, but numerator excludes those working or studying.

c. Minimum acceptable salary.

Because both groups responded in proportion to their membership in the original base-year sample, the findings imply that among secondary school leavers in Colombia one year after graduation, roughly one-third go on to advanced schooling, one-third opt for the labor market, and the remaining third either work and study part-time (10 percent of that group) are seeking work (11 percent), do not participate in the labor market (7 percent), or are not interested in further training (5 percent). This breakdown applies to both INEM and control graduates.

It thus appears that the pattern of experiences within the first year after graduation is fairly universal for Colombian high school graduates, regardless of type of school attended. The implication is that differences in secondary schools have little effect on postsecondary school opportunities within the time frame studied. If students entering INEM and non-INEM schools had radically different capabilities and backgrounds to begin with, one might conclude that INEMs play a significant role in equalizing opportunities for very different groups of youth. However, the analyses of base-year data reported earlier in this chapter revealed no major distinctions between INEM and control students, except that the former had somewhat lower socioeconomic status and ability.

Explaining the Decision to Work or Study

To predict whether a respondent will be employed full-time (or, alternatively, study full-time), we construct a dummy variable having a value of one if working full-time (or studying full-time), and zero if not. Thus the dependent variable is interpreted as the probability of working (or studying).

Because the dependent variable is dichotomous, probit analysis is used instead of multiple linear regression analysis. The estimates can be interpreted in the same way as ordinary regression estimates: the sign of the coefficient indicates a positive or negative effect of the corresponding independent variable, and the t-value indicates whether the effect is statistically significant. But unlike in multiple regression, the magnitude of the effect depends on the values of all the other independent variables, because the model assumes there is a nonlinear functional relationship between the dependent and independent variables. Hence the "marginal effect" of one independent variable—that is, the effect on the dependent variable of a small change in the independent variable—can be estimated by setting all other variables at selected values or, as in this study, at their means (see Moock and Leslie, forthcoming).

Findings from this type of nonlinear regression analysis can be used to

Table 5-38. *Main Target Occupations for 1982 Job-Seekers, Colombia, 1981 Cohort*
(percent)

| | INEM | | Control | | |
Occupation	Academic	Vocational	Academic	Vocational	Total
Accountant	12	37	12	39	100
Office messenger	18	40	13	29	100
Salesperson	24	40	10	26	100
Secretary	9	28	15	48	100
Teacher	12	39	11	38	100

Table 5-39. *Marginal Effect of Variables on the Probability of Studying Full-Time One Year after Secondary School, Colombia, 1981 Cohort*

Independent variable	Marginal effect	t-value
Out-of-school factors		
Male	0.004	0.41
Age	−0.042	0.55
Family owns business	−0.001	0.25
Books owned by household	0.004	0.45
Father's education	0.017	1.21
Family income	−0.001	0.16
Father blue-collar	0.002	0.89
Father nonmanual employee	−0.008	1.23
Father is employer	−0.002	0.60
Verbal aptitude	−0.046	1.38
Math aptitude	−0.024	0.73
School factors[a]		
INEM		
Academic	−0.001	0.30
Agricultural	−0.001	0.67
Commercial	0.002	0.61
Industrial	0.0002	0.06
Social services	0.002	1.39
Control		
Academic	0.007	1.39
Agricultural	−0.0002	0.61
Commercial	0.003	0.67
Industrial	−0.003	0.67
Social services	0.002[b]	2.06
Test score		
Academic	0.103[b]	2.15
Agricultural	0.058	1.37
Commercial	0.019	0.41
Pedagogical[c]	−0.016	0.41
Social services	−0.100[b]	2.09
Labor market factors		
Labor force participation rate	0.252[b]	1.97
Per capita income	−0.156[b]	3.08
Constant	−0.242	1.49
D-value	0.020	
Sample size	2,666	
Chi square	43.69	

a. Curriculum program categories are evaluated in relation to the pedagogical program (the omitted category).

b. Statistically significant at the 5 percent level or better. Maximum likelihood estimation by the probit procedure of the Choice Program, courtesy of Eric Swanson, the World Bank.

c. Pedagogical score relates only to control students; INEM schools do not offer teacher training.

determine whether or not secondary school students' vocational and academic achievement performance or their curriculum programs actually influence their ability to secure employment over and above the impact of family background, sex, age, innate ability, and other control factors. Independent variables in the probit analysis included many of the out-of-school influences discussed previously. In addition, several variables tapping the regional level of per capita income and participation in the labor force were included, so as to control for geographic differences in economic activity that might affect an individual's ability to find employment. Finally, measures of test scores, both vocational and academic, were included in the analysis. Cognitive scores are important because they provide an indication of the degree to which what is learned in school influences ability to find a job or to continue with education.

Table 5-39 shows that only a few of the variables significantly affect the probability that a student will continue with full-time study. The age and sex of the respondent have no effect on the decision to study full-time. Academic test score was the single most powerful school-related predictor of full-time study. According to the "marginal effect" of the academic test score, other things being equal, each additional point scored on the academic achievement test (near the mean value) is associated with a 10 percent increase in the probability that an individual will study full-time after secondary school. This should not be surprising, because postsecondary enrollments depend primarily on evidence of academic merit.

The survey also found that graduates who have done well in social studies tend to continue with full-time study. Labor market factors are also good predictors of students' decision to study full-time. In particular, the higher the local per capita income, the lower the likelihood students will continue education beyond secondary school. This is not unexpected because relatively high postsecondary earnings would imply higher forgone earnings for those who decide to continue studying, thus providing a disincentive to enter the university.

The results of a similar probit procedure attempting to isolate the factors associated with whether a student will be employed full-time one year after graduation are reported in table 5-40. No single variable is statistically related to the probability of full-time employment after graduation.

Relation between School Type, Cognitive Skills, and Earnings

A path model was fitted to postsecondary students working full-time in 1982. Father's education in years and a composite score representing verbal and nonverbal aptitude were treated as independent of school type (INEM or control); two alternative achievement scores (academic and

Table 5-40. *Marginal Effect of Variables on the Probability of Working Full-Time One Year after Secondary Graduation, Colombia, 1981 Cohort*

Independent variable	Marginal effect	t-value
Out-of-school factors		
Male	0.002	0.19
Age	0.105	1.22
Family owns business	−0.004	0.98
Books owned by household	−0.021	1.83
Father's education	−0.005	0.32
Family income	0.007	0.94
Father blue-collar	0.002	0.68
Father nonmanual employee	0.009	1.20
Father is employer	0.003	1.02
Verbal aptitude	−0.042	1.09
Math aptitude	−0.032	0.86
School factors[a]		
INEM		
Academic	0.001	0.04
Agricultural	−0.001	0.50
Commercial	−0.002	0.53
Industrial	0.001	0.29
Social services	−0.002	1.07
Control		
Academic	−0.006	1.08
Agricultural	0.003	1.01
Commercial	0.001	0.14
Industrial	0.004	0.73
Social services	0.001	0.40
Test score		
Academic	−0.064	1.18
Agricultural	0.006	0.13
Commercial	−0.012	0.26
Pedagogical[b]	0.037	0.83
Social services	0.037	0.68
Labor market factors		
Labor force participation rate	−0.089	0.61
Per capita income	0.046	0.79
Constant	−0.205	1.10
D-value	0.009	
Sample size	2,666	
Chi square	25.71	

a. Curriculum program categories are evaluated in relation to the pedagogical program (the omitted category).

b. Pedagogical score relates only to control students; INEM schools do not offer teacher training.

Source: Maximum likelihood estimation by the probit procedure of the Choice program, courtesy of Eric Swanson, the World Bank.

industrial) and earnings one year after graduation from secondary school also were part of the model.

Estimates of the model using academic achievement as an intermediate variable are provided in figure 5-8. The model is fitted to the data for all graduates with earnings in 1982, because all of them had been exposed to academic subjects. No one factor, even academic achievement, was shown to have a significant effect on earnings. Neither did the link between school type and earnings reveal any advantage of INEM over control schools in this context. This reinforces the previous finding that earnings differences between INEM and control graduates are slight.

Figure 5-9 shows the results of the same model using scores on industrial instead of academic achievement tests as an intermediate variable. In contrast to the first model, industrial achievement has a significant impact on earnings. Scores on commercial, social services, and agricultural achievement tests, however, have no such effects (not shown in figure).

Figure 5-8. *Path Model with Academic Achievement Scores Used as Intermediate Variable, Colombia, 1982 Survey of 1981 Cohort*

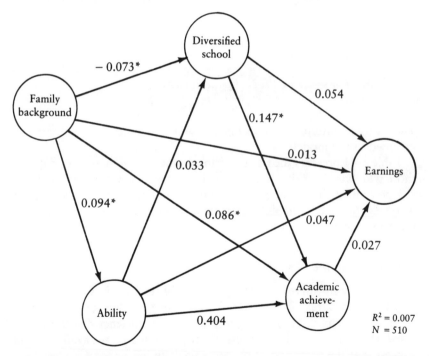

*Statistically significant path at the 10 percent level.

Figure 5-9. *Path Model with Industrial Achievement Scores Used as Intermediate Variable, Colombia, 1982 Survey of 1981 Cohort*

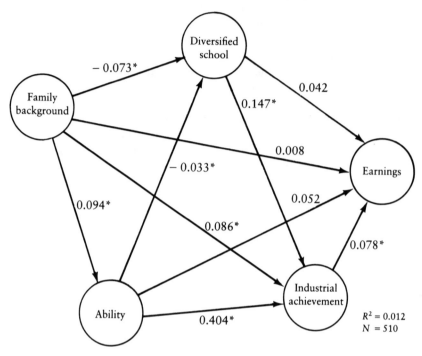

*Statistically significant path at the 10 percent level or better.

The overall pattern is not changed when part-time wage earners are included in the model.

Table 5-41 presents the results of an earnings function fitted to data for those who were working full-time in 1982. Its explanatory power is low (13 percent of the variance in earnings). Difference in local per capita income is the only variable whose coefficient is statistically significant at the 5 percent level of probability.

Summary of the 1982 Tracer Survey

The follow-up survey of secondary school students in Colombia was taken one year after they graduated. This allows for only a partial testing of the set of hypotheses relating to the external efficiency of INEM diversified schools compared with control schools. However, the available data suggest that the provision of prevocational studies:

- Has not decreased the private demand for postsecondary formal education, nor has the introduction of INEMS
- Has not resulted in prevocational-stream graduates entering training courses in a pattern different from academic-stream graduates
- Has slightly increased the propensity of prevocational students to enter full-time employment immediately after graduation from secondary school[1]
- Has not given graduates of prevocational programs access to jobs that are different from those taken by graduates of academic programs (similarly, there are no significant differences based on type of school attended)
- Has not led prevocational graduates to acquire employment earlier than academic graduates (in fact, unemployment rates were slightly higher among INEM graduates)
- Has not led to higher initial earnings for prevocational students (although the average earnings for graduates of INEM and non-INEM schools are virtually the same, the average earnings of academic program graduates from both school types are higher than those of graduates from all prevocational programs).

The Class of 1978 Three Years Later

Given the long time required to obtain data for longitudinal studies, it was decided to seek some early indications of the labor market destination and performance of secondary school graduates by a survey of pre-1981 students.

After selecting the sample of schools and students for the 1981 cohort, a target sample of 2,000 students who had graduated from the same schools in 1978 was randomly chosen from the school records. Attempts were made to locate these graduates for the administration of a special questionnaire. Of the 2,000 selected, 1,826 were interviewed. The questionnaire elicited retrospective information on the graduates' further education and occupational records between 1978 and the fall of 1981 when the interviews took place. The questionnaire also sought the graduates' opinion on the usefulness of the courses they had taken and included questions designed to measure the degree to which they had adapted to "modern" values and attitudes. The questionnaires were completed by personal interviews at the home of each selected graduate.

1. This is significant only for control schools. If those studying and working are added, this difference disappears, but then graduates from control schools as a whole appear slightly more likely to be employed.

Table 5-41. *The Determinants of 1982 Full-Time Labor Earnings, Colombia, 1981 Cohort*

Variable[a]	Coefficient	t-value
Out-of-school factors		
Male	−615.281	0.96
Age	−21.228	0.15
Family owns business	−44.152	0.06
Books owned by household	−1.010	0.19
Father's education	87.971	1.06
Log of family income	88.460	0.50
Father blue-collar	405.605	0.50
Father nonmanual employee	−410.076	0.69
Father is employer	−1,346.744	1.49
Verbal aptitude	32.610	1.04
Math aptitude	−4.052	0.14
School factors		
INEM		
Academic	466.616	0.41
Agricultural	3,558.104	0.88
Commercial	−1,465.604	1.37
Industrial	192.290	0.15
Social services	−730.687	0.58
Control		
Academic	−936.234	0.96
Agricultural	487.142	0.40
Commercial	−417.407	0.41
Industrial	−740.477	0.70
Social services	5,255.244	1.87
Test score		
Academic	49.475	1.38
Agricultural	−19.145	0.65
Commercial	28.598	0.88
Pedagogical[b]	−21.985	0.79
Social services	−32.195	0.88
Labor market factors		
Labor force participation rate	−179.504	1.47
Per capita income	4.068[c]	3.46
Constant	−7,382.444	1.30
R^2	0.13	
Sample size	274	

a. The omitted school subject is pedagogy. The omitted father occupation is farmer.

b. Pedagogical test score relates only to control students; INEM schools do not offer teacher training.

c. Statistically significant at 5 percent or better.

Table 5-42. *Distribution of the Sample by School Type and Subject, Colombia, 1978 Cohort*
(number of graduates)

Curriculum	School type		
	INEM	Control	Total
Academic	181	277	458
Agricultural	76	150	226
Commercial	184	181	365
Industrial	213	156	369
Pedagogical	—	250	250
Social services	120	38	158
Total	774	1,052	1,826

— Not applicable.

This data set was used to test the same hypotheses related to diversification as were postulated with the 1981 cohort. The exception was achievement tests; none of the cognitive tests given the 1981 cohort had been administered to the 1978 group while still in school. (For a more comprehensive analysis of the 1978 cohort, see Psacharopoulos and Zabalza 1984a and 1984b.)

The 1978 sample yielded a total of 1,826 observations distributed by type of school and subject as shown in table 5-42. The effective sample of INEM students corresponds to 14 percent of the total enrollment in the eleventh-year class of INEM schools in 1978. Data for the 1978 cohort confirm that the INEM schools draw students from the lower socioeconomic groups (see table 5-43).

Destination of Graduates

Table 5-44 compares the activities of graduates immediately after leaving school with what they were doing three years later in 1981. In general, the table shows rather little change over the three-year period, but there is a surprising increase in those who classify themselves as students. However, a cross-tabulation of initial postsecondary experiences against 1981 activities shows that the graduates actually changed their direction a good deal during the three-year span. The variety of destinations is illustrated in figure 5-10.

Two points are worth noting regarding the overall destination of the 1978 cohort. First, graduates are likely to remain in their initial destination (such as work rather than study) for at least three years. Hence, by studying the initial destination of graduates, one can to a large extent

Table 5-43. *Mean Socioeconomic Characteristics of Students by Type of School, Colombia, 1978 Cohort*

Characteristic	INEM	Control	Overall
Father's years of schooling	9.6	9.9	9.7
Mother's years of schooling	9.4	9.7	9.6
Father's monthly income (pesos)	16,674	19,001	18,022
Family monthly income (pesos)	26,426	30,027	28,440
Number of dependents in family	1.4	0.9	1.1
Primary school repeater (percent)	25.8	20.3	22.7
Secondary school repeater (percent)	15.9	24.6	20.9
Urban born (percent)	90.3	85.5	87.5

predict their longer-term destination. Second, for those who continue to study, a three-year follow-up cannot fully evaluate their performance in the labor market. For these reasons, it probably would be unprofitable to poll the 1981 cohort before 1986.

Postsecondary Education and Further Training

When the 1978 cohort was interviewed in 1981, 50.8 percent of the sample reported they were studying full-time or part-time. There were significant differences among students in the likelihood that they would still be a student in 1981, which depended upon the type of school attended or the subject studied. As shown in table 5-45, INEM students who had been in the academic stream had the highest probability that they would be continuing to study three years after graduation (75 percent of them did so). Those least likely to have continued their studies were agricultural graduates of non-INEM schools (only 20 percent did so).

Table 5-44. *First Destination of 1978 Graduates and Their Status in 1981, Colombia, 1978 Cohort*
(percent)

Activity	First destination, 1978	1981 status
Study	26.3	28.8
Work and study	26.2	22.1
Work	36.4	36.7
Other than above[a]	11.1	12.4
Total	100.0	100.0

a. Includes those who are not participating in the labor force and those who are looking for work.

Table 5-45. *Percentage of Students Continuing to Study in 1981, by School Type and Curriculum, Colombia, 1978 Cohort*

Curriculum	INEM		Control		Total sample	
	Full- and part-time	Full-time	Full- and part-time	Full-time	Full- and part-time	Full-time
Academic	75.1	56	53.8	38	62.2	45
Agricultural	44.7	35	20.0	15	28.3	22
Commercial	44.0	18	59.7	25	51.8	22
Industrial	51.6	29	48.1	30	50.1	29
Pedagogical	—	—	54.8	19	54.8	19
Social services	45.0	25	58.3	25	47.2	25
Overall	53.6	33	49.4	26	51.2	29

— Not applicable.

Of course, the inclination for further study is also influenced by non-school factors, such as family background. To isolate the effect of school type and curriculum on students' propensity to continue their education, a logit regression was fitted, as shown in table 5-46. Graduates of academic programs in INEM schools are the most likely to continue studying after secondary school. And a considerably greater percentage of those who study agriculture in INEMs went on to further study than their non-INEM counterparts.

As the survey indicates, a proportionately higher number of INEM graduates continue with education than do non-INEM graduates. This finding contradicts expectations about postsecondary experiences for the two groups. But INEM graduates receive a better secondary education, and that allows them to succeed in the higher education entrance examinations.

Of the 1,826 respondents, 800 had had a certain amount of further training between graduation and the time of the interview. Most of this further training took place in SENA (the national apprenticeship service), in technical institutes, in firms, and in universities, as indicated in table 5-47.

One of the aims of diversified schools is to produce graduates who will undertake additional training in the area of their specialization. It is therefore important to investigate the extent to which INEMs performed better than non-INEM schools in this respect, as well as the consistency between field of secondary school specialization and further training among both INEM and control students.

The mean duration of training and the proportion of graduates of each subject who undertook training is shown in table 5-48. The results suggest that INEMs do perform better than control schools, largely because the postsecondary training undertaken by their graduates lasts much longer

Figure 5-10. *First Destination and 1981 Status of the 1978 Cohort, Colombia*

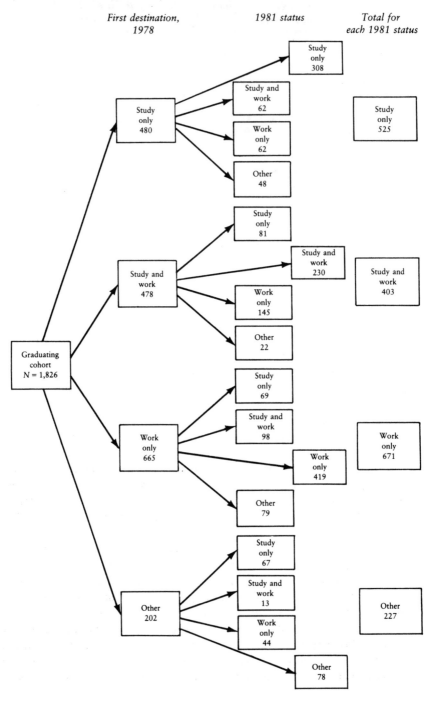

Table 5-46. *Factors Influencing the Probability of Studying Immediately after Secondary School, Colombia, 1978 Cohort*

Variable	Marginal effect	t-value
Background		
Age	4.62[a]	0.00
Male	1.62	0.58
Number of siblings	0.02	0.96
Urban born	1.76	0.66
Residence years in a city	0.54[a]	0.03
Current urban resident	−2.45	0.57
City per capita income		
(thousands of pesos monthly)	0.0001	0.73
Primary school repeater	−3.72	0.19
Secondary school repeater	0.37	0.90
Private secondary school graduate	0.27	0.94
Father's occupation[b]		
Employee	0.99	0.80
Laborer	−2.32	0.65
Self-employed	2.25	0.58
Business owner	−4.94	0.35
Father's years of schooling	0.53	0.18
Mother's years of schooling	1.04[a]	0.004
Curriculum		
Academic		
INEM	32.73[a]	0.000
Control	25.05[a]	0.000
Agricultural		
INEM	23.61[a]	0.000
Control	8.29	0.27
Commercial		
INEM	7.93	0.13
Control	11.54[a]	0.02
Industrial		
INEM	9.85[a]	0.06
Control	13.64[a]	0.01
Social services		
INEM	19.47[a]	0.000
Control	21.26[a]	0.05
D-value	0.093	
Sample size	1,712	

Note: Mean dependent variable = 26 percent.
a. Statistically significant at the 10 percent level or better.
b. Base category for father's occupation is farmer.

Table 5-47. *Location of Postsecondary School Training by School Type, 1978 Cohort*
(percent)

Training location	INEM	Control
SENA	47.3	37.9
Technical institute	29.1	25.8
Firm	9.0	9.8
University	4.2	5.1
Other	10.4	21.4
Total	100.0	100.0

than that undertaken by control graduates (forty-two weeks and twenty-nine weeks, respectively).

Graduates' further training matches their subjects of specialization in school to a much greater extent than would result from a random allocation (table 5-49). The data also show that, particularly in those subjects of specialty where the degree of congruence is highest (commercial and industrial), the difference between INEMs and control schools is not significant. However, agricultural students are more likely to enter teaching and engineering than to continue their agricultural specialization.

Labor Force Participation

Students coming from INEM schools are less likely to participate in the labor force or to hold a job three years after graduation than are control students (table 5-50). The results of standardization for other factors

Table 5-48. *Mean Duration of Postsecondary School Training and Proportion of Graduates Undertaking Training by School Type and Curriculum, Colombia, 1978 Cohort*

Curriculum	Weeks of training		Percentage of graduates undertaking training	
	INEM	Control	INEM	Control
Academic	45.0	37.0	40.7	46.7
Agricultural	25.6	14.2	34.7	49.0
Commercial	42.3	41.0	52.8	37.1
Industrial	43.2	37.4	37.8	38.6
Pedagogical	—	19.6	—	42.5
Social services	44.8	20.8	68.7	75.0
Overall	42.4	29.2	46.4	43.8

— Not applicable.

influencing the probability of employment, by means of a logit regression (table 5-51), reinforce the finding that INEMs do not specialize in producing graduates who enter the labor market directly (table 5-52).

Employment Characteristics

Of the sample of 1,826 graduates, more than 1,000 had jobs in 1981. Most were employed full-time (79 percent) and in the private sector of the economy (69 percent). Only a minority (7 percent) were self-employed. The overall mean earnings of the 1978 cohort in 1981 (10,292 pesos per month) is consistent with the mean earnings of the younger 1981 cohort in 1982 (7,552 pesos in 1981 prices), because the four years of extra labor market experience of the older group gives it substantially higher earnings in real terms. It should of course be remembered that because the two cohorts are different, their earnings are not strictly comparable. Rapid growth of earnings during the early career of graduates has been extensively documented for both advanced and developing countries (Mincer 1974; Fields and Schultz 1980).

Again there was virtually no difference between the earnings of INEM and control graduates (table 5-53). When the self-employed are excluded, academic and industrial graduates of control schools enjoy the highest earnings. The most significant difference in earnings appears between the sexes. Women from both types of school earn less than their male counterparts, and INEM women earn even less than control-school women (table 5-54).

To standardize earnings for factors other than schooling, a descriptive earnings function was fitted among those who were not self-employed (table 5-55). The explanatory power ($R^2 = 16.4$ percent) is consistent with previous findings when account is taken of the cross-sectional character of the sample and the narrow range of the age variable (the subjects were mostly aged twenty-one to twenty-three). The important findings for the purposes of this research are, first, that neither school type nor curriculum program have a significant effect on earnings. The only significant variables—such as sector of employment, job experience, and hours worked—are not related to school experience. Second, among students following the same curriculum program, there are no significant differences in earnings between INEM and control schools. The above conclusions were not modified by fitting the earnings function in alternative formulations (such as semi-log) or by including the self-employed in the study.

Table 5-56 shows mean earnings, standardized for the out-of-school factors listed in table 5-55, and the net earnings advantage of INEM graduates compared with the control group. Four out of five subject specializations show negative comparative results for the INEM group.

Table 5-49. *Relationship between Secondary School Subject and Postsecondary Specialization by School Type, Colombia, 1978 Cohort*
(percent)

Postsecondary specialization	Secondary school curriculum									
	Academic		Commercial		Industrial		Agricultural		Social services	
	I	C	I	C	I	C	I	C	I	C
Agricultural sciences	11	3	0	2	1	4	24	10	0	0
Architecture, fine arts	4	5	0	5	12	8	0	0	0	0
Economics, business administration	20	24	50	50	8	3	6	14	17	50
Education	16	22	10	5	12	11	29	24	32	29
Engineering	16	8	4	3	38	44	27	17	6	7
Health sciences	8	11	1	12	3	4	6	3	17	0
Law	8	7	10	6	3	3	10	3	4	0
Sciences	3	4	0	2	8	9	0	3	2	0
Social services, humanities	14	15	21	17	6	4	0	21	24	14
Other	0	2	4	0	0	0	0	3	0	0
Total	100	100	100	100	100	100	100	100	100	100

Note: I = INEM; C = control.

120

Table 5-50. *Labor Force Participation and Employment Rates in 1981, Colombia, 1978 Cohort*
(percent)

	INEM		Control		Total sample	
Curriculum	Labor force participation	Employment rate	Labor force participation	Employment rate	Labor force participation	Employment rate
Academic	49.2	37.0	61.4	46.2	56.6	42.6
Agricultural	63.2	50.0	78.7	58.0	73.5	55.3
Commercial	79.4	66.9	74.6	66.9	77.0	66.9
Industrial	73.7	62.9	72.4	66.7	73.2	64.5
Pedagogical	—	—	81.2	73.2	81.2	73.2
Social services	68.3	58.3	79.2	66.7	67.1	56.3
Overall	67.4	55.8	73.0	61.6	70.4	58.8

Note: A labor force participant was defined as one who was either working (full-time or part-time) or was looking for work. Employment rates are for both full-time and part-time employment.

Table 5-51. *Variables Influencing Employment in 1981,*
Colombia, 1978 Cohort

Variable	Marginal effect	t-value
Background		
Age	4.5[a]	0.000
Male	7.7[a]	0.020
Number of siblings	0.1	0.656
Urban born	0.3	0.928
Residence years in a city	−0.4[a]	0.080
Current urban resident	−2.2	0.641
City per capita income (thousands of pesos monthly)	0.02[a]	0.008
Primary school repeater	1.6	0.588
Secondary school repeater	0.1	0.962
Private secondary school graduate	−3.7	0.417
Number of postsecondary courses	6.5[a]	0.000
Father's occupation[b]		
Employee	3.8	0.399
Laborer	−2.1	0.695
Self-employed	−2.7	0.550
Business owner	5.6	0.338
Father's years of schooling	−0.2	0.578
Mother's years of schooling	−0.5	0.205
Curriculum		
Academic		
INEM	−40.4[a]	0.000
Control	−29.9[a]	0.000
Agricultural		
INEM	−25.1[a]	0.000
Control	−15.1[a]	0.049
Commercial		
INEM	−11.9[a]	0.030
Control	−1.2	0.824
Industrial		
INEM	−18.1[a]	0.001
Control	−11.8[a]	0.050
Social services		
INEM	−22.6[a]	0.000
Control	−12.4	0.318
D-value	0.105	
Sample size	1,690	

Note: Mean dependent variable = 58.8 percent.
a. Statistically significant at the 5 percent level or better.
b. Farmer is the reference occupational category.

Table 5-52. *Adjusted Probabilities of Working in 1981 by School Type and Curriculum, Colombia, 1978 Cohort*
(percent)

Curriculum	INEM	Control	INEM advantage
Academic	34.1[a]	43.9[a]	−9.8
Agricultural	49.2[a]	59.0[a]	−9.8
Commercial	62.4[a]	71.8	−9.4
Industrial	56.4[a]	62.2[a]	−5.8
Pedagogical	—	73.2	—
Social services	51.7[a]	61.5	−9.8

— Not applicable.
Note: Based on logit reported in table 5-51.
a. Significantly different from pedagogy (reference category).

Table 5-53. *Mean 1981 Labor Earnings by School Type and Curriculum, Colombia, 1978 Cohort*
(monthly pesos)

Curriculum	INEM		Control		Total sample	
	All graduates	Excluding self-employed	All graduates	Excluding self-employed	All graduates	Excluding self-employed
Academic	9,844	9,297	10,375	10,193	10,191	9,882
Agricultural	12,322	9,630	9,145	9,340	10,109	9,420
Commercial	9,904	9,811	10,155	9,874	10,028	9,842
Industrial	11,834	11,262	11,957	11,713	11,888	11,460
Pedagogical	—	—	9,526	9,495	9,526	9,495
Social services	8,862	8,921	9,050	9,050	8,898	8,895
Overall	10,534	10,001	10,142	10,016	10,300	10,002

Table 5-54. *Mean 1981 Labor Earnings by School Type and Sex, Colombia, 1978 Cohort*
(monthly pesos)

Sex	INEM	Control	Total sample
Male	11,473	10,822	11,131
Female	8,913	9,543	9,332
Overall	10,534	10,142	10,292

Table 5-55. *Determinants of Postsecondary Students' Labor Earnings in 1981, Colombia, 1978 Cohort*

Variable	Coefficient	t-value
Background		
Male	1,247[a]	3.45
Age	266[a]	3.10
Number of siblings	−37	0.75
Urban born	−44	0.09
Residence years in a city	−17	0.61
Current urban resident	712	1.35
City per capita income		
(thousands of pesos monthly)	1	1.07
Primary school repeater	243	0.76
Secondary school repeater	−143	0.41
Father's occupation[b]		
Employee	−215	0.45
Laborer	−521	0.89
Self-employed	127	0.25
Business owner	1,128	1.74
Father's years of schooling	123[a]	2.47
Mother's years of schooling	−3	0.05
Postsecondary characteristics		
Private secondary school graduate	244	0.52
Study in 1981	847[a]	2.80
Number of postsecondary courses	50	0.52
Duration of training courses	5	1.01
Months in present job	33[a]	3.42
Private sector employee	−1,323[a]	4.18
Full-time worker	1,054[a]	2.49
Weekly hours worked	62[a]	4.22
Curriculum[c]		
Academic		
INEM	−560	0.81
Control	37	0.06
Agricultural		
INEM	131	0.14
Control	−769	0.99
Commercial		
INEM	−231	0.40
Control	64	0.11
Industrial		
INEM	153	0.24
Control	770	1.23
Social services		
INEM	−836	1.23
Control	−551	0.49
Constant	−2,635	0.96
R^2	0.164	
Sample size	884	

Note: Excludes self-employed. Mean dependent variable = 10,002.
a. Statistically significant at the 5 percent level or better.
b. Farmer is the reference category.
c. Set of curriculum-specific dummies. Reference group is pedagogical graduates.

Table 5-56. *Adjusted Mean Earnings in 1981*
by School Type and Curriculum, Colombia, 1978 Cohort
(monthly pesos)

Curriculum	INEM	Control	INEM advantage (percent)
Academic	9,488	10,109	−6.1
Agricultural	10,178	9,522	6.9
Commercial	9,816	10,137	−3.2
Industrial	10,199	10,834	−5.9
Pedagogical	—	10,085	—
Social services	9,211	9,304	−1.0

Note: Based on table 5-55.

Returns to Investment in Secondary Schooling

Differences in mean earnings across school types and curriculum programs have only low levels of significance. In the following analysis, however, these means are compared with education costs, and rough estimates of rates of return are calculated. Because we are dealing with a cohort three years after graduation, we can approximate a more valid "flat equivalent" earnings differential at age twenty-two and hence use the shortcut rate of return method (see figure 5-11, and Psacharopoulos 1981b). Monthly earnings by school type and curriculum program were given for the 1978 cohort in table 5-54. Annual social costs for the 1981 cohort, including earnings forgone, were presented in table 5-20. From these data, approximate rates of return were estimated for each secondary school curriculum program and school type by the formula,

$$r = \frac{12\,(\overline{Y}_i - \overline{Y}_p)}{6\,(12\,\overline{Y}_p + C_i)}$$

where $\overline{Y}_i$ is the mean monthly earnings of graduates of the i type of secondary curriculum, $\overline{Y}_p$ is their forgone monthly earnings while studying (measured by the mean earnings of primary school graduates), and C_i is the direct annual unit cost of the i type of secondary curriculum. The results are shown in table 5-57.

Vocational education in general appears to have slightly higher returns when provided by INEM schools, but the returns to academic education are higher in control schools. Given the limitations of the earnings and cost data and the simplifying assumptions of the shortcut formula, the differences in the rates of return between INEM and control schools cannot be regarded as significant. Although some curriculum programs appear to be more profitable than others, the differences are not great enough to conclude that the introduction of prevocational tracks reduces the economic efficiency of secondary schooling. Conversely, there is no evidence to suggest that their introduction increases economic efficiency.

Incidence of Job Search

Eighteen percent of the 1978 cohort reported they were seeking work in 1981, with a very small overall difference between INEM and control schools (table 5-58). Most of those looking for a job either were already employed or were studying. When such cases are excluded, the overall unemployment rate among the 1978 cohort in 1981 was 6 percent, with a negligible overall difference between INEM and control schools. The unemployment rate was especially pronounced among control-school agricultural graduates (17.3 percent).

Table 5-59 reports the results of a logit regression explaining the prob-

Figure 5-11. *Flat-Earnings-Equivalent Assumption for Approximating the Returns to Education*

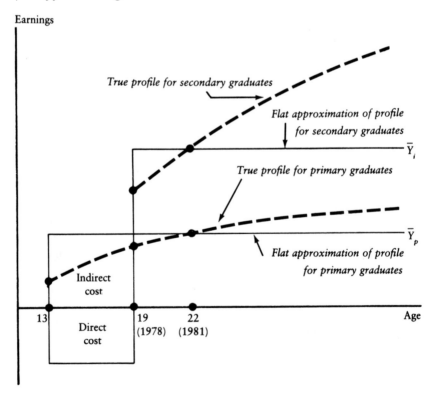

Table 5-57. *Approximate Social Rates of Return*
to Investment in Secondary Education by Curriculum
and School Type, Colombia, 1978 Cohort
(percent)

Curriculum	INEM	Control
Academic	7.7	9.3
Agricultural	9.1 ⎫	7.2 ⎫
Commercial	8.4 ⎬ 8.8[a]	9.3 ⎬ 8.3[a]
Industrial	9.2 ⎪	9.9 ⎪
Social services	7.2 ⎭	7.2 ⎭

Note: Based on adjusted earnings, table 5-56.
a. Average of agricultural, commercial, industrial, and social services.

ability of looking for a job in 1981 among labor market participants. The findings indicate that graduates of the academic and agricultural programs (from either INEM or control schools) were much more likely than other graduates to be seeking a job. According to table 5-60 (after adjustment for out-of-school factors), control-school industrial graduates were the least likely to be seeking a job in 1981.

Duration of Job Search

The 1978 graduates spent an average of fourteen weeks before starting their first job (table 5-61). Those coming from INEM schools obtained jobs

Table 5-58. *Job Search and Unemployment Rates in 1981*
by School Type and Curriculum, Colombia, 1978 Cohort
(percent)

	INEM		Control		Total sample	
Curriculum	Search rate	Unemploy- ment rate	Search rate	Unemploy- ment rate	Search rate	Unemploy- ment rate
Academic	15.5	3.9	18.4	6.1	17.3	5.2
Agricultural	17.1	9.2	24.0	17.3	21.7	14.4
Commercial	17.9	8.2	13.8	3.9	15.9	6.0
Industrial	21.1	4.7	14.1	1.9	18.2	3.5
Pedagogical	—	—	17.2	4.0	17.2	4.0
Social services	19.2	5.0	16.7	4.0	18.4	4.8
Overall	18.4	5.8	17.4	6.2	17.8	6.0

— Not applicable.
Note: Search rate includes those who might be studying or working, or both, while looking for a job. Unemployment rate refers to those who are strictly looking for a job and neither working nor studying at the same time.

Table 5-59. *Determinants of the Probability*
of Looking for a Job in 1981, Colombia, 1978 Cohort

Variable	Marginal effect	Significance
Background		
Male	−7.74[a]	0.01
Age	−1.03	0.16
Number of siblings	0.22	0.58
Urban born	−0.07	0.98
Residence years in a city	0.12	0.60
Current urban resident	5.77	0.15
City per capita income		
(thousands of pesos monthly)	−0.02[a]	0.01
Primary school repeater	0.17	0.94
Secondary school repeater	1.40	0.62
Private secondary school graduate	−1.45	0.74
Number of postsecondary courses	−1.76[a]	0.05
Duration of training courses	−0.01	0.86
Father's occupation[b]		
Employee	1.6	0.68
Laborer	5.73	0.20
Self-employed	1.24	0.75
Business owner	−5.65	0.32
Father's years of schooling	0.11	0.76
Mother's years of schooling	−0.63	0.12
Curriculum[c]		
Academic		
INEM	17.13[a]	0.001
Control	13.44[a]	0.001
Agricultural		
INEM	13.2[a]	0.04
Control	11.97[a]	0.05
Commercial		
INEM	7.41	0.12
Control	−1.81	0.73
Industrial		
INEM	9.65[a]	0.07
Control	1.74	0.78
Social services		
INEM	7.9	0.16
Control	−1.66	0.88
D-value	0.048	
Sample size[d]	1,168	

Note: Mean of the dependent variable = 17.8 weeks.
a. Statistically significant at the 5 percent level or better.
b. Farmer is the reference category.
c. Reference group is pedagogical graduates.
d. Refers to labor force participants.

Table 5-60. *Standardized Probability of Looking for a Job in 1981 by School Type and Curriculum, Colombia, 1978 Cohort*
(percent)

Curriculum	INEM	Control
Academic	25.6[a]	22.7[a]
Agricultural	19.9[a]	26.8[a]
Commercial	16.9	10.3
Industrial	14.4[a]	8.4
Pedagogical	—	10.6
Social services	17.1	11.1
Overall		16.4

— Not applicable.
Note: Based on table 5-59.
a. Significantly different from the pedagogical control.

one week sooner than the control group; however, school type and curriculum program are statistically insignificant in explaining job search duration (table 5-62).

Inspection of the minimum acceptable salary among those looking for a job reveals that job-seekers had a reservation wage much higher than the actual wages of their classmates who were already employed (table 5-63). Clearly, most of the job-search activity among the respondents was to improve their current economic situation.

Conclusions from Surveying the 1978 Cohort

The evidence from the earlier cohort largely corroborates the conclusions about external efficiency reached on the basis of studying the 1981 cohort. In particular:

Table 5-61. *Weeks Looking for First Job by School Type and Curriculum, Colombia, 1978 Cohort*
(percent)

Curriculum	INEM	Control	Total sample
Academic	11.0	12.7	12.1
Agricultural	20.1	23.8	22.3
Commercial	13.0	13.1	13.0
Industrial	12.4	12.1	12.3
Pedagogical	—	13.0	13.0
Social services	15.9	23.6	18.4
Overall	13.6	14.5	14.2

Table 5-62. *Determinants of Duration of Search for First Job after Secondary School Graduation, Colombia, 1978 Cohort*

Variable	Coefficient	t-value
Background		
Age	−0.33	0.69
Male	1.27	0.68
Number of siblings	0.29	1.09
Urban born	1.75	0.72
Residence years in a city	0.48[a]	2.93
Current urban resident	6.31[a]	2.22
City per capita income		
(thousands of pesos monthly)	−0.01[a]	2.51
Primary school repeater	−1.46	0.82
Secondary school repeater	1.04	0.56
Private secondary school graduate	0.65	0.24
Father's occupation[b]		
Employee	−0.80	0.29
Laborer	1.44	0.45
Self-employed	−3.97	1.44
Business owner	−1.88	0.51
Father's years of schooling	0.35	1.32
Mother's years of schooling	−0.70[a]	2.50
Curriculum[c]		
Academic		
INEM	−2.77	0.74
Control	−0.33	0.10
Agricultural		
INEM	6.07	1.42
Control	4.63	0.95
Commercial		
INEM	0.02	0.009
Control	0.85	0.25
Industrial		
INEM	−1.12	0.35
Control	−1.63	0.46
Social services		
INEM	4.65	1.28
Control	8.04	1.10
Constant	30.72	—
R^2		0.091
Sample size		579

Note: Mean of the dependent variable = 14.2 weeks.
a. Statistically significant at the 5 percent level.
b. Reference group is farmer.
c. Reference group is pedagogical graduates.

Table 5-63. *Reservation Wage of Those Looking for a Job in 1981, Colombia, 1978 Cohort*
(monthly pesos)

Subject	INEM	Control	Total sample
Academic	14,988	10,618	12,167
Agricultural	13,500	12,971	13,115
Commercial	13,678	12,739	13,285
Industrial	14,423	15,191	14,683
Pedagogical	—	13,125	13,125
Social services	11,000	10,000	10,793
Overall	13,713	12,480	13,019

— Not applicable.

- The simple examination of unstandardized data suggests that earnings differences between graduates from INEMs and from traditional (control) schools are not very large. Any differences observed seem to be attributable largely to the higher earnings of self-employed people.
- The raw data on employment status suggest that INEMs have not noticeably changed the employment pattern produced by the traditional school system. If anything, the data suggest that INEMs (particularly in the case of males) have accentuated the propensity of high school graduates for higher education. (The detailed results by sex are given in Psacharopoulos and Zabalza 1984a.)
- INEMs do not differ from traditional schools in the proportion of their graduates who enroll in Colombia's best universities, nor in the proportion who are unemployed after three years.
- When earnings are adjusted for influences other than differences in secondary schooling, the conclusions of the descriptive analysis are largely maintained. Overall, the data do not support the hypothesis that INEMs generate an earnings structure different from that generated by traditional schools.
- Although male earnings grow significantly with labor market experience, female earnings show hardly any growth at all. Tenure on the job seems to be a significant determinant of earnings for women but not for men. Male graduates who specialized in agricultural studies earn significantly less than other male graduates, while female graduates who specialized in commercial studies earn significantly more than women graduates working in other fields.
- When data on employment status were standardized to take into account the influence of variables that determine the relative attractiveness of work versus study, the main differences found for women

were not between INEMs and traditional schools, but between different subjects of study. For men, there were statistically significant differences between INEMs and traditional schools.

• Male INEM graduates, in particular those who followed an academic curriculum, are much more likely to end up studying full-time than are their counterparts from traditional schools. Graduates following a commercial curriculum in traditional schools are, however, much more likely to be working full-time than their peers from other curriculum programs. For graduates of other programs, the probability of "working only" is higher, and that of "studying only" lower, for INEM graduates than for control graduates.

Our overall conclusion is that INEMs have not increased the propensity of high school graduates to enter the labor force. In fact, where a significant difference can be identified, INEMs have tended to produce graduates who opted for further studies, rather than for working immediately after graduation. INEMs have not influenced earnings, but a final conclusion on this must await the availability of data from university graduates, since INEMs have sent a greater proportion of their graduates to universities than have traditional schools.

Table 5-64. *Mean and Standard Deviation of Selected Variables, Colombia, 1981 Cohort*

Variable	Mean	Standard deviation
Base-year sample (N = 8,050)		
Background		
Male	0.509	0.501
Current urban residence	0.873	0.333
Age	18.5	1.750
Number of siblings	5.17	2.84
City labor force participation rate (percent)	15.10	18.10
City per capita income (pesos per month)	1,041	862
Family income (pesos per month)	27,007	47,036
Father's occupation		
Blue-collar	0.132	0.339
Nonmanual employee	0.365	0.482
Self-employed	0.252	0.434
Farmer	0.131	0.337
Employer	0.110	0.314
Father's years of schooling	6.46	3.60
Ability		
Verbal aptitude	51.12	9.09
Math aptitude	51.36	9.65
Attitudes		
Individual "modernity" score	19.40	6.32
Plans further full-time education	0.254	0.473
Expects private sector job	0.096	0.240
Expected earnings upon graduation (pesos)	10,754	7,017
Expected waiting time to first job (weeks)	16.10	14.3
Achievement score (nonstandardized)		
Academic	11.78	4.67
Agricultural	4.27	2.40
Commercial	4.47	2.41
Industrial	7.24	3.85
Pedagogical	3.68	2.20
Social services	5.90	2.75
School type and curriculum		
INEM	0.404	0.491
Academic	0.108	0.311
Agricultural	0.022	0.145
Commercial	0.119	0.324
Industrial	0.108	0.310
Social services	0.047	0.212

(*Table continues on the following page.*)

Table 5-64 *(continued)*

Variable	Mean	Standard deviation
School type and curriculum (continued)		
Control		
Academic	0.183	0.386
Agricultural	0.046	0.210
Commercial	0.121	0.326
Industrial	0.117	0.322
Pedagogical	0.095	0.214
Social services	0.034	0.181
Other school-related variables		
Repeated primary school	0.237	0.426
Per pupil annual school expenditure	628.565	1,125.60
Private student expenditure	1,874	626
Student-teacher ratio	18.85	4.94
Private school graduate	0.194	0.395
1982 Follow-up (N = 4,925)		
Destination		
Studying	0.374	0.484
Working	0.297	0.457
Working and studying	0.104	0.305
Looking for work	0.312	0.463
Further schooling		
Full-time university study	0.194	0.396
Other coursework	0.174	0.373
Postsecondary training	0.256	0.437
Labor market outcomes		
Salaried employment	0.265	0.417
Self-employment	0.067	0.250
Earnings per month (pesos)	9,650	4,086
Hours worked	41.9	13.15
Weeks waited for first job	24.47	33.09
Weeks worked	64.14	56.09
Sector of economic activity		
Agriculture	0.018	0.105
Construction	0.053	0.067
Commercial/financial	0.426	0.465
Mining/industry	0.117	0.276
Public services	0.037	0.062
Social services	0.269	0.317
Transport	0.031	0.052

Table 5-65. *Zero-Order Correlation Matrix among Selected Variables, Colombia, 1981 Cohort*

Variable	(1)	(2)	(3)	(4)	(5)	(6)	(7)	(8)	(9)	(10)	(11)	(12)	(13)	(14)
1. Verbal ability	1.00													
2. Mother's education	0.15	1.00												
3. Father's education	0.17	0.59	1.00											
4. Father's income	0.02	0.11	0.14	1.00										
5. Father is employer	0.04	0.05	0.00	0.06	1.00									
6. Academic achievement	0.42	0.12	0.12	0.03	0.03	1.00								
7. Agricultural achievement	0.19	0.03	0.03	0.01	0.00	0.42	1.00							
8. Commercial achievement	0.09	0.02	0.03	0.03	0.02	0.24	0.23	1.00						
9. Industrial achievement	0.12	0.03	0.03	0.00	0.02	0.40	0.45	0.22	1.00					
10. Earnings in 1982	-0.01	-0.02	0.03	0.01	-0.04	0.04	0.00	0.01	0.03	1.00				
11. Hours worked	0.01	0.01	-0.02	0.03	-0.01	0.01	0.04	0.01	0.01	0.17	1.00			
12. Weeks worked	0.05	0.01	0.01	-0.03	-0.01	-0.01	0.01	-0.04	-0.05	-0.05	0.02	1.00		
13. Looking for work	0.01	0.01	0.02	-0.01	0.01	-0.02	-0.03	0.01	-0.01	0.15	0.02	-0.02	1.00	
14. INEM graduate	-0.06	-0.16	-0.12	-0.09	-0.04	0.04	0.11	0.11	0.17	0.02	0.01	0.01	-0.04	1.00

Table 5-66. *Means and Standard Deviations*
of Selected Variables, Colombia, 1978 Cohort
(Number surveyed = 1,826)

Variable	Mean	Standard deviation
Background		
Male	0.521	0.499
Age	21.859	1.864
Number of siblings	5.608	2.838
Father's years of schooling	9.775	3.302
Father's occupation		
Farmer	0.117	0.322
Laborer	0.111	0.315
Employee	0.354	0.478
Professional	0.297	0.457
Business owner	0.086	0.281
Family income (pesos)	28,440	32,516
Urban born	0.875	0.330
School type and curriculum		
INEM	0.427	0.494
Academic	0.250	0.433
Agricultural	0.123	0.329
Commercial	0.199	0.400
Industrial	0.202	0.401
Pedagogical	0.136	0.343
Social sciences	0.086	0.281
1978 destination		
Studying	0.262	0.440
Working and studying	0.261	0.439
Working	0.364	0.481
Self-employed	0.025	0.158
Earnings	5,405	3,748
Hours worked	39.054	14.235
Weeks to find job	14.157	17.784
1981 Status		
Studying	0.287	0.452
Working and studying	0.220	0.414
Working	0.367	0.482
Self-employed	0.039	0.195
Earnings	10,292	5,474
Hours worked	40.205	12.403
Looking for work	0.177	0.382
Weeks looking	27.254	30.596

Table 5-67. *Zero-Order Correlation Matrix among Selected Variables, Colombia, 1978 Cohort*

Variable	(1)	(2)	(3)	(4)	(5)	(6)	(7)	(8)	(9)	(10)	(11)	(12)	(13)	(14)
1. Male	1.00													
2. Age	0.09	1.00												
3. Urban born	-0.03	-0.16	1.00											
4. Years city resident	0.04	0.08	0.23	1.00										
5. Resident of big city	0.03	-0.16	0.09	0.15	1.00									
6. City per capita income	-0.07	-0.27	0.18	0.14	0.78	1.00								
7. INEM graduate	0.16	-0.06	0.07	0.09	0.13	0.22	1.00							
8. Repeated primary school	-0.00	0.17	-0.01	0.09	-0.01	-0.02	0.07	1.00						
9. Father is farmer	0.04	0.23	-0.31	-0.22	-0.23	-0.30	-0.13	-0.00	1.00					
10. Father is employee	-0.01	-0.11	0.07	0.02	0.05	0.08	0.03	-0.03	-0.03	1.00				
11. Student in 1981	-0.01	-0.28	0.07	-0.04	0.09	0.18	0.04	-0.06	-0.11	0.03	1.00			
12. Worker in 1981	0.03	0.13	-0.01	0.00	0.06	0.06	-0.06	0.04	0.00	0.02	-0.32	1.00		
13. 1981 earnings	0.16	0.06	0.02	0.02	0.11	0.11	0.04	0.03	-0.04	0.00	0.02	0.00	1.00	
14. Private sector employee	0.08	-0.11	0.02	-0.01	0.19	0.23	0.16	-0.03	-0.13	-0.03	0.01	0.00	-0.02	1.00

137

6. The Tanzania Case Study

WITH A PER CAPITA INCOME of $300 a year, Tanzania faces far greater constraints on its economic development than does Colombia, which is semi-industrialized. Tanzania has an agrarian economy, and most people live and work in the countryside. During the 1970s, gross domestic product (GDP) increased at an annual average rate of 5 percent. With 51 percent of the population of working age, Tanzania's labor force grew at an average yearly rate of 2.7 percent. In 1978 agriculture accounted for 53 percent of GDP (down 6 percent from 1960); manufacturing stood at 10 percent (up 4 percent from 1960); and the service sector stood at 36 percent (also up 4 percent from 1960). During the same period, agriculture's percentage of the total labor force decreased by 6 percent, from 89 to 83 percent; industry's percentage rose from 4 to 6 percent; and services' share increased from 7 to 11 percent.

Nonetheless, Tanzania remains heavily dependent on agriculture; more than half of the farm product is still derived from subsistence farming. The country has an abundance of labor and considerable uncultivated land, but it is critically short of capital, both physical and human. As in most other African nations, well-trained manpower in the modern sector has been in short supply since independence.

Background of the Study

A major feature of Tanzania is its planned economy and socialist form of production, which stress the public over the private sector, the operation of state enterprises, and government control of wages. Ever since the Arusha Declaration and President Julius Nyerere's statement spelling out in detail the concept of "Education for Self-Reliance" (see Nyerere 1967, 1977), political ideology has dictated the role of education in national development. In order for decentralized socialism to succeed in abolishing poverty, integrating a nation with a diverse tribal heritage, and achieving national self-reliance, Tanzania's policymakers decided that education had to accomplish two goals. First, it must impart useful knowledge and skills; second, it must give a practical orientation to learning. The fact that

96 percent of all primary school students received no further schooling suggested that primary education should be terminal—geared to the overall needs of a rural life and the manual skills suitable for rural employment, and fostering attitudes favorable to manual work. Primary schools were also expected to help support themselves by planting cash crops, raising chickens, and vegetable gardening. (Mbilinyi 1974a; Dodd 1969; Boesen, Madsen, and Moody 1977; Mmari 1976a, 1976b).

Diversification and Self-Reliance

The goals of secondary schools, however, were conceived very differently. At independence, Tanzania's acute shortage of skilled manpower forced the educational system to train a local cadre as quickly as possible to manage the public sector and replace the skilled expatriate work force. Because of that need, policies were focused on secondary and higher education, which historically had offered traditional academic curricula.

Tanzania's public secondary education system at first glance appears to be elitist and highly circumscribed. Those who complete it are supposed to be guaranteed appropriate jobs by the government, and the curriculum is geared to preparing graduates for work in specific economic sectors. It includes agricultural, commercial, technical crafts, and home economics subjects.

Government policy attempted to fine-tune the supply of and demand for educated workers so that the country could attain self-sufficiency in qualified manpower. Because the state controls a large part of the economy and, hence, the demand for educated labor, the public school system was permitted to expand only as much as the projected growth in demand for educated labor.

The content of Tanzanian education, like its goals, is also influenced by socialist philosophy. As expressed by President Nyerere, self-reliance refers not only to self-sufficiency in the skills and knowledge needed to achieve economic independence, but also to the attitudes and social values needed to promote national development. For example, invidious distinctions between town and country, or mental and manual work, were considered counterproductive. Likewise, it was thought that schools should not stress individual welfare, but, rather, cooperative effort and the welfare of the group.

Educators were directed to encourage behavior and attitudes conducive to the concept of self-reliance. Education was expected to stress the virtues of rural life, and thus help to slow migration to towns. At the same time, attempts were made to distribute government services more evenly throughout the country. Schools were directed to play down any distinction between work and education: work is not for the uneducated, and theory without practice is useless. Both academic knowledge and practical experience in the local environment were to be considered of equal value.

Education's role in fostering social change thus came to be viewed as critical. The curriculum became the centerpiece of an education policy designed to link education to work, skills to jobs, and graduates to job openings. Primary schools were to teach crafts and skills useful in the rural community, where more than 80 percent of the children would eventually live after leaving school. At the secondary level, diversified education was to prepare students for work and for advanced training in broadly defined economic sectors such as commerce, agriculture, and industry. As a consequence of this policy, it would seem that no public secondary school place would be created if manpower planning did not warrant it.

Hence, a major test of whether a diversified curriculum prepares students for their post-school experiences is whether students trained in a specific vocational curriculum are eventually placed in training and employment situations that utilize the skills they have acquired in school.

Educational System

A general view of Tanzanian education by scholars studying the system has been that, at the time of independence in 1961, the country had inherited "an underresourced school system, racially differentiated, urban in bias, elitist in form and culturally distant from Tanzanians themselves, which had to face up to two sets of potentially inconsistent demands. The needs of the new state for manpower related to development goals had to be balanced against the demands of parents for some tangible benefit of independence through increased educational opportunities" (Williamson 1979, p. 115).[1]

Secondary education in Tanzania consists of a four-year cycle (Forms I to IV), followed by a two-year cycle (Forms V and VI), as shown in figure 6-1. Tanzania has a very steep educational pyramid; for example, in 1980 only 4 percent of the 14–17 year-old cohort was enrolled in Forms I to IV in public schools (see figure 6-2 and table 6-1). The 4 percent secondary school participation rate is in sharp contrast to the 25 percent participation rate in Colombia (see figure 5-2) and represents one of the major differences between the two countries' systems of education. Stiff selection, based on merit tests, is in part responsible for the particular shape of Tanzania's pyramid. Because of a strict one-to-one correspondence of enrollment to job placement, secondary education is prevented from ex-

1. See also Austen (1968), Cameron and Dodd (1970), Court (1976), Furley and Watson (1977), Mbilyini (1974b), Sanyal and Kinunda (1977), Nyerere (1967), and Omari (1984).

Figure 6-1. *Flow Chart of the Tanzanian Educational System*

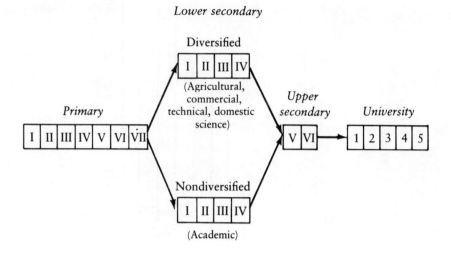

panding more rapidly than the number of suitable job openings. Unless enrollment is controlled, policymakers fear that a glut of unemployed educated manpower will result.

Students are selected to Form V on the basis of equity and merit. To qualify for university entry, students must (1) complete Form VI with at least minimum university requirements, (2) participate in a one-year national service (military) training program, (3) work for at least two years before joining the university (except for female and engineering students, who have been exempted[2]) and (4) demonstrate a commitment to serve the people in the course of their work.

During the four years spent in lower secondary school, students are assigned to, or allowed to choose from, one of four vocational curricula: commerce, agriculture, technical trades, and home economics. Vocational courses supplement the academic course load, and the amount of time devoted to all subjects—vocational and academic—is prescribed by the Ministry of Education. Considerable time is spent on vocational subjects: between 25 and 40 percent of the course-work periods a week are spent on the vocational field of concentration during the fourth year alone.

Tanzania has proceeded far in institutionalizing vocational subjects

---

2. This is considered to be a temporary measure to compensate for the social and education disadvantages suffered by Tanzanian women in the past, and to ensure that expensive technical equipment and teaching capacities at the university are fully utilized during the transition to the new system.

Figure 6-2. *Educational Pryamid, Tanzania, 1961, 1971, and 1980*

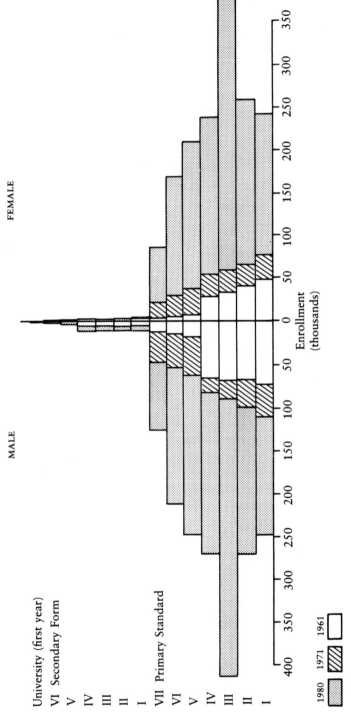

University (first year)
VI Secondary Form
V
IV
III
II
I

VII Primary Standard
VI
V
IV
III
II
I

FEMALE

MALE

Enrollment
(thousands)

1980 1971 1961

Source: Tanzania, Ministry of National Education, Sectoral Planning Department.

142

Table 6-1. *Enrollment Data for Public Schools by Grade and Sex, Tanzania, 1961, 1971, and 1980*

| | Male | | | Female | | | | | | Total |
| | | | | 1961 | | 1971 | | 1980 | | 1980 |
Grade	1961	1971	1980	Number	Percent	Number	Percent	Number	Percent	1980
University (first year)	70	624	693	6	8	75	11	216	24	909
Secondary school form										
VI	251	1,240	1,230	25	9	196	14	407	25	1,645
V	211	1,354	1,340	25	11	254	16	413	25	1,761
IV	1,121	5,274	6,550	482	30	1,170	25	2,770	25	9,320
III	1,540	5,375	5,908	548	26	1,947	27	2,737	32	8,645
II	2,514	5,426	5,827	1,019	29	2,197	29	2,785	32	8,612
I	2,967	5,554	5,887	1,229	29	2,016	27	2,960	33	8,847
Primary school standard										
VII	11,322	46,563	123,749	—	—	23,939	34	86,954	41	210,703
VI	13,061	54,011	210,534	—	—	31,256	37	167,445	43	377,973
V	14,737	63,300	246,579	—	—	39,308	38	209,329	46	455,908
IV	65,152	82,396	269,474	30,239	32	55,850	40	237,363	47	506,837
III	65,553	89,616	413,125	34,787	35	59,689	40	383,375	48	706,500
II	67,647	98,954	268,827	41,345	38	67,636	41	257,609	49	526,436
I	72,773	111,018	246,827	48,613	40	79,873	42	240,038	49	486,865

along with the academic curriculum. Its diversified education system produces, at the end of four years, students with a general knowledge not only of academic subjects but also of a particular vocation. From there, students can pursue more highly specialized training, either on the job or in other formal training programs run by the government or private institutions. The primary purpose of Tanzania's diversified vocational system is thus *not* to prepare students for the university. Nor does the system try to provide vocational training without a meaningful academic education.

Sampling Procedures

With fewer than 200 secondary schools and 18,000 Form IV (twelfth-grade, lower secondary) students in Tanzania, a random sample was made of one-third of all schools and approximately 25 percent of all Form IV students in the 1981 graduating class. The relatively large sample ensures sufficient numbers for statistical comparisons among subgroups (such as region, sex, employment in publicly or privately owned enterprises), and it compensates for unavoidable attrition in follow-up surveys. Furthermore, in order to compare schooling outcomes across the major vocational curricula, it was necessary to ensure representative subsamples of the school population: those coming from agricultural, commercial, and technical streams and a control group of nonvocational (academic) schools. The home economics stream was not included in the study because it was offered by only a few schools, and was not fully implemented even where it was available. So that the schools chosen would be fairly representative of schools throughout the country, a large ratio (1:3) of sampled to total schools was adopted.

The sample was stratified by first selecting schools and then selecting students within schools. Enrollment data for Form IV students attending secondary schools around the country were obtained from Ministry of Education lists. It was then possible to determine the overall size of the population of the Form IV class of 1981 and the percentage studying in each curriculum. Schools were selected according to their field of specialization and whether they were publicly or privately run. All technical schools, which are the fewest in the nation, were selected outright. With the help of Ministry of Education officials, random samples were made of commercial, agricultural, and academic schools. Once each subcategory of schools was established with a representative mix of schools by curriculum, researchers proceeded to test all Form IV students in each selected school, unless the total number exceeded 125, in which case a random selection of students was made.

The result was a sample of students and schools that closely approximated the distribution of the total student population among the commercial, agricultural, technical, and academic curricula. The eventual sample of more than 4,000 students represents about one-quarter of the eligible population of Form IV students (table 6-2). Secondary schools in Tanzania are widely scattered throughout the nation (figure 6-3); many are boarding schools located far from towns. The twelve regions of the country surveyed in this study account for three-quarters of all schools in the nation. The uneven distribution of schools follows the location of early missionary centers, where formal education was introduced (Ishumi 1974). (Descriptive statistics of the Tanzania sample are provided in tables 6-51 and 6-52.)

Socioeconomic Profile of Form IV Students

Data gathered on selected mean characteristics of the sample of 4,181 students in the twelve regions confirm that the regions of Arusha, Kilimanjaro, Iringa, and Morogoro and the coastal regions of Tanga and Dar es Salaam are advantaged areas, in the sense that their incomes per capita are not in the lowest quartile of regional per capita incomes in Tanzania, and that they have fewer mothers and fathers who are illiterate. Dodoma, Mtwara, and Pwani are disadvantaged by the same measures of family background (see table 6-3).

In large-scale studies, it is typical that measures of father's occupation, income, and education significantly correlate. For secondary school students in Tanzania, these correlations are also significant and indicate the tendency for education to be linked with occupational placement in the modern sector and wage employment.

The measurement of socioeconomic background or status is important for two reasons. First, equity concerns demand that we test whether differences in socioeconomic status arise across curricula. Second, to the extent that students in Tanzania are differentially recruited to a given

Table 6-2. *Sample Distribution by Curriculum, Tanzania, 1981 Cohort*

Curriculum	Students	Schools
Academic	1,025	13
Agricultural	1,380	18
Commercial	1,284	19
Technical	492	7
Total	4,181	57

Table 6-3. *Selected Characteristics of Students in the Sample by Region, Tanzania, 1981 Cohort*
(percent)

Region	Sample size (number)	Born in same region[a]	Mother's education low[b]	Father's education low[c]	Father's income low[d]	Father a farmer[e]	Private school[f]	Regional GDP[g]
Arusha	317	51	54	41	19	47	38	763
Dar es Salaam	428	45	51	35	19	24	24	3,838
Dodoma	267	18	74	58	33	51	8	415
Iringa	344	58	53	52	27	40	33	519
Kagera	213	33	76	55	31	49	7	504
Kilimanjaro	1,096	56	57	39	26	44	39	674
Mara	81	21	62	46	15	17	40	400
Morogoro	328	37	60	33	21	40	39	566
Mtwara	117	54	67	44	24	62	0	460
Pwani	245	27	75	49	28	60	0	617
Singida	99	19	56	36	25	51	0	439
Tanga	577	55	55	39	30	39	33	730

a. Percentage of students attending schools in the same region in which they were born.
b. Percentage of mothers with less than three years of education.
c. Percentage of fathers with less than three years of education.
d. Percentage of fathers in lowest quartile of income.
e. Percentage of fathers who farm for living.
f. Percentage of students attending private schools.
g. Gross domestic product (GDP) per capita in 1973 Tanzanian shillings.

educational stream on the basis of their socioeconomic backgrounds, and to the degree that the various social groups differentially prepare their children for successful competition in school, the results of schooling must be corrected to allow for these out-of-school influences. In this way, we can avoid attributing to schools alone, learning outcomes that are in fact due to family circumstances.

In table 6-4, a set of common measures of family background, generally accepted as indicators of social well-being, reveals some differences among groups with respect to certain variables. For example, commercial students have the most educated mothers in the sample (4.9 years), while technical students have the least educated mothers (3.4 years). Students

Figure 6-3. *Location of the Schools Surveyed, Tanzania*

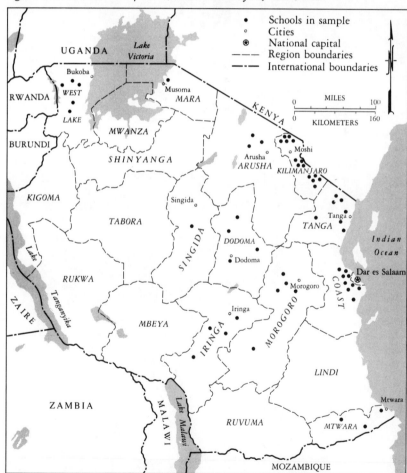

Table 6-4. *Socioeconomic Characteristics of Secondary School Students by Curriculum, Tanzania, 1981 Cohort*

| | | Percentage of fathers | | | | | Percentage |
Curriculum	Father's income (shillings)[a]	In wage employment	Farmers	Father's education (years)[a]	Mother's education (years)[a]	Number of books at home[a]	of families using English at home
Academic	7,181	54	45	5.9	4.4	37	15
Agricultural	6,656	50	48	5.7	4.0	33	15
Commercial	7,834	50	31	6.6	4.9	44	23
Technical	7,088	60	47	5.2	3.4	33	14

a. Mean values.

from high-income families tend to go to commercial schools, while those from low-income families are drawn to agricultural schools.

The questionnaire recorded how frequently English is spoken in the home, because it was assumed that families communicating in English, rather than in Kiswahili or some other East African language, probably represented "elite" households. Twenty-three percent of the commercial students come from families using English frequently, compared with 15 percent of students pursuing other courses.

Primary School Attrition and Secondary Selection

How do the socioeconomic backgrounds of incoming secondary school students compare with those of primary school graduates who did not obtain sufficiently high marks in their final examination to be accepted into secondary school?

In Tanzania it was found that children of educated parents stand a much better chance of getting into secondary school, even under a system of meritocratic selection. On the basis of 1969 census data on population distributions for paternal education, indices of the representativeness of the sample of both public and private school students were calculated (table 6-5). The indices show that the children of parents with higher levels of education are overrepresented in public secondary schools by a factor of six in relation to their percentage in the total population. The index is still higher for private school children. If the distribution of parental education in Tanzania has changed since the census, it has undoubtedly shifted

Table 6-5. *Selectivity Indices for Students in Public and Private Secondary Schools, Tanzania, 1981 Cohort*

	Father		Student		Selectivity index[a]	
Education (years) (1)	In total population (percent) (2)	Public school (percent) (3)	Private school (percent) (4)	Public school (5)	Private school (6)
0	70	11	26	0.16	0.37
1–4	20	37	22	1.85	1.10
5–8	7	40	32	5.70	4.60
8+	2	12	20	6.00	10.00

Source: Cols. (1) and (2): World Bank data based on 1969 census data. Cols. (3) and (4): our study sample.

a. Selectivity index = percentage in school ÷ percentage in total population.

upward, and this would imply slightly lower representation indices for children of educated parents.

A second method of assessing the degree of selectivity of secondary students is to compare the number of students from farm backgrounds in the entire school-age population with those in the sample. Approximately 90 percent of all Tanzanians live and work in rural areas, and of that percentage about 90 percent are engaged in strictly farm-related work. On this basis, about 80 percent of all Tanzanian children in any age cohort should have fathers engaged in farming. Normally, however, by the end of primary school, disproportionate numbers of rural children will have dropped out of school because they are needed for agricultural work. If 20 percent of rural students drop out before completing primary school, one would expect about 75 percent of secondary school students to come from homes in which fathers are farmers, if little selectivity by social class occurred at entrance to secondary school.

In our secondary school sample, however, only 47 percent of the students had fathers engaged in farming. By extrapolating backwards to the number of farm children in the population who entered lower secondary school (Form I), we can be reasonably sure that students with a farming background are underrepresented in secondary schools in proportion to their number at the end of primary school, and that this reflects inequality of selection by socioeconomic background.

Distribution of Students by Sex

Another way to measure equity is to examine sex distributions in the student sample. Relatively few females are enrolled in all levels of the education system. In the entire Form IV secondary school population, and in our sample, only about 35 percent of the students are females. This is mainly because historically fewer secondary schools were built for females than for males. Within the sample, one can note whether the percentages of females studying various curricula are similar or dissimilar, especially in the public schools, where close to 35 percent of the students should be female if the system is selecting equally across curricula.

Among all public school students, 32 percent are females, but across curriculum tracks, the figures are quite skewed. Only 7 percent of female students are enrolled in technical courses, compared with 24 percent in the agricultural curriculum, 52 percent in the commercial, and 38 percent in the academic. There are also some wide disparities in the representation of girls in the curricula of private schools (table 6-6).

Overall, female-to-male enrollment rates are far from the 50 percent parity found in the population at large, but the ratios are similar to the male-female ratio found in Standard VII classes (last year of primary

Table 6-6. *Enrollment by Secondary Curriculum, Sex, Parental Education, and School Ownership, Tanzania, 1981 Cohort*

Curriculum and school ownership	Enrollment as percentage of curriculum group		Father's education (years)	
	Male	Female	Male	Female
Academic				
Public	62	38	5.2	6.4
Private	66	34	6.5	6.8
Agricultural				
Public	76	24	5.4	7.1
Private	65	35	7.2	7.5
Commercial				
Public	48	52	5.9	6.7
Private	56	44	6.5	7.3
Technical				
Public	93	7	4.8	6.4
Private	99	1	6.0	7.2

school). A few disparities in these proportions can be found between public and private schools, although by curriculum, much greater differences arise in commercial and technical programs (and undoubtedly domestic science).

Public versus Private Schools

Still another way to look at Form IV enrollment variations is to compare students attending public and private schools. Private schools in Tanzania are generally not as popular as the state-run public schools. Public schools have no fees, most offer boarding facilities, and, best of all, their students have a very good chance of going on to Form V, a teacher training course, or a government service job. Because entry into the public schools is principally determined by an examination taken in the last year of primary school, students accepted into state schools are already considered among the country's elite.

Private schools, in contrast, are viewed as second-choice institutions for those who cannot get into public schools. Children of affluent parents who are not admitted into public schools attend these schools in disproportionate numbers. Not only are the fees considerable, but students cannot automatically expect government employment after graduation. Transfers to public schools are impossible.

A comparison of public and private school enrollments indicates that, as expected, private schools are attended by children of higher-income families (table 6-7). As shown below, these students perform less well in achievement tests than their public school counterparts, and this difference may partly explain why they are in private schools to begin with. However, many children who do well in the primary school final examination are not admitted to public schools because Tanzania has a regional quota system. Table 6-7 also indicates that private school students tend to have more educated parents than public school students. Indeed, it is commonly believed that educated parents who work in the modern urban wage sector of the economy, but whose children do not gain entrance to state schools, are more willing than other groups to pay for private schooling in order to secure secondary education for their children.

Although there are no major social class differences across curricula, certain types of schools may appeal to students of different backgrounds. A cursory inspection of seventeen public schools judged to be "elite" in the eyes of Tanzanian parents, on the basis of the quality of teaching staff or the high proportion of graduates going on to Form V, showed that such schools do not draw students disproportionately from socioeconomic backgrounds of higher status. Meritocratic selection procedures appear to have successfully negated social influences in these schools.

In summary, although distinctions of sex, region of birth, socioeconomic background, and innate ability undoubtedly contribute to some degree of educational inequality in Tanzania, it appears that the state-run secondary school system is relatively free of social class bias.

Measures of Students' Ability

Two measures—one of verbal ability, the other of quantitative ability—were used to test whether students of high innate intelligence fall disproportionately into any one curriculum. Because Form IV students are by definition a very select group to begin with, any differences in ability that arise across curricula represent second-order variations. The ability tests were designed to measure thinking with numbers and associated word

Table 6-7. *Parental Income and Level of Education by Type of School Students Attend, Tanzania, 1981 Cohort*

Type of school	Father's education (years)	Mother's education (years)	Father's monthly income (shillings)
Public	5.6	4.0	6,713
Private	6.8	5.3	7,594

problems and were intended for use as control measures for innate ability (non-curriculum-based knowledge) and more general learning skills. (For examples of test items, see Psacharopoulos and Loxley 1984.) The test results reveal significant differences across the four curricula in favor of technical students (table 6-8).

When further divided by sex, state or private school ownership, and parental education, the results suggest that recruitment into the technical track is the most selective. Possibly, the science curriculum demands more proficiency with numbers, as well as with words, than do other curricula. Males significantly outperform females on both measures, which is somewhat surprising because one would expect females—being underrepresented in the school population—to have been more strictly selected for ability.

State schools apparently do far better than private schools in recruiting talent, according to our measures of aptitude. A primary reason for this is that state schools are generally looked upon as high-caliber institutions in Tanzania. The state-private school distinction also helps explain why commercial schools appear to do most poorly: twice as many commercial students as other students are enrolled in private schools, and their lower mean ability as a group dampens the average ability scope of students in the commerical curriculum as a whole. The differences in mean ability between males and females and between public and private schools are of the order of five points, or half the standard deviation (highly significant).

To complete the profile of Form IV students by curriculum, we asked students a series of questions about their attitudes and opinions. Eighty-three percent of all respondents, regardless of curriculum, had started

Table 6-8. *Mean Ability Score by Selected Student Characteristics, Tanzania, 1981 Cohort*

Characteristic	Verbal aptitude	Quantitative aptitude
Sex		
Male	52	52
Female	46	46
School ownership		
Public	52	52
Private	46	45
Curriculum		
Academic	51	51
Agricultural	51	51
Commercial	43	48
Technical	52	54

Note: Test scores are standardized to a mean of 50 and standard deviation of 10.

primary school in the same year; thus, age in the sample is fairly homogeneous. With a similar degree of uniformity, 85 percent of all students claimed to be studying the subject of their choice. Seventy percent of agricultural and technical students and 80 percent of commercial and academic students planned to apply for Form V. No significant differences arose across curricula in students' own assessment of their academic performance in secondary school. Forty-five percent of all students considered their schoolwork "above average," and 55 percent of all students, regardless of curriculum assessed the quality of English spoken in their classrooms as "above average."

Internal Efficiency of Schools

One of the more important functions of diversified curricula is to facilitate further training for occupational specialization and the transmission of cognitive skills that will later enhance the graduate's labor market performance. Better cognitive performance in school should make a person more productive on the job, even if productivity is not reflected in higher wages and salaries because of a government wage cap. Thus, it is important to examine the extent to which schooling in the different curricula improves cognitive performance.

Cognitive Achievement

As discussed in chapter 4, special vocational achievement tests in commerce, agriculture, and technical trades were prepared by the National Institute of Education at the University of Dar es Salaam. Test items were based on questions closely tied to secondary school curricula. Reliability for these tests was high enough (in the mid-0.60s) to warrant confidence that the tests were indeed measuring knowledge in the specific field of concentration. No academic achievement test was administered because achievement scores in languages (English and Kiswahili), math, and science were already available from the Form IV individual examination booklets.

Performance scores on four achievement tests, distributed by curriculum, sex, and public or private school ownership are provided in table 6-9. The scores are normalized to a mean of 50 and a standard deviation of 10. Figure 6-4 displays in the form of a bar graph standardized performance in these four subjects. Students do best in their own specialization; males do better than females in agriculture, technical, and academic subjects, although not in commerce; and public school mean scores exceed those of private schools in all subjects.

Table 6-9. *Mean Achievement Score by Selected Student Characteristics, Tanzania, 1981 Cohort*

	Test score			
Characteristic	Academic	Agricultural	Commercial	Technical
Sex				
Male	52	51	50	51
Female	47	49	51	47
School ownership				
Public	52	52	51	52
Private	46	46	49	46
Curriculum				
Academic	52	50	49	50
Agricultural	50	53	48	50
Commercial	49	47	54	47
Technical	50	50	48	57

Note: Academic test refers to mathematics, Kiswahili, and English. All test score comparisons between groups are statistically significant at the 0.0001 level.

Boldface scores are in the students' own area of specialization.

Having observed mean test score differences across curricula, we employed regression analysis to see which groups performed better relative to the academic control group, once a set of background characteristics were controlled for. The findings for each of five achievement tests—three vocational and two academic—are presented in table 6-10. The control variables include sex, age, parental characteristics, and natural ability. Each vocational curriculum dummy is based on the omitted comparator group of academic-track students. The coefficients of the dummy variables represent points gained or lost on a test relative to the reference group of academic-track students.

In practically all cases, private school students scored significantly below public school students. For each vocational test, the group trained in the subject of that test did better than the others, as expected. The regression findings simply confirm previous observations of the mean scores, when out-of-school characteristics as independent variables were not controlled for.

Effect of Course Time on Achievement

Having observed differences in test performance across the various subjects, we examined the effect on achievement of variations in time devoted to different courses. The measurement in this case is based on the number of class periods per week attended by individual students in Form IV.

Figure 6-4. *Academic and Vocational Test Scores by Curriculum, Tanzania, 1981 Cohort*

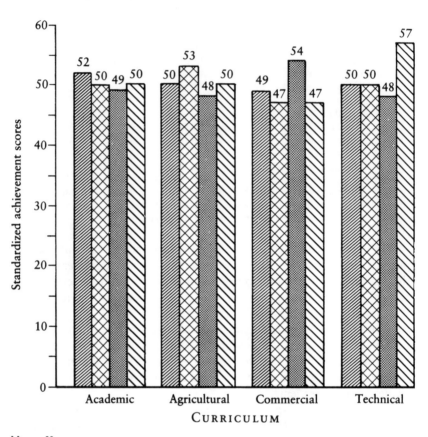

Mean = 50
Standard deviation = 10

Achievement test

Table 6-10. *Vocational and Academic Achievement as a Function of Curriculum and Selected Socioeconomic Characteristics, Tanzania, 1981 Cohort*

Independent variable	Vocational test score						Academic test score			
	Agricultural		Commercial		Technical		English		Math	
	Coefficient	t-value	Coefficient	t-value	Coefficient	t-value	Coefficient	t-value	Coefficient	t-value
Background										
Male	0.134	0.37	−0.379	0.10	1.692[a]	4.93	2.413[a]	7.24	2.986[a]	9.38
Age	−0.140	1.09	−0.317[a]	2.38	−0.277[a]	2.32	−0.636[a]	5.47	−0.277[a]	2.49
Books at home	−0.002	0.37	−0.002	0.46	−0.008	1.87	0.20[a]	4.64	0.002	0.51
Urban born	0.480	1.20	1.793[a]	4.34	0.912[a]	2.44	−0.468	1.29	−0.911[a]	2.63
Father's education	−0.005	0.09	0.108[a]	2.01	0.002	0.04	−0.050	1.06	−0.065	1.45
Log of father's earnings	0.129	1.23	0.063	0.58	0.008	0.08	−0.112	1.17	0.032	0.36
Father self-employed	0.946[a]	2.84	0.821[a]	2.38	0.345	1.11	0.143	0.48	0.573[a]	1.99
Father farmer	−0.392	0.96	−0.089	0.21	−0.142	0.37	0.276	0.74	−0.730[a]	2.06
Father blue-collar	0.634	1.16	0.202	0.36	0.829	1.63	−0.263	0.53	−1.077[a]	2.28
Father white-collar	0.108	0.21	0.194	0.35	−0.260	0.53	−0.203	0.43	−1.071[a]	2.35
Father professional	1.502[a]	2.69	2.137[a]	3.70	0.927	1.78	−0.024	0.05	−0.185	0.38
Verbal aptitude	0.227[a]	12.91	0.147[a]	8.08	0.196[a]	11.96	0.265[a]	16.63	0.198[a]	12.97
Math aptitude	0.108[a]	6.17	0.094[a]	5.19	0.233[a]	14.28	0.267[a]	16.88	0.432[a]	28.56
Private school	−2.961	8.09	−2.474[a]	6.54	−2.402[a]	7.03	−3.292[a]	9.92	−0.004	0.01
Curriculum										
Agricultural	1.608[a]	4.11	−1.131[a]	2.79	−0.967[a]	2.65	−2.240[a]	6.31	−0.468	1.38
Commercial	−2.604	6.51	5.431[a]	13.11	−1.897[a]	5.07	−2.274[a]	6.26	−1.559[a]	4.50
Technical	−1.606[a]	3.05	−1.138[a]	2.09	5.264[a]	10.69	−4.049[a]	8.47	−1.924[a]	4.21
Constant	35.880[a]	12.30	42.176[a]	13.96	33.872[a]	12.42	37.620[a]	14.21	23.377[a]	9.24
R^2	0.18		0.13		0.28		0.33		0.39	
Sample size 3,903										

Note: Curriculum dummy variables are evaluated relative to students in the academic track (omitted reference category). The occupational groups listed are evaluated relative to those not listed.

a. Statistically significant at the 5 percent level or better.

157

Table 6-11. *Percentage of Time Spent on Core Courses,*
by Curriculum, Tanzania, 1981 Cohort

Curriculum	Official syllabus	Student assessment
Academic	100	100
Agricultural	28	20
Commercial	32	27
Technical	42	26

Sources: Tanzanian Ministry of Education (1980), and Diversified Secondary Curriculum Study.

The core courses in academic subjects include civics taught in Kiswahili, languages (Kiswahili and either English or French), sciences (chemistry, biology, physics, and mathematics), and social sciences (geography and history). Academic streams emphasize strictly academic material, and students often get a heavy dose of English, math, and science.[3] The core courses taken by the vocational students depend upon the curriculum they are following. Essentially, those in commerce take business education, which includes commerce, economics, bookkeeping, typewriting, and office routine. Commerce students often take additional social science courses, such as geography and history. Technical core subjects include mechanical, civil, and electrical engineering, designed to prepare students for jobs as trainee craftsmen in these areas and, if they are able to pass the examination at the Form IV level, for a technical college or the Form V science stream. Agriculture students take core courses in the introduction to agriculture, soil science, animal science, crop production, and agro-mechanics.

The official course syllabus for Form IV students dictates that technical students spend nineteen periods a week on technical subjects, out of a total of forty-five periods. The figures for agriculture are ten and thirty-six periods, respectively; for commerce, about fourteen and thirty-nine. Academic students take academic subjects exclusively. A comparison of the survey figures and the students' own assessments of the time devoted to different courses in Form IV is shown in table 6-11. Apparently, in the Tanzanian secondary education system, wide deviations occur between scheduled and actual course loads. These are probably a result of insufficient teachers or facilities, or only partial implementation of diversification.

3. Although the official number of periods for the core curriculum is the same for all curricula, including the academic track, students can take optional subjects such as additional mathematics, arts, foreign languages, and music.

Regressions were fitted separately for each curriculum using three academic scores (math, English, and Kiswahili), with the score in the curriculum for which the student was registered as the dependent variable. Again, a host of out-of-school characteristics were included in the set of independent variables to serve as controls so that any effect of sex, age, or ability was removed before the impact of the specific course-time-exposure variable was assessed. The findings for agriculture students are presented in table 6-12; results for technical, commercial, and academic students, respectively, are contained in tables 6-13, 6-14, and 6-15.

The findings reported in these tables highlight several important effects of course-load distribution on learning. (Note that it is the amount of class time specifically devoted to courses rather than the undifferentiated total number of course hours that affects test scores.) First, in practically all cases, related courses have a powerful and significant impact on the test in the subject they complement. For example, in table 6-12, the figures show that exposure to commerce and science has a positive effect on math achievement. Second, it appears that in different curricula combinations of courses affect learning in different ways, depending on the subject tested. To use commercial students as an example, table 6-14 reveals that social studies courses aid commercial students in learning math and English; commerce courses, as expected, aid these students in learning commerce skills, but apparently at the expense of English learning. Language and social studies courses have some surprising effects on test performance. For academic students (table 6-15) language courses do not aid learning in English, Kiswahili, or math, whereas social studies courses affect performance positively in these academic areas. For commerce students (table 6-14) a different pattern is revealed: language courses negatively affect math performance and have no effect on commerce. For agriculture students, language courses have a negative effect on agriculture and on math test scores (see Karweit 1983).

Effect of Date of Implementation on Achievement

Do students attending schools that have a relatively long history of offering a given curriculum specialization perform better than students in schools that introduced it later? The survey data show that student scores in schools that established a specialization before 1977 are indeed higher than those of students in schools that began to diversify after 1977.

When exam date (pre-1977 = 0 and post-1977 = 1) and course periods in individual vocational subjects are included in regressions on vocational test scores by curriculum (table 6-16), we are able to observe more fully how "time on task" affects learning. In table 6-16, each regression is run only for students majoring in the given subject area. For example, in the

Table 6-12. *Effects of Class Time on Achievement, Agricultural Students, Tanzania, 1981 Cohort*

	Test score							
	English		*Mathematics*		*Kiswahili*		*Agriculture*	
Independent variable	*Coefficient*	*t-value*	*Coefficient*	*t-value*	*Coefficient*	*t-value*	*Coefficient*	*t-value*
Background								
Male	2.654[a]	4.40	3.927[a]	6.44	4.998[a]	8.17	-1.539[a]	2.08
Age	-0.474[a]	2.39	-0.384	1.92	-0.486[a]	2.42	0.080	0.33
Books at home	0.019[a]	2.57	0.001	0.14	0.009	1.19	-0.003	0.32
Urban born	-1.232	1.93	0.084	1.13	-1.853[a]	2.86	0.220	0.28
Father's education	0.002	0.03	-0.144	1.82	-0.118	1.49	0.180	1.87
Log of father's earnings	-0.068	0.47	0.187	1.29	-0.039	0.27	0.472[a]	2.67
Father self-employed	0.327	0.64	0.730	1.41	0.044	0.08	0.160	0.25
Father farmer	-0.711	1.17	-0.608	0.99	-0.766	1.25	0.589	0.79
Father blue-collar	0.373	0.43	-0.302	0.34	-0.464	0.52	0.031	0.02
Father white-collar	-0.420	0.48	-1.610	1.83	-2.108[a]	2.39	0.604	0.56
Father professional	-2.025[a]	2.29	-0.753	0.84	-1.486	1.66	1.770	1.63
Verbal aptitude	0.212[a]	8.29	0.181[a]	6.99	0.173[a]	6.66	0.234[a]	7.43
Math aptitude	0.266[a]	10.24	0.433[a]	16.47	0.248[a]	9.43	0.087[a]	2.75
Private school	-5.458[a]	7.30	-1.802[a]	2.38	-6.992[a]	9.22	-3.382	3.69
Class time periods								
Agriculture	-0.416[a]	4.11	-0.498[a]	4.86	0.086	0.83	0.749[a]	6.02
Commerce	0.174	1.46	-0.307[a]	2.54	0.278[a]	2.30	0.011	0.07
Language	-0.258	1.74	-0.160	1.07	-0.120	0.80	-0.448[a]	2.46
Science	0.572[a]	8.12	0.405[a]	5.68	0.143[a]	2.00	0.174[a]	2.01
Social studies	0.069	1.01	-0.094	1.37	0.449[a]	6.49	-0.064	0.76
Constant	30.362	6.38	23.571[a]	4.89	32.289[a]	6.68	27.437[a]	4.70
R^2	0.37		0.43		0.37		0.18	

Sample size 1,252

a. Statistically significant at the 5 percent level or better.

Table 6-13. *Effects of Class Time on Achievement, Technical Students, Tanzania, 1981 Cohort*

	Test score							
	English		Mathematics		Kiswahili		Technical	
Independent variable	Coefficient	t-value	Coefficient	t-value	Coefficient	t-value	Coefficient	t-value
Background								
Male	2.405	1.44	0.549	0.30	1.889	1.13	−0.180	0.10
Age	−0.152	0.43	−0.730	1.93	−0.248	0.71	−0.469	1.23
Books at home	0.028[a]	2.05	0.020	1.30	0.023	1.64	−0.002	0.14
Urban born	−3.278[a]	2.04	−4.366[a]	2.50	−3.464[a]	2.15	−3.151	1.79
Father's education	−0.135	0.98	−0.109	0.73	−0.114	0.82	−0.075	0.50
Log of father's earnings	0.060	0.20	0.058	0.18	0.026	0.08	−0.005	0.01
Father self-employed	1.413	1.52	−0.257	0.25	1.253	1.35	0.514	0.50
Father farmer	−1.639	1.56	−1.408	1.23	−1.739	1.65	0.061	0.05
Father blue-collar	−0.148	0.11	0.498	0.33	−1.059	0.78	0.938	0.63
Father white-collar	−2.315	1.46	−3.846	2.23	−1.716	1.08	−2.893	1.67
Father professional	−0.216	0.11	−1.738	0.82	−0.864	0.44	1.051	0.49
Verbal aptitude	0.213[a]	3.85	0.227[a]	3.78	0.173[a]	3.13	0.099	1.63
Math aptitude	0.220[a]	4.41	0.324[a]	5.96	0.289[a]	5.78	0.430[a]	7.88
Private school	−15.395[a]	11.04	−8.184[a]	5.39	−19.956[a]	14.29	−5.573[a]	3.65
Class time periods								
Agriculture	−1.621	1.50	−0.280	0.23	1.456	1.34	−0.399	0.33
Commerce	0.399	0.29	1.100	0.75	−2.331	1.73	−0.687	0.47
Language	0.052	0.17	−0.791[a]	2.39	0.680[a]	2.24	0.350	1.05
Science	0.090	0.54	0.901[a]	5.04	−0.414[a]	2.51	−0.165	0.92
Social studies	0.032	0.08	0.572	1.30	−0.840[a]	2.08	0.225	0.51
Technical	−0.255	1.24	−0.070	0.81	−0.239	0.53	0.143	1.09
Constant	28.468[a]	3.40	31.938[a]	3.51	35.519[a]	4.24	38.634[a]	4.22
R^2	0.49		0.45		0.57		0.32	
Sample size 457								

a. Statistically significant at the 5 percent level or better.

Table 6-14. *Effects of Class Time on Achievement, Commercial Students, Tanzania, 1981 Cohort*

| | Test score | | | | | | | |
| | English | | Mathematics | | Kiswahili | | Commercial | |
Independent variable	Coefficient	t-value	Coefficient	t-value	Coefficient	t-value	Coefficient	t-value
Background								
Male	4.069[a]	6.906	1.765[a]	3.737	2.913[a]	4.938	−0.004	0.007
Age	−0.832[a]	3.682	−0.175	0.970	0.917	0.873	−0.251	1.052
Books at home	0.026[a]	3.353	0.001	0.246	0.007	0.957	−0.008	1.011
Urban born	−0.857	1.360	−1.653[a]	3.272	−0.385	0.611	−0.205	0.309
Father's education	−0.134	1.441	−0.002	0.036	0.005	0.063	0.087	0.890
Log of father's earnings	0.066	0.336	0.145	0.918	0.166	0.839	0.363	1.735
Father self-employed	−0.545	0.974	0.318	0.709	−0.232	0.415	−0.383	0.648
Father farmer	1.591[a]	2.212	−0.514	0.893	0.486	0.675	−0.124	0.164
Father blue-collar	−0.483	0.532	−1.282	1.759	0.046	0.051	−0.742	0.772
Father white-collar	0.703	0.870	−0.008	0.013	0.534	0.661	0.524	0.614
Father professional	0.390	0.443	0.482	0.682	−0.285	0.324	−0.114	0.123
Verbal aptitude	0.218[a]	6.714	0.160[a]	6.141	0.173	5.322	0.127[a]	3.696
Math aptitude	0.191[a]	6.084	0.350[a]	13.872	0.170[a]	5.406	0.209[a]	6.285
Private school	−5.808[a]	8.975	1.716[a]	3.310	−5.677[a]	8.763	−2.158[a]	3.155
Class time periods								
Agriculture	1.234	1.834	1.305[a]	2.419	0.770	1.143	0.310	0.436
Commerce	−0.207[a]	3.119	0.079	1.500	−0.065	0.982	0.246[a]	3.510
Language	−0.010	0.099	−0.248[a]	2.820	0.310[a]	2.821	0.008	0.077
Science	0.004	0.067	0.195[a]	3.624	−0.221[a]	3.286	−0.065	0.922
Social studies	0.440[a]	7.754	0.154[a]	3.401	0.102	1.811	0.061	1.020
Constant	40.779[a]	7.648	21.750[a]	5.089	27.588[a]	5.168	39.008[a]	6.919
R^2	0.36		0.39		0.24		0.13	
Sample size	1,024							

a. Statistically significant at the 5 percent level or better.

162

Table 6-15. *Effects of Class Time on Achievement, Academic Students, Tanzania, 1981 Cohort*

	Test score					
	English		*Mathematics*		*Kiswahili*	
Independent variable	*Coefficient*	*t-value*	*Coefficient*	*t-value*	*Coefficient*	*t-value*
Background						
Male	-0.100	0.16	5.025[a]	7.70	-3.449[a]	5.33
Age	-0.198	0.93	0.041	0.18	-0.195	0.86
Books at home	0.016[a]	2.10	0.013	1.62	0.013	1.55
Urban born	-0.991	1.44	-1.035	1.40	-2.344[a]	3.20
Father's education	0.091	1.04	-0.004	0.05	0.188[a]	2.01
Log of father's earnings	-0.207	1.12	-0.172	0.86	-0.194	0.98
Father self-employed	-0.083	0.14	0.181	0.30	0.605	1.02
Father farmer	0.077	0.11	-1.192	1.60	0.606	0.82
Father blue-collar	-0.660	0.71	-0.988	0.99	-0.136	0.13
Father white-collar	-1.601	1.71	-1.907	1.90	-0.818	0.82
Father professional	0.114	0.11	-0.987	0.95	0.965	0.94
Verbal aptitude	0.318[a]	11.03	0.166[a]	5.36	0.221[a]	6.90
Math aptitude	0.234[a]	7.77	0.432[a]	13.55	0.221[a]	6.90
Private school	-0.180	0.30	1.483[a]	2.30	-2.471[a]	3.87
Class time periods						
Agriculture	-0.179	1.26	-0.281	1.84	0.210	1.39
Commerce	-0.134	0.69	-0.487[a]	2.32	0.614[a]	2.96
Language	-0.035	0.45	-0.142	1.68	-0.016	0.20
Science	2.398[a]	9.75	1.286[a]	4.87	0.888[a]	3.39
Social studies	0.414[a]	6.12	0.390[a]	5.37	0.420[a]	5.85
Constant	24.138[a]	4.90	16.245[a]	3.07	27.598[a]	5.27
R^2	0.45		0.48		0.32	
Sample size 922						

a. Statistically significant at the 5 percent level or better.

Table 6-16. Influence of Exam Date and the Number of Course Periods on Learning for Vocational Students, Tanzania, 1981 Cohort

Independent variable	Achievement score							
	Agricultural		Commercial		English		Technical	
	Coefficient	t-value	Coefficient	t-value	Coefficient	t-value	Coefficient	t-value
Background								
Male	0.47[a]	2.5	−0.13	0.7	2.74[a]	6.0	0.21	0.4
Age	0.01	0.6	0.03	0.9	0.99[a]	6.2	0.10	0.6
Household possessions	0.16[a]	2.3	−0.10	0.5	0.07	0.8	−0.10	0.5
Log of father's income	0.25[a]	2.2	0.27[a]	2.5	0.01	0.7	−0.13	0.9
English spoken in home	−0.11	0.6	−0.13	0.8	−0.19	0.9	−0.02	0.8
Books at home	−0.00	0.5	−0.01	0.7	0.01[a]	2.5	−0.00	0.7
Father professional	0.17	0.8	0.13	0.9	−1.60[a]	2.5	0.17	0.7
Father self-employed	0.09	0.7	0.09	0.8	−0.15	0.6	0.15	0.9
Father white-collar	−0.25	0.4	0.17	0.8	−0.92	0.7	−0.67	1.0
Father blue-collar	−0.19	0.5	−0.09	0.9	−1.70[a]	2.4	−0.07	0.8
Father's education	0.04	1.0	0.04	0.7	−0.07	0.5	−0.01	0.4
Mother's education	−0.05	0.2	−0.01	0.9	−0.19[a]	2.5	−0.02	0.7
Verbal aptitude	0.19[a]	9.0	0.09[a]	4.5	0.93[a]	16.0	0.11[a]	2.2
Math aptitude	0.10[a]	4.2	0.19[a]	7.7	1.13[a]	16.0	0.41[a]	8.5
Exam date after 1977	−0.02[a]	2.0	−0.06[a]	2.0	−0.03	0.5	−0.05[a]	4.6
Class time periods								
Agriculture	0.21[a]	8.0	—		—		—	
Commerce	—		0.05[a]	2.5	—		—	
English	—		—		−0.25	0.8	—	
Technical	—		—		—		−0.05	0.6
Constant	0.22		6.56		−32.9		2.37	
R²	0.175		0.132		0.306		0.280	
Sample size	1,380		1,284		4,181		492	

Note: The reference occupational category is farmer.
a. Statistically significant at the 5 percent level or better.

agriculture equation, only the 1,380 students majoring in agriculture are included. The same is true for the 492 technical students and the 1,280 commerical students. All commercial, technical, and agriculture students are included with the academic students in the regression for English, because everyone takes that subject. The exam date variable is significantly negative for each of the three specialized biases; in other words, schools that offered a specialization and were prepared to offer exams in that subject prior to 1977 produce students with significantly higher scores in their bias subject. Students in those schools do not have higher English scores, however, and their academic performance is not significantly better. The variable representing the course periods in the specialization is positive and significant for agriculture and commerce, but not for technical and English achievement scores.

In summary, students attending schools which specialized before 1977 do significantly better in agriculture, commerce, and technical subjects.

Effect of School Quality on Achievement

To what extent do school expenditures and related quality indicators improve test scores? A breakdown of selected private and public school expenditures by curriculum is presented in table 6-17.

Achievement scores in vocational and academic subjects were regressed on a block of school quality inputs, along with the previous list of out-of-school independent variables. Table 6-18 presents the results, with scholastic achievement in English, commerce, agriculture, and industrial arts used as the dependent variables. As can be seen, school inputs differentially affect learning outcomes. As the number of students per teacher increases, test scores in English decrease. Teachers' educational levels are significantly related to test scores in commerce, but not in other subjects.

Table 6-17. *Annual School Expenditure per Student by Curriculum, Selected Items, Tanzania, 1981 Cohort*
(shillings)

Expenditure	Academic	Agricultural	Commercial	Technical
Government-supplied				
Teacher salaries	1,050	1,441	1,185	1,378
Materials	441	352	230	763
Family-supplied				
Textbooks	172	156	210	150
Writing supplies	120	96	121	108
Fees	748	340	811	399

Note: Expenditures are for both public and private schools.

Table 6-18. *Achievement as a Function of Background and School Factors, Tanzania, 1981 Cohort*

Independent variable	Technical		Agricultural		Commercial		English	
	Coefficient	*t-value*	*Coefficient*	*t-value*	*Coefficient*	*t-value*	*Coefficient*	*t-value*
Background								
Male	2.031[a]	4.80	0.477	1.02	0.321	0.68	2.385[a]	5.78
Age	−0.255	1.82	−0.271	1.76	−0.345[a]	2.23	−0.447[a]	3.27
Books at home	−0.003	0.67	0.006	1.17	0.005	0.89	0.018[a]	3.63
Urban born	−0.010	0.02	0.231	0.45	1,419[a]	2.79	−0.613	1.36
Father's education	−0.055	0.98	−0.118	1.90	0.024[a]	0.38	0.007	0.13
Log of father's earnings	−0.107	0.97	−0.059	0.49	−0.157	1.30	−0.020	0.18
Father self-employed	0.278	0.77	0.952[a]	2.41	0.853[a]	2.15	0.619	1.77
Father farmer	−0.215	0.49	−0.208	0.43	0.027	0.05	−0.185	0.43
Father blue-collar	0.783	1.34	0.442	0.69	0.338	0.52	−0.666	1.17
Father white-collar	0.038	0.06	1.079	1.69	0.069	0.10	−0.295	0.52
Father professional	0.708	1.10	1.781[a]	2.53	2,158[a]	3.06	0.009	0.01
Verbal aptitude	0.190[a]	9.75	0.220[a]	10.29	0.126[a]	5.89	0.250[a]	13.17
Math aptitude	0.233[a]	12.37	0.137[a]	6.65	0.091[a]	4.40	0.262[a]	14.27

School

	(1)		(2)		(3)		(4)	
Curriculum								
Agriculture	−2.275[a]	5.15	−0.385	0.79	−4.616[a]	9.49	−2.802[a]	6.51
Commercial	−1.923[a]	3.52	−3.261[a]	5.45	2.861[a]	4.76	−3.936[a]	7.40
Technical	4.937[a]	8.02	−2.877[a]	4.25	−3.000[a]	4.42	−5.453[a]	9.08
Private school	−1.753[a]	3.59	−2.554[a]	4.77	0.092	0.17	−1.575[a]	3.31
Teacher education	0.122	1.36	−0.135	1.37	0.357[a]	3.62	0.095	1.09
Per student expenditure	0.74E-03[a]	4.56	0.55E-03[a]	3.07	0.29E-04	0.16	0.16E-03	1.05
Student/teacher ratio	−0.007	0.28	−0.046	1.68	−0.027	0.97	−0.119[a]	4.87
Teacher salaries	−0.001[a]	3.41	−0.001[a]	2.47	−0.51E-04	0.11	0.27E-03	0.69
Academic periods	0.015[a]	1.99	0.008	0.97	−0.001	0.21	0.003	0.46
Constant	31.997[a]	8.68	42.304[a]	10.46	41.767[a]	10.29	34.243[a]	9.53
R^2	0.32		0.19		0.15		0.37	

Sample size 2,803

Note: The occupational groups listed are evaluated relative to those not listed.

a. Statistically significant at the 5 percent level or better.

Teacher salaries and per student expenditure are inversely related to technical and agricultural scores. The time devoted to academic subjects has a significant effect on technical scores only. In sum, there is no clear overall pattern for the effect on achievement of common indicators of school quality.

A convenient method of evaluating the effectiveness of the vocational programs is presented in table 6-19. This table shows that higher mean scores are obtained by vocational students on measures of vocational learning than on academic subjects. These scores are derived from the regression equation after adjustment for background characteristics and measures of ability (see table 6-10). In all cases, the gains in vocational learning are obtained at the expense of some English language achievement. Because the government's policy objective is to develop vocational skills, however, it may be concluded that the curriculum design does meet its intended goal.

Modernity Attitudes

As discussed in previous chapters, schools are believed to influence the values and attitudes of students and make them more "modern." Such changes toward modernity are judged to contribute to national and economic development. To measure psychological modernity, students were asked to agree or disagree (on the Lickert scale[4]) with hypothetical behavioral statements relating to a variety of day-to-day situations. These items were intended to elicit choices that would identify persons as either "traditional" or "modern" in their value orientation and outlook. For example, the following statement asked students to agree or disagree: "Success depends more on luck than on hard work." Presumably, less traditional individuals will believe less in fate and more in the results of their own labor and thus view change as something they can control. Another statement reads: "If I were given a choice of 20 shillings today or 40 shillings next month, I would take my 20 shillings today." The modern individual might be more inclined to disagree with the statement, deferring present consumption for future greater investment. A final example states: "The only people one really can trust are one's family and relatives." Modern individuals probably are more inclined to view outsiders as trustworthy. In all, twenty-one questions were asked. The coefficient of reliability for the sample was equal to 0.75, which indicates that the items seemed to measure a single concept of what we call individual modernity.

---

4. A Lickert scale measures the respondent's reaction to a question along a continuum from less to more: (1) disagree strongly, (2) disagree, (3) no opinion, (4) agree, (5) agree strongly. The scale is extensively used in opinion and attitude surveys.

Table 6-19. *Achievement Score Gains: Vocational Curriculum Compared with Academic Control, Tanzania, 1981 Cohort*

Curriculum	Achievement test	Gain
Technical	Technical	5.26
	English	−4.05
Commercial	Commerce	5.43
	English	−2.27
Agricultural	Agriculture	1.61
	English	−2.24
Academic	Commerce	−2.74
	Technical	−4.09
	Agriculture	−2.24

Note: All achievement score differences are statistically significant at the 5 percent level or better. Background and ability are held constant.

The mean score of the modernity scale by selected characteristics of the education system is presented in table 6-20. Technical students enrolled in public schools outscore all others. Although not shown in the table, differences in parental education among students in the various curricula were not significantly associated with differences in modernity.

Of course, the question remains whether the modernity attitudes preexisted or were formed by the type of school attended. In order to control for ability and other out-of-school characteristics, a regression was fitted with modernity score as the dependent variable and the various curricula as a

Table 6-20. *Mean Modernity Score by Curriculum and Type of School, Tanzania, 1981 Cohort*

Curriculum and school ownership	Mean modernity score
Agricultural	5.9
Public	6.1
Private	5.0
Technical	6.3
Public	6.5
Private	5.6
Commercial	5.6
Public	6.0
Private	5.0
Academic	5.8
Public	6.0
Private	5.4

series of independent dummies. The results show that, after controlling for background characteristics, very few modernity differences survive among curriculum programs, although private school students score significantly lower than public school students on modernity (table 6-21).

When students are compared on the basis of whether they wish to pursue formal education, those desiring to enter Form V are much more modern than those who do not expect to continue with their studies. This is equally true for all curricula.

School Experience and Expectations

Do curriculum programs differentially alter a student's view about occupations or his expectations about the job he will eventually take? As vocational students invest more and more time in specialized subjects, they

Table 6-21. *Individual Modernity as a Function of School and Out-of-School Characteristics, Tanzania, 1981 Cohort*

Independent variable	Coefficiency	t-value
Background		
Male	0.323	0.84
Age	−0.008	−0.06
Books at home	0.015[a]	3.00
Urban born	−0.728	−1.74
Father's education	−0.046	−0.85
Log of father's earnings	0.029	0.27
Father self-employed	−0.791[a]	−2.28
Father farmer	0.186	0.43
Father blue-collar	−0.641	−1.13
Father white-collar	−0.500	−0.91
Father professional	−0.996	−1.71
Verbal aptitude	0.199[a]	10.89
Math aptitude	0.120[a]	6.62
Curriculum		
Agriculture	0.529	1.29
Commercial	0.669	1.60
Technical	0.973	1.77
Private school	−1.453[a]	−3.80
Constant	34.101[a]	11.20
R^2	0.11	
Sample size	3,903	

Note: Academic bias is the omitted reference category.
a. Statistically significant at the 5 percent level or better.

may come to realize that those special subjects are of limited value outside certain occupations. One might expect these students to be prepared to continue with their specialized course of training so as not to lose the advantage they have built up in the course work already completed. In contrast, students taking only academic courses have invested most of their time in general subjects that facilitate entry to many kinds of employment. The expectation is that these students would therefore be less likely to tie themselves to any specialized occupational field.

In the survey, students were asked to examine a list of sixteen occupations and to rate each in terms of its importance in Tanzania. Ratings varied from very important to unimportant. For some students, importance may have implied personal social prestige, rather than value to the nation, but in every case students rated occupations on the basis of their own perceptions. The occupations were chosen from existing lists used to tap occupational expectations elsewhere in Africa (see Foster 1966) and were hierarchically ranked from professional-managerial, clerical, and skilled labor down to unskilled manual work. A few new items were introduced so that the scale fit more neatly with the occupational categories found in Tanzania (such as, party worker and youth worker).

Differences in how Tanzanian students within the various tracks viewed the importance of specific occupations is reported in table 6-22. Because most of the findings are of only borderline statistical significance, it is likely that students in the sample, regardless of their curriculum, viewed the Tanzanian occupational structure in much the same way. It appears that clergy, sales persons, and youth leaders were not highly valued, while most students, regardless of track placement, listed agricultural scientist, nurse, and school teacher as highly valuable and useful occupations.

Depending on the school enrolled in or the course of instruction, students may view their own prospective careers differently. For example, more than 70 percent of all students (72 percent of agricultural, 71 percent of technical, 81 percent of commercial, and 82 percent of academic) planned to apply for admission to Form V (upper secondary school), even though fewer than 20 percent of all Form IV graduates would eventually be accepted (table 6-23). Sixty-six percent of agricultural students planned to apply for employment training upon completion of Form IV. Comparable figures for technical, commercial, and academic students were 69 percent, 55 percent, and 53 percent, respectively. Although the differences are relatively small, agricultural and technical students appear to be slightly more interested in pursuing careers in their training fields than in pursuing traditional academic course work in Form V. Academic students planned to apply for Form V in large numbers (which is to be expected, given their stream's close link to the university curriculum), but many planned to apply for jobs and nonuniversity training programs as well, perhaps as a form of insurance in case they were not accepted into Form V.

Table 6-22. *Percentage of Students Asserting that a Given Occupation Is of Importance for Tanzania, 1981 Cohort*

	Curriculum			
Occupation	Agricultural	Technical	Commercial	Academic
Agricultural scientist	87	82	82	84
Auto mechanic	57	65	53	59
Building trades	34	55	34	40
Clergy	19	19	22	31
Customs inspector	40	44	47	44
Farm manager	62	53	52	54
Government clerk	44	35	45	44
Lawyer	55	55	62	61
Nurse	79	65	77	80
Party worker	46	53	47	52
Police Officer	66	59	70	67
Primary school teacher	76	74	72	76
Sales worker	24	22	31	27
Secondary school teacher	76	78	74	75
University professor	69	74	69	68
Youth leader	38	39	38	35

Note: Figures refer to percentages responding that the occupation is of "above average importance" and "very important."

With regard to the choice of sector of employment (public sector exclusively, versus parastatal or private), little difference was evident across curricula, with more than 50 percent of all respondents planning to seek public sector employment.

Students also were asked to select from a list of thirteen job training areas their first, second, and third choices for a career after graduation. The list included two agricultural choices (farming and veterinary training), three commercial (secretarial training, hotel management, and bookkeeping), three technical (electrical, mechanical, and automotive training), and two academic (teacher and cultural officer training), along with some miscellaneous categories (tailoring, food technology, and day care), which were used as distractors. These choices were then grouped to reflect the four broad fields of agricultural, commercial, technical, and academic pursuits, so that it was possible to compare student occupational choices with their curriculum program.

As first choice, agriculture students selected their own field 53 percent of the time, technical students picked their specialization 75 percent of the time, and commerce students chose theirs 59 percent of the time. Academic students seemed to scatter their choices more widely; only 22 percent wished to pursue such traditional academic courses as teacher training or cultural affairs training (table 6-24).

Table 6-23. *Post-Graduation Plans and Expectations,*
Tanzania, 1981 Cohort
(percent)

Characteristic	Curriculum			
	Academic	*Agricultural*	*Commercial*	*Technical*
Plans to apply to				
Form V	82	72	81	71
Employment training	53	66	55	69
Plans to enter				
Self-employment	22	19	16	14
Salaried employment	5	6	6	4
Salaried employment in				
Government service	60	69	59	61
Parastatal	34	25	32	35
Private sector	6	6	9	4
Expectations				
Starting salary (shillings a month)	852	824	833	856
Weeks to get a job	23	23	21	21

Like the Colombian secondary school cohort examined in chapter 5, Tanzanian students were asked to state their earnings prospects with and without a Form IV education. The perceived value of a Form IV education indicates how realistically students view education's worth in the labor market.

Expected mean earnings by curriculum bias are listed in table 6-25. The first column refers to expected earnings if students dropped out of Form IV and immediately went to work. The second column refers to expected earnings from employment on the assumption that students would complete Form IV a few months after the survey was made. The difference between columns 1 and 2 represents the value attributed to a Form IV certificate. The third column refers to what students hoped to be earning in five years' time. (In every case students were asked to discount for effects of inflation.) There are few differences in expected initial earnings across curriculum programs, a finding undoubtedly due to the government's egalitarian pay policy.

Comparing Costs with Outcomes

The unit costs for Tanzania's secondary schools are more easily calculated than was the case for Colombia. In Tanzania, each school has only one area of specialization, and hence expense accounts can be differentiated. The assumptions underlying the cost comparisons are briefly de-

Table 6-24. *First, Second, and Third Career Choices by Curriculum, Tanzania, 1981 Cohort*
(percent)

| | | | | | Career choice | | | | | | | |
| | Academic | | | Agricultural | | | Commercial | | | Technical | | |
Curriculum	First	Second	Third	First	Second	Third	First	Second	Third	First	Second	Third
Academic	**22**	**24**	**34**	33	26	21	25	28	24	20	22	21
Agricultural	12	17	41	**53**	**45**	17	18	20	21	17	18	21
Commercial	12	19	26	14	22	16	**59**	**45**	**31**	15	14	17
Technical	11	16	35	6	8	6	8	13	17	**75**	**63**	**42**

Note: This table summarized thirteen specific job choices in four general areas; students from each curriculum ranked three of the four. Figures in boldface indicate choices in the student's own field of specialization.

174

Table 6-25. *Expected Monthly Earnings by Curriculum, Tanzania, 1981 Cohort*
(shillings)

| | Without Form IV certificate (1) | With Form IV certificate | |
| | | Upon graduation (2) | In five years (3) |
Curriculum			
Academic	798	852	1,763
Agricultural	735	824	1,675
Commercial	746	833	1,831
Technical	776	856	1,763

scribed below, and the detailed calculations are to be found in Hinchliffe (1983).

Unit Costs by Curriculum

Estimates of forgone earnings, relevant to both private and social costs, have been based on students' expected earnings without a Form IV diploma. Other data in the study suggest that students generally overestimate earnings by about 20 percent. As a result, we have reduced the stated levels of earnings forgone by that amount. The final figure of 624 shillings a month is consistent with findings of a 1980 survey of wage employment in Tanzania, where twenty-one- and twenty-five-year-old primary and secondary school leavers were earning a monthly average wage of 596 and 745 shillings, respectively. (Special tabulations from the survey are described in Knight and Sabot 1981.) Annual per student capital costs, have been calculated directly from World Bank appraisal reports for education diversification projects in Tanzania. Recurrent school costs were reported in some detail on the questionnaires. Data on private expenditures by school curriculum and ownership (state or private) and by item (textbooks, fees, and so forth) were available, as were data on school expenditures for salaries, materials, and room and board for both state and private schools.

Annual private and social costs by school curriculum are presented in table 6-26, while table 6-27 converts a number of the cost sets into indices, with the unit cost of the academic track set at 100. Total social costs of each type of school are dominated by forgone earnings; and differences in these according to curriculum are not statistically significant. The variations in total social costs by curriculum therefore appear small—the average for vocational schools is only 3 percent above that for the academic schools. In contrast, total recurrent costs in state schools are 14

Table 6-26. *Annual Average Cost of Secondary Schooling per Student, Tanzania, 1981*
(shillings)

Item	Curriculum			
	Agricultural	Technical	Commercial	Academic
Recurrent cost				
Borne by individual				
State schools	749	854	1,114	1,112
Private schools	1,328	1,129	1,556	1,065
Private school fees	1,987	1,981	1,841	2,226
Borne by rest of society				
State schools	2,700	2,409	2,046	1,776
Private schools	—	—	—	—
Total recurrent cost				
State schools	3,449	3,263	3,160	2,888
Private schools	3,315	3,110	3,397	3,291
State schools				
Total direct cost[a]	5,798	5,612	5,509	5,237
Total social cost[b]	13,290	13,104	13,001	12,729

— Not applicable.
a. Including capital costs.
b. Including forgone earnings.

percent higher in the diversified schools than in those offering only academic subjects. In the case of government-financed recurrent costs, the diversified schools are on average 34 percent higher.[5]

Whether differences in costs between diversified and nondiversified schools are regarded as significant depends on the type of cost considered. Total social costs show little variation. The implications for public expenditure, however, are substantial.

Cost-Effectiveness of Cognitive Achievement

To compare the costs and achievements of different curricula, the same procedure was followed as in Colombia. The comparison is limited to

5. Secondary school costs have also been estimated by the Tanzania Ministry of National Education (1979a). These estimates differ in major ways from those based on our questionnaire, for two main reasons. First, the ministry figures cover a much wider set of components, some of which, it can be argued, are incidental to teaching. Second, ministry figures are all accounting costs, whereas those used in the present study reflect social opportunity costs. When these two factors are taken into account, the two estimates of the costs of commercial schools are virtually the same; the difference is 8 percent. For technical schools, however,

Table 6-27. *Indices of Annual Private and Social Costs per Student for State and Private Schools, by Curriculum, Tanzania, 1981*
(academic cost = 100)

	Curriculum			
Item	Agricultural	Technical	Commercial	Academic
Private direct expenditure				
State schools	67	77	100	100
Private schools	102	95	106	100
Private direct cost				
State schools	67	76	100	100
Private schools	125	106	146	100
Government financed				
Recurrent cost	152	136	115	100
Recurrent and capital cost	122	115	106	100
Total recurrent social cost				
State schools	119	112	109	100
Private schools	101	95	103	100
State schools				
Total recurrent and capital social cost	111	107	105	100
Total social cost (including forgone earnings)	104	103	102	100

public schools, which have the most relevance for government policymakers. Because most secondary schools would continue to be academically oriented if diversification had not been introduced, the academic stream has been treated as a control group to contrast with vocational students.

Table 6-28 presents average annual recurrent costs by curriculum program, along with achievement scores in both academic and vocational subjects. Test score means have been adjusted to remove the influences of innate ability, sex, age, and other nonschool factors potentially influencing educational achievement.

Annual costs per student are higher in all vocational schools than they are for the academic control group: 13 percent higher for technical students, 19 percent for agricultural students, and 9 percent for commercial students. How do such increased costs translate into achievement improvements?

The adjusted mean achievement scores in table 6-28 have a mean of 50

substantial differences remain; ministry estimates are 40 percent greater than those obtained from our questionnaire.

Table 6-28. *Recurrent Costs and Achievement Scores*
in Public Schools, Tanzania, 1981 Cohort

| | | Cost | Adjusted mean achievement score | | | | |
| | Annual unit cost (shillings) | difference, diversified/ control (percent) | Academic | | Vocational | | |
Curriculum			Math	English	Agri- culture	Com- merce	Tech- nical
Academic (control)	2,888	—	**51**	**52**	52	50	52
Agricultural	3,449	+19	52	52	**54**	—	—
Commercial	3,160	+ 9	49	51	—	**55**	—
Technical	3,263	+13	55	51	—	—	**58**

Note: Means are for public school students only, and adjustments have been made to remove the effects of ability and out-of-school characteristics on achievement.

Scores in boldface are those for students' area of specialization.

and a standard deviation of 10. An advantage of ten points means that 34 percent of the group in question outscore the control group (see figure 5-5). For example, agriculture students scored 54 on the agriculture test, while academic students averaged only 52. The two-point difference in favor of agricultural students corresponds to a 0.2 difference in standard deviation and indicates that about 7 percent more agricultural students than academic students score above the sample mean. For 19 percent more resources per student, agricultural schools are able to boost agricultural achievement by about 7 percent; at the same time, math achievement is raised by 3 percent, and English achievement is not raised at all. For the extra resources committed, gains in agricultural knowledge seem modest, while the academic skills acquired are neither better nor worse than those obtained by academic students in the control group.

Comparisons can also be made between technical and control students. For 13 percent more resources, technical schools can boost technical achievement by 0.6 standard deviation, or 23 percent—a rather large impact. In return for the additional resources, math achievement is raised by 16 percent, though English achievement drops by about 4 percent. The technical stream appears to be cost-effective in raising technical and math achievement levels, at virtually no loss to English skills.

Students in commercial schools cost 9 percent more on average to educate than those in the control group. In return, commercial achievement is raised by 0.5 standard deviation, or about 19 percent. Although commercial schools appear to sacrifice academic skills for commercial skills, the loss is small.

Thus, it appears that technical schools, though costing more than control schools, yield a substantial increase in both academic and vocational knowledge over that of the academic control group. Likewise, both agricultural and commercial students gain in vocational knowledge as the result of higher per student costs, but they show little or no increase in academic knowledge relative to the control group.

The Class of 1981 One Year Later

Of the 1981 base-year sample (4,181 students), a total of 2,426 returned the follow-up questionnaire distributed one year after graduation—a response rate of nearly 60 percent. This response rate was expected when the original 1981 sample was designed. Although it appears low by U.S. or European standards of survey research, the figure is highly satisfactory by developing nations' standards, particularly given the conditions in Tanzanian rural areas (long distances, poor roads and transportation, limited postal service, and the movement of students back and forth between rural and urban areas).[6]

Response Rate

Because fewer than two-thirds responded, however, it is essential to determine whether there were any differences in the characteristics between those who did and did not respond. Response bias arises when the missing cases are not a random subsample of the original sample. If missing cases are randomly distributed by key sample characteristics, however, the omission is of little consequence because it simply leaves a smaller but still random sample of the original population.

To detect any systematic response differences, selected characteristics of the base-year sample, follow-up respondents, and follow-up nonrespondents were compared. According to table 6-29 there are no significant differences between respondents and nonrespondents based on sex, aptitude, curriculum bias, and father's education or employment. Slight differences arise regarding public school graduates and the urban born. The latter, who constituted only 18 percent of the 1981 base-year cohort, responded to the 1982 follow-up in greater numbers than expected. But when response rates by region are compared, only three regions (the Dar es Salaam area, Dodoma, and Arusha) significantly deviate from their expected response rates.

The discrepancy in the Dar response rate is mitigated by the fact the capital contained less than 10 percent of the 1981 base-year sample to begin with. The nine remaining regions, including the two most populous

6. A Land Rover was secured to trace sample participants in the countryside.

Table 6-29. *Base-Year Cohort, Follow-up Respondents,*
and Nonrespondents by Selected Background Characteristics,
Tanzania, 1981 Cohort
(percent)

Characteristic	1981 base sample	1982 respondents	1982 non-respondents
Curriculum			
Agricultural	32.8	32.2	33.9
Technical	11.6	11.5	12.1
Commercial	30.2	30.6	30.9
Academic	25.3	25.6	23.1
Male	65.7	66.0	67.8
Public school graduate	72.3	74.3	69.8
Urban born	17.9	19.8	15.6
Applied to Form V in 1981	76.9	76.2	77.5
Top quartile scorer (math aptitude)	25.0	25.9	23.7
Top quartile scorer (english)	25.0	26.5	23.5
Top quartile scorer (math)	25.0	25.6	24.3
Father secondary school graduate	14.9	16.2	13.9
Father professional/manager	10.1	10.7	9.3
Father farmer	41.9	41.6	42.3

in the sample (Kilimanjaro and Tanga), had response rates in the 1982 follow-up identical to those observed in the 1981 base year.

Post-Form IV Opportunities

The major post-Form IV avenues available to graduates are:

- Entry into Form V—a preferred option because it is likely to lead to university and a professional career
- Placement in teacher training or other public sector training, which may lead to a career in a government ministry
- Salaried employment or self-employment in the private sector
- Looking for a job (particularly a teaching, clerical, or technical job in the public sector—very rarely in farming) or further training
- Being voluntarily inactive.

The last two groups might include individuals who scored low on their Form IV examinations, private school graduates who were never led to expect public sector employment in the first place, or those who for personal reasons never desired further training or immediate employment.

As mentioned previously, Tanzania's secondary school system is tied closely to estimated needs for manpower in the public sector. Originally, students admitted into public secondary schools were expected to enter public sector or parastatal employment upon graduation. With the expansion of secondary education, however, that objective has been reviewed, and it is now understood that public school graduates will also work in the private sector or be self-employed.

Even on its present scale, the secondary education system has not been able to place all its graduates. (Placement is defined here as government assignment of students to Form V, further training, or full-time public sector employment.) Ntuah (1981) reports that only 10 percent of Form IV graduates in 1977–78 obtained suitable further education or employment in fields related to their secondary education. In addition, he found that 31 percent of the 1977 cohort were unemployed two years after graduation, and that more than 43 percent of the 1978 cohort had not found jobs or further training one year after graduation. Ministry of Manpower statistics reveal that from 1978 to 1981, more than one-third of all Form IV graduates were never placed (posted to Form V, given teacher or other public sector training, or employment). A fair number of those not placed undoubtedly came from private schools, whose students are often not considered in government manpower forecasts and whose standards are generally lower than those of public schools.

Graduate Destinations

By comparing the destinations of graduates from diversified and control schools, it is possible to see whether the diversification of secondary education has had any impact on graduates' career opportunities. As in the case of Colombia, we asked whether diversification:

- Reduces private demand for upper secondary education
- Raises the probability of postgraduate labor force participation
- Reduces unemployment and the time spent seeking work
- Raises the initial earnings of those working
- Raises the social rates of return to investment in schooling.

Answers to these questions help assess whether diversification of the secondary curriculum has its intended effects, at least during the early career of graduates.

The first question in the 1982 follow-up survey asked students to indicate the activity which most nearly described how they spent the preceding month—whether they were in school, further training, salaried employment, or self-employment or were looking for work or a place in further education. Only one individual marked the category of "other" than the above activities. Clearly, virtually all 1981 graduates saw their future in terms of competitive employment, absorption into government

Table 6-30. *The 1982 Activity of Form IV Graduates,*
Tanzania, 1981 Cohort
(percent)

1982 activity	1981 Form IV curriculum				
	Academic	Agricultural	Commercial	Technical	Overall
Form V	27.5	25.3	34.2	33.3	29.5
Training	45.0	45.1	35.9	39.4	41.6
Working	14.1	13.7	14.2	17.4	14.4
Looking for work	13.4	15.8	15.7	9.8	14.5
Total	100.0	100.0	100.0	100.0	100.0

service, or further education. Form IV graduates represent a select competitive group who are not likely to choose to remain without a job or a
place in further education or training.

Table 6-30 shows the distribution of Form IV graduates among activities, and figure 6-5 illustrates their various destinations by curriculum.
Curriculum appears to make no major difference to graduates' initial
destination. Technical students, however, are more likely than others to be
employed and less likely than others to seek schooling or training or be
unemployed (not shown in figure). Consequently, one can infer that with
the possible exception of technical students, all Form IV graduates stand
nearly the same chances of landing a job.

Figure 6-5. *Distribution of Respondents by 1982 Activity,*
Tanzania, 1981 Cohort

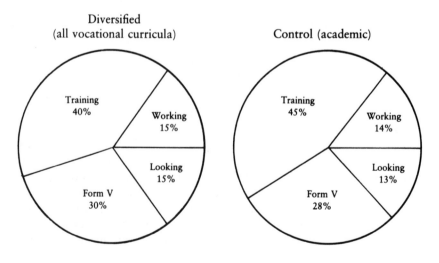

Diversified
(all vocational curricula)

Training 40%
Working 15%
Looking 15%
Form V 30%

Control (academic)

Training 45%
Working 14%
Looking 13%
Form V 28%

The 1982 activities of Form IV public and private school graduates by curriculum are listed in table 6-31. Private school graduates appear to have been placed in almost equal proportions to the public school graduates, which implies that government recruitment procedures have not discriminated against them.

Table 6-32 relates graduates' current activities to their achievement scores in school. In general, graduates who are self-employed or are looking for work, schooling, or training—all of whom constitute the residual of unplaced—do not appear to have been low achievers.

Table 6-31. *Graduate Destination by Form IV Bias and School Ownership, Tanzania, 1981 Cohort*
(percent)

Form IV curriculum and 1982 activity	Form IV school	
	Public	Private
Academic		
Form V	28	27
Training	44	46
Salaried employment	8	10
Self-employed	8	2
Looking for training	8	6
Looking for work	5	9
Agricultural		
Form V	28	20
Training	46	48
Salaried employment	9	7
Self-employed	5	7
Looking for training	7	13
Looking for work	7	5
Commercial		
Form V	36	37
Training	45	29
Salaried employment	7	13
Self-employed	7	8
Looking for training	8	12
Looking for work	8	5
Technical		
Form V	33	35
Training	38	45
Salaried employment	15	6
Self-employed	4	4
Looking for training	5	6
Looking for work	4	4

Table 6-32. *Achievement Score by Curriculum and 1982 Activity, Tanzania, 1981 Cohort*

Form IV curriculum and 1982 activity	Academic		Vocational			Non-verbal Aptitude
	Math	English	Agri-cultural	Com-mercial	Tech-nical	
Academic	51	53	52	51	51	51
Form V	52	53	54	51	53	52
Training	51	53	51	50	50	50
Salaried work	52	50	53	52	52	50
Self-employed	51	55	48	48	50	49
Looking for training	52	53	51	51	51	51
Looking for work	52	50	54	52	52	51
Agricultural	51	51	53	48	50	51
Form V	52	51	53	48	51	52
Training	51	51	53	48	50	51
Salaried work	49	51	51	46	49	50
Self-employed	49	51	52	47	49	48
Looking for training	51	50	54	49	49	51
Looking for work	52	53	54	46	49	54
Commercial	47	47	47	54	47	47
Form V	46	47	47	54	47	47
Training	48	49	47	53	48	48
Salaried work	47	45	48	54	47	47
Self-employed	46	47	46	56	44	48
Looking for training	47	47	45	56	46	46
Looking for work	47	46	48	54	47	48
Technical	53	50	50	48	57	55
Form V	52	51	50	48	56	55
Training	51	50	51	49	56	53
Salaried work	57	54	51	47	59	58
Self-employed	53	54	52	50	58	57
Looking for training	52	49	47	49	54	52
Looking for work	56	48	48	48	52	56
Overall	50	50	50	50	50	50

ENROLLMENT IN FORM V

At completion of Form IV in 1981, well over 80 percent of students reported they had applied to Form V. As noted, only a small fraction of Form IV graduates have sufficiently good examination results to be selected for Form V. To what extent does the probability of going on to further education relate to the type of school attended and its specialization?

The follow-up survey of the 1981 cohort provides information on the way students were actually selected into Form V—whether on the basis of high academic achievement, as measured by Form IV examination results

Table 6-33. *Form V Major Subject by Form IV Curriculum,*
Tanzania, 1981 Cohort
(percent)

Form V subject	Form IV curriculum				
	Academic	Agricultural	Commercial	Technical	Overall
Academic	**71.6**	79.3	79.6	81.8	77.9
Agricultural[a]	1.2	**5.3**	4.6	0.0	3.4
Commercial	9.9	10.6	**9.6**	10.2	10.0
Technical	17.3	4.8	6.3	**8.0**	8.7
Total	100.0	100.0	100.0	100.0	100.0

Note: Figures in boldface indicate students who continued to study in their Form IV field of specialization.

a. Refers to those enrolled in the MATI and LITI agricultural and livestock training institutes.

and the course content, or of nonschool factors such as sex, age, and socioeconomic background.

The follow-up survey asked those who were currently attending Form V to list the courses they were taking. Such courses were clustered into three major fields: technical (civil or electrical engineering), commercial (commerce or principles of accounting), and agricultural. An agricultural stream in Form V was not officially adopted until the 1983-84 school year, so the students polled by the study were those taking courses in the training institutes run by the Ministry of Agriculture and the Ministry of Livestock.[7] All students not in these three fields were considered to be in the "academic" stream.

The survey included a cross-tabulation of pre- and post-Form IV subjects (table 6-33). Seventy-eight percent of all those in Form V took academic subjects (math, history, languages, and social and physical sciences) exclusively and were evenly distributed by Form IV curriculum. Of the remaining 22 percent of respondents, students pursuing technical courses in Form V were drawn mostly from the Form IV academic track, and many of those majoring in agricultural sciences had majored in commerce in Form IV. Even though diversification was not fully implemented at the time of the survey, the continuity between Form IV and Form V subject specialization seems rather loose.

We examined test scores for graduates of each curriculum in two categories: those who stayed in their same Form IV field of specialization

7. Although these courses are not strictly equivalent to Form V level, graduates of them receive a diploma in the appropriate field, just as the Form VI leavers do.

and those who moved into academic streams. Among agricultural students math, English, Kiswahili, and agriculture scores did not vary between the two groups. Presumably, students who pursue some agricultural courses in Form V are selected for reasons other than examination results in that subject, since only 5 percent of those who finished Form IV and had above average achievement scores in agriculture stayed in that field in Form V. For the two groups of commercial students, there were no differences in math, English and Kiswahili scores. Students who remained in commerce after Form IV, however, obtained significantly higher scores in commercial achievement tests. Thus, staying in commerce is related to better scores in that subject—which means that recruitment into Form V commercial subjects is based in part on achievement in Form IV commercial studies. Among technical and academic Form IV students, no differences emerge on test scores between those who pursued academic and nonacademic careers in Form V.

Among Form V students, 58 percent said they were studying the curriculum of their first choice. This statistic varies by field: agriculture, 56 percent; commerce, 79 percent; technical, 62 percent; and academic track, 51 percent.

Form V students were also asked about their occupational expectations. Seventy-one percent wanted to pursue professional or managerial careers rather than jobs in agriculture, technical fields, and commerce. By field, the figures are 68 percent for agriculture, 40 percent for commerce, 100 percent for technical, and 77 percent for the academic bias.

An examination of the number of academic and vocational courses taken in lower secondary school by students who went on to Form V reveals no significant differences. This is also the case for students' nonverbal ability.

The selection of students for Form V appears to be essentially unrelated to the subjects they studied in lower secondary school, with the possible exception of commercial students. More than three-quarters of Form V students pursued academic courses—whatever their Form IV course may have been. The remainder, who specialized in nonacademic courses, did not differ significantly from academic students in terms of innate ability, socioeconomic background, scholastic attainment in Form IV, occupational expectations, or forgone and expected earnings. In short, although ability, achievement, social class, and other characteristics may be an important determinant of obtaining a place in Form V, once accepted, a student's choice of a particular curriculum program does not appear to be contingent on past performance or previous field of study.

Table 6-34 presents schooling expenses and expected labor market outcomes among those in Form V. Again, no major differences arise on any of the characteristics. The rather lengthy (thirty-six weeks on average)

Table 6-34. *Monthly School Expenses, Expected Earnings,*
and Weeks to Find Employment by Students Enrolled in Form V,
Tanzania, 1981 Cohort

Form IV curriculum	Expected weeks to find work	Expected earnings (shillings)	Current schooling expenses (shillings)	Earnings forgone (shillings)
Academic	31	2,116	245	603
Agricultural	37	2,534	224	715
Commercial	38	2,491	251	611
Technical	36	2,263	205	568
Overall	36	2,381	236	632

waiting period to obtain employment is described as "normal" by Tanzania government officials because of the time necessary to process the examination results and place the graduates.

FURTHER TRAINING

The group of nearly a thousand Form IV graduates placed in training programs (including teacher training) constituted 42 percent of the 1982 follow-up respondents. When this group is subdivided according to Form IV curriculum and the graduate training program, a pattern emerges as shown in table 6-35.

Nearly half of the group was engaged in teacher training, most of them coming from Form IV agricultural and commercial curricula. Those who entered teacher training did not come disproportionately from the academic track. The most interesting result in this table is the small proportion of commerical graduates and the high proportion of technical

Table 6-35. *Further Training in 1982 by Form IV Curriculum,*
Tanzania, 1981 Cohort
(percent)

1982 training	1981 Form IV curriculum				
	Academic	Agricultural	Commercial	Technical	Overall
Agriculture	7.5	5.4	11.1	6.7	7.6
Clerical occupations	10.2	8.4	5.6	21.2	9.5
Primary school teaching	47.9	55.8	59.1	45.2	53.3
Other	34.3	30.4	24.2	26.9	29.5
Total	100.0	100.0	100.0	100.0	100.0

graduates who took clerical training courses. This would seem to imply that post-Form IV clerical courses are not seen as adding to a commercial student's job opportunities, but that a substantial proportion of technical students who opt for further training expect to find openings in the clerical field. Finally, the proportion of agricultural graduates taking agricultural training courses is slightly lower than the proportion of graduates of other curricula studying agriculture.

There were no sex differences by type of further training. But, when public and private school graduates were compared, it was found that public school graduates were more likely than their private school counterparts to continue in the field they studied in Form IV.

Occupational expectations of trainees revealed that the largest proportion (44.4 percent) expected to become teachers. Eleven percent expected to enter clerical occupations, with technical and academic students preferring such roles.

Two other questions were designed to elicit how contented respondents were with their post-Form IV training program. On the question whether, given a choice, graduates would prefer to work, be in school, or continue in training, 70 percent expressed satisfaction with training, 25 percent had a desire to go on to Form V, and only 5 percent would have preferred to be employed. No significant differences were found in such opinions by Form IV track or between public and private schools. However, slightly more males than females preferred work (7 percent compared with 4 percent). On the question whether, given the choice, respondents would prefer a form of training different from their current one, 35 percent expressed a desire to change; agriculture students had the highest percentage (41 percent) wishing a change, and technical students the lowest (25 percent). Respondents did not vary in their opinions according to sex and public-private school background.

When questioned about the number of weeks they expected to wait before obtaining employment and their expected earnings from initial employment, students evidenced no significant differences by Form IV curriculum (table 6-36). To an outside observer, the expected waiting period appears unusually long, but this is accepted as normal because Form IV graduates must await placement by the government.

EMPLOYMENT

Nine percent of the respondents had found salaried employment one year after graduation, and another 5 percent were self-employed. A comparison of their jobs and earnings allows some conclusions about whether one curriculum offered any advantage over another to graduates in the labor market. Because self-employment and salaried employment differ

Table 6-36. *Labor Market Expectations of Those in Training in 1982, Tanzania, 1981 Cohort*

Form IV curriculum	Expected number of weeks to find employment	Expected monthly earnings (shillings)	Monthly training expenses (shillings)	Forgone earnings while in training (shillings)
Academic	31	1,264	236	690
Agricultural	35	1,279	231	673
Commercial	32	1,175	222	680
Technical	36	1,172	247	769
Overall	33	1,254	229	683

substantially, the two groups are treated separately. And because the government sets wages in Tanzania, those in public employment are distinguished from those in the private sector.

Of the graduates in salaried employment, 48 percent were in government, 12 percent were in private, and the rest were in parastatal employment (table 6-37). By economic sector, 29 percent were in commerce, 9 percent were in agricultural jobs, and 17 percent were in manufacturing, with the remaining 45 percent in all other sectors. Most respondents had found their jobs after waiting six months. They worked, on average, forty-four hours a week and earned 726 shillings a month before taxes.

When these workers were studied on the basis of their Form IV curriculum, we found that 20 percent of agricultural students went into private sector employment and that 57 percent of technical graduates went into government work, as did 55 percent of commercial graduates. Thus, it appears that agricultural students are not as readily hired into the public sector as students from other specialties. Moreover, agriculture graduates' private sector activities do not necessarily include farming because one-third of them work in commercial or secretarial occupations.

Among all respondents in salaried employment, half are in public sector clerical jobs, with no differences by Form IV curriculum or public-private school background. Females, however, are twice as likely as males to end up in private sector employment. No significant differences emerge in earnings and hours worked by curriculum bias.

The self-employed were working on average 42 hours a week and earning twice as much as those engaged in salaried employment. Twenty-three percent worked on their own farms, and another 48 percent were engaged in family agricultural help. Those who owned their own farms worked significantly fewer hours a week than those who worked on farms as laborers—38 and 44 hours, respectively. The remaining 30 percent earned their living from personal services, odd jobs, or nonfarm businesses. This group waited longer than the others before deciding to enter self-employment (35 as opposed to 28 weeks). Self-employed commercial graduates earned substantially less than those coming from other specialties. Females were significantly less likely to be earning their living from "kibarua," or odd jobs, than were males. On measures of the socioeconomic background, innate ability, and modernity of self-employed graduates no differences were found by Form IV track.

In the light of government equalizing wage controls, it is of interest to examine how respondents perceived their earnings prospects as they progressed through the various educational, training, and employment programs, and what they in fact earned as secondary school graduates in the public and private sectors of the economy.

Table 6-38 presents expected and actual earnings for respondents in the 1982 follow-up on the basis of their Form IV curriculum. Reports of students' expected earnings before and at the time of Form IV graduation were obtained from the base-year survey, while the expected earnings cited in the follow-up survey are on the assumption that any schooling or

Table 6-37. *Selected Characteristics of Those Employed in 1982, Tanzania, 1981 Cohort*

| Characteristic | Form IV curriculum | | | | |
	Academic	Agricultural	Commercial	Technical	Overall
Economic sector and employer (percent)					
Government	49	34	55	57	48
Parastatal	40	46	35	37	40
Private sector	11	20	10	6	12
Agriculture	5	12	7	10	9
Manufacturing	10	18	25	14	17
Commerce	30	40	20	21	29
Administration and services	55	30	48	55	45
Salaried employment	57	60	60	69	62
Self-employment	43	40	40	31	38
Those in salaried employment					
Weeks waiting for job	26	29	27	33	28
Hours worked	42	44	45	42	44
Monthly earnings (shillings)	762	736	710	699	726
Those in self-employment					
Weeks waiting for job	39	38	32	20	35
Hours worked	44	38	39	42	42
Monthly earnings (shillings)	1,532	1,676	1,252	1,560	1,504
Sample size	83	101	100	45	329

Table 6-38. *Expected Monthly Earnings at Three Levels of Education and 1982 Actual Earnings by Sector of Employment, Tanzania, 1981 Cohort*
(shillings a month)

| Form IV curriculum | Expected earnings | | | Actual earnings | | | |
	Without Form IV	With Form IV	With post-Form IV studies	Public sector	Private sector	Self-employ-ment	All sectors
Academic	792	883	1,252	746	787	1,532	1,065
Agricultural	755	830	1,325	722	776	1,676	1,100
Commercial	754	852	1,356	697	820	1,252	932
Technical	773	844	1,247	702	580	1,560	892
Average	766	852	1,307	716	777	1,504	1,013

training activity in the interim will have been successfully completed. Actual earnings were computed from follow-up data. Expected and actual earnings differed somewhat by Form IV curriculum, but with only a low level of statistical significance.

LOOKING FOR SCHOOLING OR WORK

About 7 percent of the respondents were looking for full-time schooling or further training and another 6 percent were looking for work. These respondents constitute a residual group who had neither been placed in any public sector activity nor found a job in the private sector at the time of the follow-up. Only one person wished to remain inactive. The ratios of males to females and public to private school graduates in this residual category are similar to those who were already placed in further training or jobs (tables 6-39 and 6-40). Therefore, no particular group is disproportionately looking for work or training.

Of those looking for work only, 65 percent were looking exclusively for government employment, and 29 percent were seeking employment in parastatals; only 6 percent were interested in private sector work. The attraction of government employment varies little across Form IV curricula, sex, or public-private school affiliation, which further suggests that those still looking are actually hoping for placement in government jobs. The notable exception is technical school graduates, who seek private employment in greater proportion to other students. About half of those looking for work were interested in secretarial or accounting positions, regardless of their curriculum in 1981. All but 15 percent started looking

Table 6-39. *Characteristics of Those Looking for Schooling or Training in 1982, Tanzania, 1981 Cohort*

	Form IV curriculum				
Characteristic	Aca-demic	Agri-cultural	Com-mercial	Tech-nical	Over-all
Sex (percent)					
Male	61	67	40	100	59
Female	39	33	60	0	41
Form IV school (percent)					
Public	80	75	48	79	67
Private	20	25	52	21	33
Family income (shillings a month)	5,934	7,841	7,280	6,040	7,048
Sample size	48	62	58	16	184

for jobs sometime in 1982, although all the private school graduates in the group (24 percent) started looking as early as 1981.

Of those looking for work 70 percent were supported by families and 30 percent by odd jobs. Among those supported by families, there was a slight preponderance of Form IV agricultural graduates, males, and private school graduates. On average, they expected to wait eleven more weeks before finding a job, which 50 percent described as secretarial or clerical in nature. The minimum acceptable monthly salary averaged 957 shillings. There were no significant differences among job-seekers with respect to ability and family background.

Likewise, among the 7 percent looking for training a year after graduating from Form IV, little difference could be discerned between males and females, public and private school graduates, or curricula. Twenty-three percent were looking for training in clerical-commercial subjects, 17 percent in agriculture, 14 percent in trades, 10 percent in teaching, 8 percent in a profession, and 27 percent training in other occupations.

It is interesting that those still looking for work put "minimum acceptable earnings" at a much higher level than the salaries of their counterparts who were already working. The data are summarized in table 6-41, together with the amounts that those who were in training and in school expected to earn once they entered the labor market.

As a group, those looking for work or training did not vary by aptitude or social class from the entire 1981 sample, and within the group the variations in achievement as measured by national examination scores were also similar to those found for the entire 1981 sample: technical students did better in math, academic and agricultural students did better in English, and students in each curriculum did best in their respective

Table 6-40. *Characteristics of Those Looking for Employment in 1982, Tanzania, 1981 Cohort*

Characteristic	Form IV curriculum				
	Aca-demic	Agri-cultural	Com-mercial	Tech-nical	Over-all
Sex (percent)					
Male	77	79	47	92	69
Female	23	21	53	8	31
Form IV school (percent)					
Public	66	89	68	83	76
Private	34	11	32	17	24
Expected sector of employment (percent)					
Public	97	96	91	82	93
Private	3	4	9	18	6
Weeks looking for job					
In current search	32	32	28	16	31
Additional expected	11	11	9	8	11
Reservation wage (shillings a month)	859	944	1,051	958	957
Source of financial support (percent)					
Family	70	73	70	64	70
Other sources	30	27	30	36	30
Sample size	35	53	47	12	147

specialty. In conclusion, those graduates who did not immediately go on to Form V, training, or employment do not noticeably differ from other graduates on the basis of their Form IV curriculum.

UNEMPLOYMENT

One of the main goals of diversification was to provide sufficient training so that graduates of agricultural, technical, and commercial curricula would experience a shorter period of unemployment than they might otherwise have encountered after graduating from an academic school. However, the data in table 6-42 do not show that this has happened. One year after graduation, 13 percent of academic students were still looking for either work or training while the percentages for technical, commercial, and agricultural students were 10, 16, and 16, respectively. Academic graduates did not believe that they had to wait any longer for some activity than other students. Form IV graduates in Form V or in training courses also showed no differences by curriculum in the period they expected to have to wait before obtaining work once they entered the labor force.

Table 6-41. *Actual and Expected Monthly Earnings of Form IV Leavers, Tanzania, 1981 Cohort*
(shillings)

	Form IV curriculum			
Monthly earnings	Academic	Agricultural	Commercial	Technical
Actual in 1982[a]	762	736	710	699
Expected				
Those looking for work	859	944	1,051	958
Those in training	1,264	1,279	1,175	1,172
Those in school	2,116	2,534	2,491	2,263

a. Those in salaried employment.

Predicting Post–Form V Destinations

Having examined several descriptive dimensions of the sample, we turned to the question of how school and background characteristics affect the decision to study, work, obtain further training, or look for work. What characteristic most encourages a move into upper secondary education? Is it high grades, the type of lower secondary school attended, or the previous curriculum track? As noted above, 27 percent of graduates in the follow-up survey entered Form V. We wanted to know whether test scores in the vocational secondary school curriculum helped students to get accepted into Form V. It is especially interesting to see how, in a centrally monitored system such as Tanzania's, merit, school type, curriculum, and socioeconomic background affect the eventual destination of graduates.

To do this, we applied logit analysis, using control variable for family background, sex, age, scholastic achievement, vocational scores, curricu-

Table 6-42. *Unemployment Rates in 1982 and Expected Periods of Job Search, Tanzania, 1981 Cohort*

	Form IV curriculum			
Item	Academic	Agricultural	Commercial	Technical
Unemployment rate (percent)	13	16	16	8
Expected weeks to find work				
Those looking	10	11	9	9
Those in Form V	38	34	36	38
Those in training	31	35	32	36

lum, and measures of school quality, all of which might potentially affect the probability of entry into Form V. The findings reported in table 6-43 reveal that six variables affect entry into full-time study (statistical significance at the 0.10 percent level or better): being male, coming from a commercial-track high school (either private or public), coming from a school with a lower level of English usage, having scored higher on the technical test, and having scored lower on the modernity test. Test scores in academic subjects do not influence entry, and the technical achievement score barely affects selection into Form V ($t = 1.6$).

Access to Training

More than 40 percent of the 1981 Form IV graduating class went on to further training, primarily teacher training. Using a logit model, we again found only six variables that significantly predicted access to further training (table 6-44): attending a public agricultural school, attending a school with high-quality resources, coming from a curriculum program with few vocational courses, scoring high in English achievement or individual modernity, and having a less-educated mother. Such factors increased the chances for selection into government-sponsored training. At the margin, higher English and modernity scores, along with an agricultural curriculum, helped students get into training program. Surprisingly, more vocational course work hurts rather than helps students in gaining entrance to further training.

Entry into Salaried Employment

About 10 percent of the 1982 respondents were in salaried employment (excluding those who were self-employed), most of them in public or parastatal jobs. Some countervailing tendencies can be noted in table 6-45. Graduation from a public technical school aids in finding employment, whereas graduation from a public commerical school makes it more difficult to find employment. Salaried workers tended to have scored lower in English, taken more vocational courses, graduated from poorer quality schools, and privately spent more on schooling than the rest of the 1982 respondents.

When self-employed workers are added to salaried employees, the combined group represents 15 percent of the 1982 sample. The only difference regarding the prediction of employment status is that in the combined group males are less likely to land jobs in 1982. The explanation for this is that the self-employed are predominantly female graduates who reside on farms.

Table 6-43. *Maximum Likelihood Estimates of the Determinants of Form V Selection in 1982, Tanzania, 1981 Cohort*

Variable	Marginal effect	t-value
Background		
Male	0.086[a]	3.50
Age	0.011	1.30
Urban residence	0.019	0.70
Books in home	0.001	0.20
English usage in home	0.023	1.20
English usage in school	−0.042[a]	1.60
Mother's education	0.014	0.20
Father's education	0.002	0.50
Father professional	0.011	0.30
Father white-collar	0.023	0.70
Father blue-collar	0.040	1.20
Father teacher	0.052	1.20
Father's income	0.001	0.30
Regional GNP	0.001	0.30
School quality index	0.034	1.00
Modernity score	−0.011[a]	2.50
Achievement score		
Agricultural	0.002	0.50
Commercial	0.002	0.40
Technical	0.006[a]	1.60
Math	0.001	0.20
English	0.001	0.40
Form IV school		
Academic private	0.034	0.60
Agricultural public	−0.029	0.70
Agricultural private	−0.086	1.40
Commercial public	0.064[a]	1.70
Commercial private	0.087[a]	1.50
Technical public	0.018	0.40
Technical private	0.072	0.80
Private school expenditure	0.001	0.20
Teachers' salaries	0.001	0.20
School maintenance expenditure	0.002	0.30
Science periods	0.017	0.70
Vocational periods	0.001	0.80
Sample size	1,722	
D-value	0.026	
Mean dependent variable		0.208

a. Significant at the 10 percent level or better.

Table 6-44. *Maximum Likelihood Estimates of the Determinants of Recruitment into Training Programs in 1982, Tanzania, 1981 Cohort*

Variable	Marginal effect	t-value
Background		
Male	−0.028	1.00
Age	0.001	0.50
Urban residence	0.001	0.20
Books in home	0.001	1.00
English usage in home	0.001	0.60
English usage in school	−0.001	0.40
Mother's education	−0.009[a]	2.00
Father's education	0.001	0.80
Father professional	0.024	0.70
Father white-collar	0.001	0.20
Father blue-collar	−0.003	1.00
Father teacher	0.001	0.20
Father's income	0.001	0.20
Regional GNP	−0.001	1.10
School quality index	0.008[a]	1.70
Modernity score	0.006[a]	1.60
Achievement score		
Agricultural	−0.001	0.90
Commercial	−0.001	0.50
Technical	−0.001	0.90
Math	−0.001	0.90
English	0.001[a]	1.80
Form IV school		
Academic private	−0.001	0.50
Agricultural public	0.058[a]	1.60
Agricultural private	0.073	1.30
Commercial public	0.001	0.40
Commercial private	−0.001	0.50
Technical public	0.006	0.20
Technical private	0.078	0.90
Private school expenditure	0.001	0.40
Teachers' salaries	0.001	0.40
School maintenance expenditure	0.001	0.30
Science periods	0.001	0.10
Vocational periods	−0.010[a]	3.50
Sample size	1,722	
D-value	0.028	
Mean dependent variable		0.416

a. Significant at the 10 percent level or better.

Table 6-45. *Maximum Likelihood Estimates of the Determinants of Salaried Employment One Year after Graduation, Tanzania, 1981 Cohort*

Variable	Marginal effect	t-value
Background		
Male	−0.008	1.00
Age	0.001	0.60
Urban residence	−0.004	0.50
Books in home	0.001	0.50
English usage in home	−0.008	0.90
English usage in school	0.014	1.00
Mother's education	−0.001	1.00
Father's education	−0.001	0.90
Father professional	0.003	0.40
Father white-collar	0.026	1.30
Father blue-collar	0.005	1.00
Father teacher	−0.036	1.00
Father's income	0.001	1.20
Regional GNP	0.001	0.80
School quality index	−0.006[a]	1.90
Modernity score	−0.001	0.60
Achievement score		
Agricultural	0.001	0.50
Commercial	−0.001	0.50
Technical	0.002	1.00
Math	0.001	1.00
English	−0.001[a]	1.50
Form IV school		
Academic private	0.011	0.80
Agricultural public	−0.002	0.50
Agricultural private	−0.049	1.30
Commercial public	−0.044[a]	1.70
Commercial private	−0.036	1.00
Technical public	0.041[a]	1.60
Technical private	−0.057	1.00
Private school expenditure	0.001[a]	1.70
Teachers' salaries	0.001	0.50
School maintenance expenditure	−0.001	1.20
Science periods	0.001	1.00
Vocational periods	0.002[a]	2.40
Sample size	1,722	
D-value	0.021	
Mean dependent variable		0.82

a. Significant at the 10 percent level or better.

Recruitment by the Government

As has been mentioned, recruitment into Tanzania's large public sector is based heavily on manpower planning considerations. Nearly 80 percent of the base cohort in the sample was absorbed by the government in 1982 in one way or another. As table 6-46 shows, most of the factors influencing that absorption are similar to the ones discussed in the above sections.

First, families with less-educated mothers and families with fathers who are white-collar workers were most likely to have children recruited into the public domain. Second, males and older graduates were more likely to be absorbed by the government than others in the sample. Respondents coming from poorer economic regions (areas outside Dar es Salaam and Dodoma) were more likely to have entered government-sponsored activities, as were respondents with more traditional attitudes. Finally, those who graduated from public technical and commercial schools and those who took fewer vocational courses were more likely to find themselves in government activities. With regard to achievement scores, it appears that students who scored high on technical tests or low in commercial tests stood a better chance of being selected. In short, coming from a poor region, having a father who is a clerical worker, having oneself traditional values, and being male increase one's chance of getting selected into government sector activities.

Graduates Still Seeking Placement

Twenty percent of the sample had not been placed in school, training, or work by 1982, but were seeking to participate in one of these activities (table 6-47). Respondents whose fathers were not clerical workers, mothers who were more highly educated, graduates living in high-income areas, those with more modern outlooks, high achievers on commercial and math tests, those who took more vocational courses, and those who were younger were more likely to be searching for work, training, or employment one year after graduation.

Many of these characteristics suggest that these individuals could afford to wait for a job or further training. Having higher modernity scores, which implies a willingness to take risks, and coming from wealthier regions of the nation and being younger may predispose a graduate to search longer. Those looking for training or employment opportunities may have been offered positions by the ministries of Education or Manpower, but turned them down for personal reasons.

Table 6-46. *Maximum Likelihood Estimates of the Determinants of Being Recruited into the Public Sector in 1982, Tanzania, 1981 Cohort*

Variable	Marginal effect	t-value
Background		
Male	0.050[a]	2.30
Age	0.016[a]	2.10
Urban residence	0.017	1.00
Books in home	0.001	1.00
English usage in home	0.025	1.50
English usage in school	−0.030	1.40
Mother's education	−0.010[a]	2.90
Father's education	0.006	1.40
Father professional	0.040	1.20
Father white-collar	0.066[a]	2.10
Father blue-collar	0.012	0.90
Father teacher	0.026	0.80
Father's income	0.001	0.20
Regional GNP	−0.001[a]	3.00
School quality index	−0.001	0.30
Modernity score	−0.001[a]	1.50
Achievement score		
Agricultural	−0.001	0.50
Commercial	−0.001[a]	1.50
Technical	0.001[a]	1.50
Math	−0.001	1.10
English	0.001	0.90
Form IV school		
Academic private	0.021	0.70
Agricultural public	0.024	0.80
Agricultural private	−0.046	1.00
Commercial public	0.045[a]	1.50
Commercial private	0.033	1.00
Technical public	0.078[a]	1.90
Technical private	0.099	1.30
Private school expenditure	0.001	0.50
Teachers' salaries	0.001	1.00
School maintenance expenditure	−0.001[a]	1.70
Science periods	0.002	0.90
Vocational periods	−0.004[a]	1.80
Sample size	1,722	
D-value	0.023	
Mean dependent variable		0.758

a. Significant at the 10 percent level or better.

THE TANZANIA CASE STUDY

Table 6-47. *Maximum Likelihood Estimates of the Determinants of Being Unplaced in 1982, Tanzania, 1981 Cohort*

Variable	Marginal effect	t-value
Background		
Male	−0.029	1.50
Age	−0.015[a]	2.10
Urban residence	−0.028	1.40
Books in home	−0.001	1.00
English usage in home	−0.014	0.90
English usage in school	0.001	0.70
Mother's education	0.010[a]	2.90
Father's education	−0.001	1.70
Father professional	−0.084	1.40
Father white-collar	−0.069[a]	2.40
Father blue-collar	−0.015	1.00
Father teacher	−0.009	0.50
Father's income	−0.001	0.90
Regional GNP	0.001[a]	2.30
School quality index	0.001	1.00
Modernity score	0.003[a]	2.00
Achievement score		
Agricultural	0.001	1.00
Commercial	0.003[a]	1.80
Technical	−0.001	1.00
Math	0.001[a]	1.80
English	−0.001[a]	1.90
Form IV school		
Academic private	0.019	0.70
Agricultural public	−0.009	0.90
Agricultural private	0.036	0.80
Commercial public	−0.026	0.90
Commercial private	−0.025	0.90
Technical public	−0.063	1.50
Technical private	−0.077	1.20
Private school expenditure	0.001	0.80
Teachers' salaries	0.001	0.70
School maintenance expenditure	0.001	1.00
Science periods	−0.009	0.90
Vocational periods	0.001[a]	2.30
Sample size	1,722	
D-value	0.026	
Mean dependent variable		0.123

a. Significant at the 10 percent level or better.

Summary of Logit Analysis

The best school-based strategy for getting into Form V would be to attend a commercial-track school and score well in technical subjects. Form IV graduates were more likely to be recruited into further training if they came from agricultural public schools and scored well in English tests. To obtain salaried employment, chances are better for private commercial or technical school graduates who have taken several vocational courses and (surprisingly) scored poorly on the English test. A lack of English may not be a handicap for this group of public employees because those who work in party-affiliated firms, utilities, and corporations are less likely to find foreign language ability a necessity.

Those currently unemployed may be holding out for something unusually attractive. As a rule, members of this unplaced group are high achievers, modern in attitudinal outlook, urban, and younger and wealthier than the rest of the sample. They graduated from all combinations of public and private curriculum biases except technical schools.

The Determinants of Labor Earnings

Because several hundred of the 1981 graduates sampled were actually earning wages in 1982, it is possible to test whether monthly earnings differed by curriculum. The respondents who graduated from Form IV in academic programs were used as a control group against which to compare other wage earners, but there were no differences in earnings attributable to the diversified curriculum programs (table 6-48). (The earnings by curriculum subject were adjusted for the other independent variables in the earnings function in table 6-49.)

Path Analysis

If it can be theorized that a given variable affects another either because of an expected causal link or because of some temporal ordering, path analysis can be used to test the actual relationship between given socioeconomic factors, schooling, and earnings. Following the model presented in chapter 4 and tested for Colombia in chapter 5, we examined the relationship among father's education, student ability (a composite of verbal and nonverbal), school type (diversified or control), achievement scores, and earnings one year after graduation from Form IV in Tanzania. The model hypothesizes that family background, ability, school attended, and achievement scores all influence earnings.

Table 6-48. *The Determinants of 1982 Labor Earnings, Tanzania, 1981 Cohort*

Variable	Coefficient	t-value
Background		
Male	2.01	0.09
Age	−30.07	0.42
Urban residence	−1.69	0.42
Father farmer	−22.50	0.20
Father's education	19.38	1.21
Regional GNP	0.04	0.92
Nonverbal ability	0.05	0.49
Attended private school	5.30	0.04
Achievement score		
Agricultural	10.09[a]	1.75
Commercial	−5.70	1.00
Technical	−3.97	0.50
Math	12.77[a]	1.90
English	−1.69	0.35
Work characteristic		
Self-employed	543.77[a]	4.50
Started work in 1981	−116.37	0.52
Work in private wage sector	7.15	0.06
Form IV curriculum[b]		
Agricultural	102.35	0.52
Commercial	−27.92	0.39
Technical	−110.27	0.42
Constant	2,051.48	
R^2	0.224	
Sample size	302	

a. Statistically significant at the 10 percent level.
b. Omitted school program variable is the academic control.

Figure 6-6 presents the results of the path model, with the agricultural score as the intermediate achievement variable. The model is based on the complete data which were available for 254 respondents. Neither their achievement scores nor the type of school attended had a significant effect on earnings. When the agricultural score is replaced with scores in other subjects, the results show that technical, commercial, math, and English achievement scores also do not have a significant influence on earnings (not shown in figure). Thus, the effect of the academic curriculum on earnings is no different from that of the agricultural, technical, or commercial curriculum.

Figure 6-6. *Path Model: Effect of Diversification on Achievement and Earnings, Tanzania, 1981 Cohort*

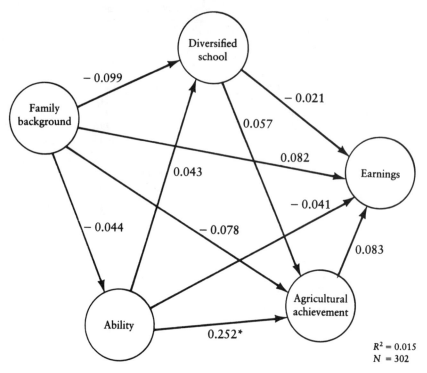

$R^2 = 0.015$
$N = 302$

*Statistically significant path.

The Returns to Education

Until the same cohort of graduates has been surveyed again some years hence, the data set for Tanzania will not permit a calculation of the social rate of return to investment in secondary education. First, only a very small fraction (14 percent) of the 1981 cohort was employed in 1982. Second, most of those employed worked in the noncompetitive public sector of the economy, and hence their earnings did not necessarily reflect the marginal product of labor. Third, the graduates were surveyed too early in their careers for their earnings to approximate the overall lifetime equivalent earnings differential assumed by the short-cut method (see the corresponding section in chapter 5, above).

Subject to these qualifications, the set of adjusted earnings reported above has been used to calculate indicative social rates of return to investment in the four curricula, but merely to summarize the different costs and benefits associated with them.

Table 6-49. *Adjusted 1982 Earnings by Curriculum, Tanzania, 1981 Cohort*

Curriculum	Mean earnings (shillings per month)	Difference from academic control (percent)
Academic	1,014	—
Agricultural	1,116	10.1
Commercial	986	−2.8
Technical	902	−10.8

Note: Monthly earnings for 302 public, private, and self-employed workers. Adjustment factors are listed in table 6-48.

Table 6-50 presents the estimated "rates of return," which highlight the cost and benefit differences among the four curricula. The academic (control) program exhibits the highest rate of return (6.3 percent) and the technical bias the lowest (1.7 percent). It should again be emphasized that the usefulness of this calculation lies more in the comparison of curricula than in the absolute level of the returns.

Conclusion

Although the follow-up survey of school leavers, made one year after graduation, allows sufficient time to test some of the hypotheses about external efficiency, others require a longer period. However, from the data available it appears that in Tanzania diversification has NOT:

- Reduced private demand for schooling beyond Form IV of secondary school
- Achieved a close correspondence between vocational curriculum and subsequent training

Table 6-50. *Indicative Social Rates of Return to Investment in Secondary Education, Tanzania, 1981 Cohort*
(percent)

Form IV curriculum	Rate of return
Academic (control)	6.3
Agricultural	5.4
Commercial	3.2
Technical	1.7
Overall	3.7

Note: Returns are based on regression-adjusted earnings (table 6-49).

Table 6-51. *Means and Standard Deviations of Selected Variables, Tanzania, 1981 Cohort*

Variable	Mean	Standard deviation
Base-year sample (sample size = 4,181)		
Background		
Male	0.668	0.047
Age	19.1	1.30
Urban residence	0.179	0.384
Number of siblings	6.36	2.720
Mother's education	4.33	3.045
Father's education	5.97	3.296
Father's annual income (shillings)	5,318	11,010
Regional per capita income (shillings)	944	980
Father farmer	0.419	0.493
Father professional	0.101	0.301
Father white-collar	0.119	0.324
Father teacher	0.060	0.237
Father blue-collar	0.101	0.302
Father otherwise employed	0.200	0.400
Father self-employed	0.526	0.499
Expectations		
Will seek private employment	0.051	0.221
Expected post-Form IV earnings (shillings a month)	836	649
Achievement score (nonstandardized)		
Kiswahili	46.500	9.499
Math	36.400	16.300
English	41.500	12.300
Commercial	6.060	2.720
Agricultural	6.140	2.590
Technical	6.940	2.999
Ability		
Verbal aptitude	10.353	3.822
Math aptitude	7.330	3.200
Modernity score	5.830	2.570
Form IV school		
Private agricultural	0.053	0.255
Public agricultural	0.277	0.447
Private technical	0.021	0.143
Public technical	0.097	0.296
Private commercial	0.129	0.335
Public commercial	0.179	0.383
Private academic	0.074	0.262
Public academic	0.170	0.402
Private expenditure per student (shillings/year)	1,759	1,292
Public teacher expenditure per student	1,045	870

Table 6-51 (*continued*)

Variable	Mean	Standard deviation
1982 Follow-up (sample size = 2,297)		
Destination		
Form V	0.295	0.456
Training	0.416	0.493
Salaried employment	0.091	0.288
Self-employed	0.053	0.224
Looking for placement	0.144	0.351
Expectations		
Expected earnings of Form V students	3,450	7,653
Expected earnings of students in training	1,282	944
Labor market outcomes		
Earnings of salaried workers	699	153
Earnings of self-employed	319	304
Satisfied with training program	0.653	0.476
Hours worked per week (salaried worker)	42.8	16.8
Hours worked per week (self-employed)	41.6	23.3
Sector of economic activity		
Public sector	0.077	0.266
Private sector	0.010	0.102
Self-employed	0.053	0.224

- Generally raised the proportion of secondary school graduates directly entering employment (although a higher proportion of technical graduates than academic students were employed in 1982—17 percent compared with 14 percent)
- Increased the likelihood that the few who are employed will obtain work in their field of specialization (however, after all students have completed their post-Form IV education and training, this situation may change)
- Reduced the amount of time needed to find work (though technical students do find employment earlier than all others)
- Raised the initial earnings of graduates of vocational programs above those of academic graduates (again, however, it is possible this finding may change when all students have entered the labor force).

An evaluation of the diversification of secondary school curricula in Tanzania must also take account of the political rationale for the

Table 6-52. Zero-Order Correlation Matrix among Selected Variables, Tanzania, 1981 Cohort

	(1)	(2)	(3)	(4)	(5)	(6)	(7)	(8)	(9)	(10)	(11)	(12)	(13)	(14)
1. Mother's education	1.00													
2. Father's education	0.66	1.00												
3. Father's earnings	0.03	0.02	1.00											
4. Father in private sector	-0.21	-0.24	0.09	1.00										
5. Father farmer	-0.27	-0.31	0.04	0.41	1.00									
6. School fees	0.17	0.14	0.03	-0.05	-0.18	1.00								
7. Expected earnings	0.01	0.00	0.03	-0.02	-0.01	0.01	1.00							
8. Verbal aptitude	-0.04	-0.03	-0.01	0.06	0.06	-0.26	-0.02	1.00						
9. Modernity score	-0.04	-0.03	0.02	0.00	0.06	-0.14	0.01	0.30	1.00					
10. Labor earnings in 1982	0.11	0.05	0.07	0.01	-0.07	0.11	-0.14	-0.05	0.08	1.00				
11. In Form V in 1982	0.02	0.02	-0.02	0.01	-0.03	-0.02	0.02	0.02	-0.04	-0.09	1.00			
12. Working in 1982	0.00	0.00	0.01	0.01	0.01	0.00	0.04	0.00	-0.02	0.03	0.03	1.00		
13. Looking for work in 1982	0.03	0.01	0.01	-0.02	0.00	0.02	0.00	0.00	0.02	0.00	-0.12	-0.09	1.00	
14. Diversified school	0.01	-0.02	-0.01	-0.01	-0.03	-0.11	-0.01	-0.04	0.01	-0.01	0.03	-0.01	0.02	1.00

innovation.[8] The previous education system was acknowledged to be elitist, inadequate, and irrelevant to Tanzania's needs. The new system, of which diversified secondary schooling is a part, constitutes one of the means of implementing the political ideology of socialism and self-reliance. By making secondary school curricula more practical, policy-makers hoped to instill positive attitudes toward work—a sense of dignity and respect for workers at all levels of skill—and to provide students with training that would enhance individual development and that of the community and the nation at large.

Difficulties in implementation may mean that diversification is not initially cost-effective, but it may still be considered worthwhile if the political objectives for which it was adopted are being realized. Thus, its value should be judged by the extent to which it advances realization of the national objectives of socialism and self-reliance and the extent to which individuals themselves profit from their educational experiences.

8. Based on Tanzania Ministry of National Education, letter to the Diversified Secondary Curriculum Study research team, January 25, 1984, pp. 19–20.

7. Summary and Conclusions

THIS STUDY has been concerned with whether the diversification of curricula in secondary schools has led to differences in postschool experiences between students who enrolled in prevocational courses and those who concentrated solely on academic programs. In chapter 4, a number of positive results of diversification were noted, including higher cognitive achievement and better labor market performance of students following diversified curricula. But the question that remains is how these outcomes relate to the higher costs involved. If, for instance, a diversified curriculum imparts cognitive skills and other attributes that are superior to those taught in a traditional program and is also judged to be cost-effective, those findings would provide some support for diversification. Similarly, if graduates of diversified programs find jobs more easily and at higher salaries than do graduates of more traditional academic programs, a case could be made in favor of any additional cost. Conversely, if the results of diversification are not significantly better than those of traditional education, yet extra costs are involved, the case for this type of curriculum reform is weakened.

The individual country findings described in detail in the previous two chapters are summarized and consolidated in the following pages in an attempt to make some initial judgments about the success of such curriculum innovation. We begin with issues of internal efficiency and look briefly at learning achievements of students in different curriculum programs. There follows a discussion of students' postschool experiences in further educational programs and in the labor market.

Internal Efficiency: Colombia

Achievement Scores and Course Hours

In Colombia, students attending the diversified Institutos Nacionales de Educacion Media (INEMs) were found to come from less affluent socioeconomic backgrounds and to have slightly lower aptitude scores than non-INEM students, regardless of curriculum. Yet their achievement scores in all vocational subjects and in academic subjects surpassed those of the non-INEM control group after socioeconomic background, natural ability, and other nonschool factors were controlled for. The results point to substantial differences in achievement by curriculum stream and school type, which cannot be attributed to out-of-school factors.

When students' learning achievements by school type and by academic and vocational specialization are considered, the following patterns emerge:

- INEM students always score much higher than non-INEM students on vocational tests in general.
- Regardless of the type of school attended, students concentrating in a particular curriculum always have higher scores on tests of their own specialization than do others not taking that subject.
- INEM students' scores are better than those of control students on academic achievement tests as well.

Apparently, not only have INEM schools been successful in raising the level of learning in vocational subjects, but they have achieved this success without sacrificing academic knowledge.

One way to test whether the learning differences between INEM and non-INEM students are due to the curriculum followed is to see whether greater exposure to vocational subjects enhances vocational test achievements. Variations between INEM and control schools in course hours were substantial and contributed heavily to explaining the higher INEM achievement scores. Because INEM schools were all developed at the same time, they offer more similar numbers of course hours in vocational subjects than do the non-INEM schools. In addition, all INEM students devote more time to their subject of specialization during their final year than do students in other schools.

Influence of Home and School

Another measure of internal efficiency concerns the relative influence of home and school on achievement scores. Previous studies have generally shown that secondary school inputs affect academic achievement less than do personal and family characteristics. Does this pattern also hold for students of vocational subjects? Vocational achievement, by its nature, may be more dependent on learning in school than is achievement in languages, the humanities, science, and mathematics.

The impact of home and school variables on test scores was measured for the entire sample. Only 20 percent of the total explicable variance in the academic achievement test (humanities and science) was attributed to school inputs. But in the vocational achievement tests school factors explained up to four times as much: 79 percent in industrial, 53 percent in commercial, 60 percent in agriculture, and 53 percent in pedagogy.

One possible reason for the large difference is that levels of innate ability, as measured by tests of verbal and numerical reasoning, do not correlate equally with achievement levels for each school subject. Even though natural ability is the most powerful out-of-school influence on performance in vocational tests, its overall impact in that area is smaller than it is on academic scores. In other words, test performance in academic subjects is more predictable from measures of aptitude than is test performance in vocational subjects. Thus, there is more room for school factors, shaped in part by government policy, to influence achievement in vocational subjects.

Unit Costs by Curriculum

The Colombia study focused on two issues: whether learning and postschool experiences differ between students pursuing an academic course and those in prevocational studies, and whether outcomes vary according to school type (INEM, non-INEM). Before trying to assess whether and how differences in outcomes are related to the resources used to produce them, it is necessary to attempt two types of cost analysis: first, a comparison of costs among the different curricula (academic, industrial, commercial, social services, and agriculture) offered within INEMs; and, second, a comparison of each of these with the non-INEM schools teaching those subjects.

The cost of schooling can be looked at from three viewpoints—society, government, and the individual (or household). The cost components that may be relevant to one or more of these are forgone output or earnings; capital costs of buildings, furniture, and equipment; and direct recurrent costs. For calculations of social costs it is immaterial how capital and recurrent costs are financed. From the viewpoint of the government or individual, however, the source of expenditure is obviously important. An analysis of recurrent costs revealed that:

- In INEMs, recurrent costs differ little among curricula.
- INEM academic and commercial tracks are more expensive than their counterparts in control schools.
- INEM agricultural and industrial curricula are significantly less expensive than their control counterparts, and the same is true for the social services but to a lesser extent.

The social costs of all curricula in both types of school are dominated by earnings forgone. Differences in social costs are thus small; they lie within a range of 12 percentage points. While control schools specializing in academic and commercial studies have costs slightly less than those of INEMS, costs of schools for agriculture, social services, and industry are higher. For capital and recurrent costs alone, again variations among INEMS are very slight. There are, however, wide differences between the average costs in INEMS and those in single- and multi-track control schools, with agriculture and industry studies being one-third and one-quarter more expensive respectively in control schools.

For total social costs, differences between school types (INEM and non-INEM) and between academic and prevocational tracks are small. For capital and recurrent costs alone, however, there are substantial differences among non-INEM schools and between them and the INEM schools. INEM academic and commercial schools are 16 and 9 percent, respectively, more expensive than their control counterparts, while INEM industrial, agricultural, and social services curricula are between 10 and 22 percent less expensive.

Cost-Effectiveness of Cognitive Achievement

To relate costs to achievement, the differences in the capital and recurrent costs of producing various types of secondary graduates are compared with the differences in the graduates' achievement. There are two relevant sets of comparisons: the first compares students following the same track in different types of school, and the second compares the control group of academic students with prevocational students.

Students in the academic track cost 16 percent more resources a year in INEM schools than in control schools. Twelve percent of INEM students in the academic track outscore control students on academic tests of achievement. In the commercial track, a 9 percent extra cost per student generates no additional academic achievement. The INEM industrial, agricultural, and social services curricula, however, are cost-effective since with less resources they produce equivalent or higher academic achievement scores.

Cognitive differences between students in INEM and control secondary schools favor INEM schools. Although INEM students come from slightly less advantaged socioeconomic backgrounds and score lower on aptitude test, their achievement scores are higher than average on the relevant vocational tests and higher than average on the academic tests in three out of five of the curricula.

A comparison of the control group of students taking academic subjects and students who have followed prevocational courses shows that INEM students do better than academic control students in the prevocational tests. Any apparent concurrent reductions in academic test performance are relatively slight in the raw data and vanish when statistical controls are introduced.

Internal Efficiency: Tanzania

Achievement Scores and Course Hours

In Tanzania, students in vocational courses always scored higher on achievement tests of their own specialization than did the academic control group. Conversely, students in vocational curricula scored below the academic control students on all academic tests.

We also tested whether students' achievement was affected by the proportion of their total course load spent on vocational subjects. The higher proportion of time spent on agriculture and commerce did appear to raise achievement in those areas, but additional course work in technical subjects did not. We also found that the earlier a school had begun teaching vocational subjects, the higher were the achievement scores of its students.

Influence of Home and School

Another issue in assessing internal efficiency is the extent to which school resources affect learning, home influences and ability. As in Colombia, the hypothesis tested was that school factors would be more powerful in predicting scores for vocational subjects than for academic subjects. Confirmation of this hypothesis would imply that vocational skills could be taught in schools more successfully than, say, on the job. In contrast to the findings in Colombia, however, in Tanzania school factors had no greater impact on vocational achievement than on achievement in academic subjects.

Unit Costs by Curriculum

In Tanzania the unit costs of secondary schooling are more easily determined than in the case for Colombia, because vocational and academic subjects are taught in different types of school and therefore separate accounts are kept.

Total social costs of each type of school are dominated by forgone earnings, and differences according to school curriculum are statistically insignificant. Because of this, the variation in total social costs by curriculum appears small—the average for vocational schools is only 3 percent above that for control schools. From the point of view of public expenditure, however, the differences in cost are substantial. Total recurrent costs are 14 percent higher in the vocational schools than in those emphasizing purely academic subjects. Government-financed recurrent costs, however, are on average 34 percent higher for the vocational schools.

Cost-Effectiveness of Cognitive Achievement

Unit costs were highest in agricultural and technical schools, and lowest in academic control schools. Differences in achievement were compared with differences in cost per student for the various curricula in order to assess the internal efficiency of schooling in Tanzania.

The unit costs for agricultural students were 19 percent higher than for academic students; math and English scores were virtually the same for the two groups; and agricultural students performed 8 percent better on the agriculture test. In this case, the increase in learning appears small relative to the higher unit cost. For technical students costs were 13 percent higher, math scores 16 percent higher, and technical test scores 23 percent higher than those of the control groups. In the commerce stream, unit costs were 9 percent above those for the academic stream and commercial students scored 19 percent higher on tests in commercial subjects.

In summary, in Tanzania all prevocational curriculum tracks are more costly than academic ones. For technical and commercial students the gains in vocational learning appear substantial; for agricultural students, they are small. For all students, there is a tradeoff between gains in the vocational subject and losses in the academic ones.

External Efficiency

The focus of this study is on the results of education in different types of secondary schools, and the relationship between these results and the costs of providing schools. One result is learning, as measured by achievement tests in both prevocational and conventional academic subjects. This was extensively discussed in chapters 5 and 6 and summarized in the previous section. Another result is the school leaver's ability to undertake further education or training and ultimately to find work. Variations in this ability associated with different forms of schooling are the subject of this section.

An important qualification at the outset is that only a minority of secondary school leavers in Colombia and Tanzania had entered the labor market within a year of graduation. As a result, the follow-up surveys conducted in each country in late 1982 can only suggest the effects of different forms of secondary schooling on the labor market performance of school leavers. Further tracing of the same cohorts is planned in order to complete the picture.

The indicators revealed by the study are therefore only tentative, but they are nonetheless important, since the main rationale for introducing vocational or prevocational studies has been to increase the economic relevance of schooling. Higher achievement scores and positive changes in attitudes toward work are not ends in themselves, but are presumed to raise the economic contribution of schooling.

There are two ways to measure the relevance or economic impact of diversified schooling. The first is to examine how closely students' post-school activities match their subject of specialization; that is, to assess the correspondence between secondary school curriculum and the content of subsequent training or education, the occupation entered, or the period of unemployment after graduation. In this approach, the success of diversified schooling would be judged by how many more jobs were filled by appropriately prepared people than would otherwise have been possible. The usefulness of the information collected, however, depends in part on the degree to which the government controls labor market placements. The more both supply and demand are controlled, the less informative is the degree of fit.

An alternative approach is to go straight to the earnings data. If, other things being equal, a graduate who has followed a vocational track earns more than one who has followed a purely academic track, and the difference in earnings at least matches any additional costs per student of providing vocational education, diversification can be regarded as contributing more to economic development than does traditional education. The validity of this approach depends on the degree to which earnings reflect actual productivity rather than, say, government policy to keep wages egalitarian.

In the rest of this chapter, the results of the tracer surveys are used to test hypotheses that graduates' careers differ according to the secondary curricula followed and, in the case of Colombia, the type of school attended. The hypotheses are:

a. Diversification reduces individual demand for postsecondary schooling.
b. Diversification leads to a closer correspondence between school curriculum and the field of postschool training.
c. Diversification leads to a higher propensity to seek work after secondary school.
d. Diversification leads to employment in the field of prevocational specialization.

   e. Diversification leads to a shorter period of job search after graduation.

   f. Diversification enables graduates to earn more initially than graduates of other programs.

Colombia

For several years Colombia has had secondary schools that concentrate on one or more prevocational subjects as well as schools that teach conventional academic subjects. What is new is the introduction in the 1970s of the INEM schools, each offering a set of prevocational subjects in addition to an academic curriculum.

If the purpose in the Colombia study were simply to compare the outcomes of studying academic and prevocational subjects, then data on all students taking each subject could be aggregated across school types. It was also important, however, to measure the effects of the new INEM schools and to identify the most appropriate ways of introducing prevocational subjects (if they should be introduced at all). Thus, data on students from INEM and non-INEM schools need to be differentiated. Where possible, therefore, outcomes were analyzed by both curriculum and school type.

The labor market in Colombia is more competitive than in Tanzania. The availability of secondary school places is not so rigidly determined by forecasts of manpower requirements, the private sector is large, and there is no government policy to narrow wage differentials. As a result, differences among graduates in finding employment, in their earnings, and in the degree of correspondence between their secondary school curriculum and their occupation will be reasonable indicative of the interaction between the effective demand for and supply of labor—and hence the demand for and supply of secondary school graduates of different curricula.

HYPOTHESES RELATING TO OUTCOMES

Respondents to the 1982 tracer follow-up were divided into those studying full time, those working full time, those combining study and work, and a residual group of the unemployed and voluntarily inactive. Exactly the same proportion (37 percent) of graduates from INEM and non-INEM schools took up further study, and a slightly higher proportion of control graduates were working (31 percent as opposed to 29 percent of INEM graduates). Thus in the choice between further study and work, there is no systematic difference between graduates of vocational and academic tracks.

The results for the hypotheses presented above are as follows:

a. Diversification reduces individual demand for postsecondary schooling.

Since there is virtually no difference in the proportions of academic and prevocational graduates from either type of school who continue studying, it appears that neither curriculum diversification nor the introduction of INEMs has reduced the desire of secondary students to continue with some type of formal education. Prevocational studies, like academic studies, seem to be used to qualify for further education. There are, however, differences between tracks and schools in the type of further education followed. A higher percentage of INEM academic students (67 percent) enter university than do the control group of academic students (61 percent).

b. Diversification leads to a closer correspondence between school curriculum and the field of postschool training.

Postsecondary education in Colombia can be at a university, at a technical institute, or in a nonaccredited program. One year after graduation, 25 percent of non-INEM graduates and 24 percent of INEM graduates were currently or had previously been enrolled in a postsecondary training program. These programs have been grouped into humanities, commercial, technical, and a residual category.

INEM graduates are more likely to follow their secondary school specialization (academic or vocational) in their postsecondary studies. But from every track, more graduates take commercial courses than any other type. Forty percent of the courses taken are commercial, and the demand for them is the same among graduates of all curricula. Among INEM graduates, those having taken industry and agriculture are more likely to take industrial courses than are the others; INEM academic graduates take humanities-related courses in a greater proportion than do other graduates. Among non-INEM graduates, the proportion of industrial graduates taking technical courses is surprisingly low.

c. Diversification leads to a higher propensity to seek work after secondary school.

As with the first hypothesis, it is assumed that with some prevocational training fewer students will demand further scooling, and that they will be less likely to require additional training. In short, they will possess appropriate attitudes and skills and be better prepared to enter the labor force.

One year after finishing secondary school, 30 percent of the graduates were working full time. So as to focus on the data more sharply, the observations for agricultural, commercial, and industrial studies are aggregated under the heading of vocational subjects.

There was virtually no difference in employment rates between academic and vocational graduates of the INEMS, or between these groups and non-INEM academic graduates. Moreover, among those who work full time, non-INEM vocational graduates have a higher propensity to be working full-time one year after graduating than do INEM vocational graduates (about 34 and 28 percent, respectively). These percentages change when those who both work and study are added to the graduates who work full time. Vocational graduates from non-INEM schools are more likely to be in some kind of employment (full- or part-time) one year after secondary school than are INEM vocational graduates (about 44 and 39 percent, respectively).

    d. Diversification leads to employment in the field of prevocational specialization.

Even if diversification of the curriculum does not lead to a higher rate of employment immediately after secondary school, it could be hypothesized that those who do work will tend to be employed in occupations and sectors that correspond with the curriculum followed. This hypothesis can be tested by examining, first, the occupational groupings and, second, the economic sectors into which INEM and control academic and vocational graduates flow.

The wide range of occupations entered by graduates has been narrowed down into six groupings: teaching, secretarial work, other white-collar jobs, vending, agricultural work, and blue-collar jobs. Neither the INEM/control nor the academic/vocational dichotomy shows any obvious pattern, except that teaching is a much less likely occupation for control graduates than for those of INEM schools. For a particular track and type of school some differences emerge. For example, INEM academic graduates are least likely to be in vending, control vocational graduates are least likely to be blue-collar workers, and control academic students are least likely to be in teaching. The occupational distribution has been further disaggregated by vocational track, and again there is very little pattern. Graduates who follow the commercial track are no more likely to work in secretarial and other white-collar jobs than are graduates from other tracks, and industrial students are no more likely to work in blue-collar jobs. Nor are there major differences in the economic sectors in which graduates of different school types or tracks are employed, except that INEM graduates are more likely to work in personal services than are non-INEM graduates.

Thus, one year after graduation there is no strong evidence that academic and vocational students enter different kinds of jobs or work in different sectors of the economy. Neither does the type of school attended appear to influence the jobs held.

e. Diversification leads to a shorter period of job search after graduation.

This hypothesis assumes that graduates with some prevocational training will have some recognizable skills and more definite ideas of the jobs they want. At the same time, employers may expect them to need less on-the-job training and therefore will consider them to be more attractive candidates than those without prevocational training. As a result, graduates of vocational curricula should have a shorter period of unemployment.

The data for Colombia do not substantiate this hypothesis. If anything, they show the reverse: those who have taken vocational courses in either INEM or control schools experience significantly longer periods of unemployment before they land their first job (26 weeks for vocational students from both types of school compared with 21 weeks for INEM and 22 weeks for non-INEM academic students). Some graduates, however, were still unemployed one year after graduation. Levels of unemployment in late 1982 were slightly higher for INEM students, and in particular for those who had followed the academic and agricultural curricula.

f. Diversification enables graduates to earn more initially than graduates of other programs.

If diversification provides prevocational training that either makes graduates more productive or reduces the amount of on-the-job training they need, the initial earnings of diversified school graduates should be higher than those of graduates who followed an academic curriculum.

The difference in average earnings between INEM and control graduates is 1 percent in favor of the latter. Before any conclusions are drawn from these figures, it should be repeated that only 30 percent of the sample was working, the range of earnings within each track and school type is very wide, and differences in the means between tracks are not statistically significant at the 0.05 level. At the very least, however, it can be said that there is no evidence to support the hypothesis that the initial earnings of prevocational students will be higher than those of academic students.

CORROBORATING EVIDENCE FROM THE 1978 COHORT

In the case of Colombia it was possible to obtain a sample of graduates from an earlier cohort (1978) to get an extended view of the external efficiency of diversified schools. By and large, the evidence from those who

have been out of school three years confirmed, and in some cases reinforced, the results obtained for the younger cohort.

- INEM graduates have a higher propensity than control school graduates to be studying three years after secondary school (54 and 49
  percent, respectively).
- INEM graduates are less likely than control school graduates to participate in the labor force three years after graduation (67 and 73 percent,
  respectively).
- School type and curriculum do not relate in any way to differences in
  earnings among those employed.
- The length of time needed to find a first job is not related to the type of
  school attended or the subjet studied.
- The incidence of unemployment three years after graduation is highest
  among those who studied agricultural and academic subjects (in either
  type of school) and those who studied industrial arts in INEM schools.
- The reservation wage of job seekers, especially those coming from
  INEM academic schools, is substantially higher than the actual wage
  rate of those employed.

In the case of the 1978 cohort we were able to estimate rough social
rates of return to investment in different types of secondary school offering
various curricula. No major differences were discovered in the returns to
education for those coming from the two types of school and various
tracks; the overall profitability to such investment was about 8 to 9
percent.

Tanzania

The tracer data on secondary school students one year after graduation
are difficult to interpret in the case of Tanzania. The government has
sought to expand secondary school enrollment strictly in line with forecasts of manpower requirements and itself hires nine out of ten graduates.
At the extreme, it can thus ensure a close fit between, say, graduates from a
technical school and jobs with a presumed technical content, regardless of
whether the graduates contribute to the national economy or whether
their education was cost-effective. Given the Tanzanian policy, anything
other than short periods of unemployment or job search and a close
correspondence between schooling, training, and work would indicate
that the government had failed to forecast manpower requirements cor-
rectly or to finance the absorption (in employment or future training) of
the planned output of graduates. The structure of earnings in Tanzania is
very much a creation of government policy: the private sector is small, and
a conscious attempt is made to narrow wage differentials in the public
sector. In these circumstances, significant differences in earnings across

curricula would be very unlikely, particularly in the first years of employment.

With these qualifications and expectations, the data from the follow-up survey are discussed below in the framework of the stipulated hypotheses.

a. Diversification reduces individual demand for postsecondary schooling.

The evidence from the Tanzania study does not support the view that the incorporation of prevocational studies into secondary school will decrease the demand for more schooling. When students in Form IV were asked whether they would apply for Form V, 72 percent of agricultural, 71 percent of technical, 81 percent of commercial, and 82 percent of academic students answered positively. Because this level of education is severely rationed, only a minority of these students were admitted in 1982: of those applying in each bias, 25 percent of agricultural, 33 percent of technical, 34 percent of commercial, and 28 percent of academic students gained places in Form V. Thus the very high private demand for postsecondary schooling does not appear to be diminished by the introduction of prevocational studies. Actual enrollment, however, is determined by the effective supply of places.

b. Diversification leads to a closer correspondence between school curriculum and the field of postschool training.

It is often argued by advocates of diversification that the additional subjects are prevocational rather than vocational. But although one should not expect graduates of these schools to be fully trained, there should be a close correspondence between the curriculum followed in school and the subject matter of subsequent training. The 1982 tracer information reveals that teacher training clearly dominates postschool training activities. The proportion of academic graduates who enter teacher training does not appear to be out of line with the rest of the graduates. One interesting result is the small proportion (6 percent) of commercial graduates and the high proportion (21 percent) of technical students who take further clerical courses. This implies that post-Form IV clerical courses are not seen as adding anything to similar studies in secondary schools, while a substantial proportion of technical students who opt for postschool training anticipate openings in the clerical field. Finally, fewer agricultural graduates (5 percent) than other graduates take postschool agricultural training courses.

Thus no close relationship has been demonstrated between school curriculum and the content of subsequent training courses.

c. Diversification leads to a higher propensity to seek work after secondary school.

One year after leaving Form IV, only 14 percent of the graduates were employed: 9 percent were in wage employment and 5 percent were self-employed. Between 27 and 30 percent entered Form V or further training immediately after Form IV (the proportion depends on the curriculum). While students from technical schools showed an above-average propensity to be employed (17 percent), those from the other two prevocational curricula behaved no differently from academic students. There were no significant differences by curriculum in the type of employment or in the earnings received. Nor were there differences in the time taken to find a job.

In addition to those already working or studying, 7 percent of the sample was looking for immediate employment and an additional 8 percent were hoping to take additional training. This means that despite the very tight control over secondary school expansion based on manpower forecasts, one in seven graduates was not placed in a job or further training one year after graduation. Technical students were underrepresented in this group—10 percent of them were unoccupied, against an overall average of 15 percent.

In short, diversification does not appear to lead to a higher propensity for work.

d. Diversification leads to employment in the field of prevocational specialization.

If the introduction of prevocational studies into secondary schools is intended to orient students more toward the world of work in general, graduates might be expected to move into occupations corresponding to the curriculum followed. Again, any comments on this are necessarily limited to only the 14 percent of the sample who were working for wages or self-employed one year after leaving Form IV.

In general, it is not possible to observe any correspondence between bias and job type. Of those who did obtain wage employment, 50 percent found public sector clerical jobs, but commercial students were no more likely to be working in clerical jobs than were academic or agricultural students. For the self-employed, however, there is a difference by curriculum. Although 21, 24, and 29 percent of the self-employed graduates from commercial, agricultural, and academic studies, respectively, were working on farms, the corresponding figure for technical students was only 9 percent. Of those looking for immediate employment, only 8 percent of the technical students expected to work in commerce, but for all other curricula the figure was between 20 and 30 percent.

Although graduates from the academic, agricultural, and commercial streams show no differences in their pattern of employment, technical graduates obtained employment more in line with their specialization.

 e. Diversification leads to a shorter period of job search after graduation.

If students are given some orientation toward specific forms of employment they ought to be more employable and more sure of the type of work they wish to do. On this assumption, graduates who had followed agricultural, technical, and commercial curricula would expect to experience a shorter period of unemployment than those in purely academic subjects. However, the data from Tanzania do not support this.

One year after graduation, 13 percent of academic students were still looking for either work or training, while the percentages for technical, commercial, and agricultural students were 10, 16, and 16, respectively. These academic graduates did not believe that they had any longer to wait for placement than did other students. Nor did those in Form V or in training courses show any difference by curriculum in the period they expected to have to wait to find employment once they entered the labor force.

 f. Diversification enables graduates to earn more initially than graduates of other programs.

On the assumption that prevocational studies make a person more employable and less in need of training on the job, it may be hypothesized that at least the initial earnings of vocational graduates will be higher than those of academic graduates. Because only 9 percent of Form IV students were in salaried employment one year after graduating, any data presented on earnings can be only approximate. The data give average monthly earnings of 709, 710, 736, and 762 shillings for technical, commercial, agricultural, and academic students, respectively, and an overall average of 726 shillings a month. Those still looking for work put their "minimum acceptable earnings" at a much higher average level of 947 shillings (ranging from 857 shillings for academic students to 1,057 shillings for commercial students).

Therefore, although only a very small proportion of school graduates were working one year after leaving secondary Form IV, the data do not support the hypothesis that initial earnings of graduates from prevocational biases will be higher than those received by other graduates.

THE RETURNS TO EDUCATION

It was argued previously that the external effects of introducing diversified secondary schooling could in principle be measured in two ways:

first, by looking at the correspondence between type of school and occupation and at such measures as the amount and length of unemployment (a manpower forecasting approach; second, by comparing the earnings of graduates of different curricula with the costs of their education. The problem with either approach in the case of Tanzania is that only a small fraction of secondary Form IV leavers were employed one year after graduation. Analyses pertaining to their labor market performance therefore need to be regarded as merely indicative.

Subject to this caveat mean earnings have been calculated and compared with cost differences to give a rough approximation of social rates of return. By any standard, the rates of return are low, ranging from 2 to 6 percent. The technical curriculum has the lowest return—a reflection of its higher unit cost. Conversely, the academic stream exhibits the highest rate of return. One should be cautious, however, in interpreting these rates as a case against all forms of secondary schooling. Not only were the data collected early in the careers of the graduates, but also the imperfections of the labor market make it difficult to assess the results. Of those secondary leavers who were employed, 88 percent were in the public and parastatal sectors, and government policy was to minimize earnings differentials. In these circumstances earnings differentials are unlikely to adequately reflect differences in productivity, and hence rates of return are poor indicators of the social profitability of educational investment. All that can be said at this point is that the first indications do not corroborate the hypothesis that the introduction of prevocational studies into secondary schooling can be justified on the grounds that the economic payoff is greater for an academic curriculum.

Concluding Remarks

The effectiveness of school reform is generally judged in two ways: first, the extent to which access to education is increased and, second, the extent to which knowledge is acquired and cognitive skills developed. In developing countries, however, the role of education in promoting economic development has been emphasized. In particular, the responsibility of schools for determining the labor market outcomes of graduates has been stressed much more than in industrialized countries. Certainly, the movement toward curriculum diversification in developing countries has centered on the hope that prevocational studies would ease students' transition from school to work by changing their attitudes and by teaching employable skills.

This study has attempted to assess the effects of curriculum diversification by measuring any increases in the access to education, by measuring and comparing students' attitudinal changes and learning achievement, by comparing postschool experiences, and by comparing the costs of education with its outcomes (graduates' activities and earnings). The last comparison is ultimately required for a thorough evaluation of the investment made in curriculum diversification, but the data on this are the most incomplete. Information on labor market experience was collected only one year after graduation. At that time many secondary school graduates were continuing their studies, many of those who were employed could be expected to change jobs, and the meaning of the unemployment figures and the eventual outcomes of job search were difficult to determine. The information on, and analysis of, postschool experiences therefore needs to be treated with a great deal of caution.

The results of the attitudinal tests are also not definitive. Even if education in prevocational subjects does change students' occupational aspirations and expectations and instills attitudes toward work that increase productivity, the effects of such changes (or even the direction) are not always obvious and may not be felt for several years.

The most comprehensive data measuring the effects of diversification are from the achievement tests administered to students at the end of their secondary schooling. Any differences in the scores by school type or curriculum could be meaningful in two situations. First, if diversification has already been accepted in principle and the question (as in Colombia) is what type of school should implement it, then differences in learning among students of the same specialization but in different types of school are relevant. Second, if differences in learning achievement influence the ability to find employment, then the knowledge and skills gained could potentially raise worker productivity, provided the labor market is organized in such a way that they would be used.

It is always difficult, if not dangerous, to derive firm policy implications on the basis of a single study of young graduates in two countries. Ideally, one might have to repeat this study in several other countries and wait years or decades until the young cohorts of graduates reach their full earning capacity. But decisions must be made now to shape a secondary educational system and provide curricula. It would be of little use to tell the policymakers to postpone these decisions, even though they must be based on intuition rather than on facts. It is probable, however, that the longer the time perspective, the looser would be the relationship between initial educational experience and subsequent occupation and earnings, and this would weaken rather than strengthen the case for diversified or prevocational curricula.

It has been argued that diversified curricula should be instituted on purely educational grounds. Educators have often suggested that a good general education should comprise both academic and manual components in the interest of developing the "whole person." This argument has merit, but a perusal of documents justifying such innovation suggests that economic considerations were the predominant impetus for the development of diversified secondary curricula, and the programs must stand or fall on whether they meet these economic objectives. Diversified programs cannot be justified on the basis of the null hypothesis that they are no better and no worse than conventional curricula. Continued implementation or expansion can be justified only on the basis of evidence that the internal or external efficiency of diversified schools is superior to that of conventional schools. The data do not support this criterion.

The findings of this study that do have clear policy implications seem to be the following:

- It must not be assumed that new structures and curricula will necessarily broaden the social basis of recruitment and make secondary schooling more accessible to the poor. Any type of school expansion would increase the enrollment rate among the less privileged social groups. The problem of equal access to educational opportunity cannot be addressed through curricular reform alone.
- Curriculum diversification is expensive; the cost per student in a diversified school can be double that in a conventional (academic) school, mainly because of the specialized equipment used. Therefore, policymakers should weigh this cost against the potential extra benefits (monetary and nonmonetary) that such schools confer to the students and to society at large.
- This study has failed to provide evidence that the measurable monetary benefits of diversification are greater than those of conventional education. *All* forms of secondary education increase the productivity of the worker, but diversified schools have not yet proven better in this respect than conventional schools.
- Another rationale for such schools—to improve the fit between the school and the world of work—is not supported by our findings. Graduates from both types of schools spend roughly the same amount of time in finding employment.
- Neither has the argument that prevocational education provides better preparation for further study been borne out by our data. Those who have specialized in a particular curriculum (such as agriculture or technical trades) in secondary school are often found to study a completely different subject (such as liberal arts) at a university.
- Diversified curricula are difficult to implement. The need for new instructional materials, teachers with new qualifications, and associated laboratories and equipment can present logistical problems that cause the reform to fail at the outset. Unless a country has the

necessary infrastructure to implement a diversified curriculum, the reform may appear only on paper and never become a reality. To put it differently, curriculum diversification requires more than new buildings and equipment; it must be accompanied by a series of software components that may well prove to be a bottleneck in implementing the reform, if reform is in fact warranted.

Paradoxically, it seems that the lower the overall level of a country's development, the weaker the case for introducing a diversified curriculum. The more developed the country, the more it may be able to afford diversification. This policy conclusion is exactly the opposite of what actually happens: the poorer the country, the greater the pressure for making the secondary school curriculum "more relevant to the world of work."

References

Ahmed, Manzoor, and Philip H. Coombs, eds. 1975. *Education for Rural Development: Case-Studies for Planners*. Prepared by the International Council for Educational Development under sponsorship of the World Bank and the United Nation's Children's Fund. New York: Praeger.

Anderson, C. A. 1983. "Social Selection in Education and Economic Development." Washington, D.C.: The World Bank, Education Department. Processed.

Armer, M., and Z. Youtz. 1971. "Formal Education and Individual Modernity in an African Society." *American Journal of Sociology*, vol. 76, no. 4, pp. 604–26.

Austen, R. A. 1968. *Northwest Tanzania under German and British Rule*. New Haven, Conn.: Yale University Press.

Bellaby, P. 1977. *The Sociology of Comprehensive Schooling*. London: Methuen.

Benavot, A. 1983. "The Rise and Decline of Vocational Education." *Sociology of Education*, vol. 56, no. 2, pp. 63–76.

Benoit, A. 1974. *Changing the Educational System: A Colombian Case-Study*. Munich: Weltforum Verlag.

Biede, K. 1970. "The Pattern of Education and Economic Growth." *Economic Record*, vol. 46 (September).

Blaug, Mark. 1973. *Education and the Employment Problem in Developing Countries*. Geneva: International Labour Office.

———. 1979. "The Quality of Population in Developing Countries, with Particular Reference to Education and Training." In P. Hauser, ed., *World Population and Development: Challenges and Prospects*. Syracuse, N.Y.: Syracuse University Press.

Blumenthal, I., and C. Benson. 1978. *Educational Reform in the Soviet Union: Implications for Developing Countries*. World Bank Staff Working Paper no. 288. Washington, D.C.

Boesen, J., B. Madsen, and T. Moody. 1977. "Ujàmaa: Socialism from Above." Uppsala, Sweden. Scandinavian Institute of African Studies. Processed.

Boudon, R. 1974. *Education, Opportunity and Social Inequality: Changing Prospects in Western Society*. New York: Wiley.

Bowles, S. 1971. "Cuban Education and the Revolutionary Ideology." *Harvard Education Review*, vol. 41, no. 4.

Breneman, D., and S. Nelson. 1981. *Financing Community Colleges: An Economic Perspective*. Washington, D.C.: Brookings Institution.

Bukhari, N. 1968a. "Issues in Occupational Education: A Case Study in Jordan."

Stanford International Development Education Center, Studies on Content and Methods of Education for Development. Stanford, Calif.: SIDEC.

―――. 1968b. "Issues in Occupational Education: A Case Study in Tunisia." Stanford International Development Education Center, Studies on Content and Methods of Education for Development. Stanford, Calif.: SIDEC.

Cameron, J., and W. A. Dodd. 1970. *Society, Schools and Progress in Tanzania.* Oxford, Eng.: Pergamon Press.

Carnoy, Martin, and J. Wharteim. 1976. *Economic Change and Education Reform in Cuba.* Baltimore, Md.: Johns Hopkins University Press.

―――. 1977. "Socialist Ideology and the Transformation of Cuban Education." In J. Karabel and A. H. Halsey, eds., *Power and Ideology in Education.* New York: Oxford University Press.

Carroll, A. B., and L. A. Ihnen. 1967. "Cost and Returns for Two Years of Post-Secondary Technical Schooling: A Pilot Study." *Journal of Political Economy,* vol. 75 (December).

Castro, C. de Moura. 1976. *Vocational Education and the Training of Industrial Labour in Brazil.* Report Studies C.20. Paris: Unesco.

―――. 1983. "High Technology in Intermediate Countries? The Case of Brazil." Brasilia: Instituto de Planejamento Economico e Social. June. Processed.

Clark, D. H. 1983. *How Secondary School Graduates Perform in the Labor Market: A Study of Indonesia.* World Bank Staff Working Paper no. 615. Washington, D.C.

Cliffe, L. 1973. "The Policy of Ujàmaa Vijijini and the Class Struggle in Tanzania." In L. Cliffe and J. Saul, eds., *Socialism in Tanzania.* Vols. 1 and 2. Nairobi: East African Publishing House.

Clignet, R., and P. Foster. 1966. *The Fortunate Few: A Study of Secondary Schools and Students in the Ivory Coast.* Evanston, Ill.: Northwestern University Press.

Cohn, E. 1979. *The Economics of Education.* Cambridge, Mass.: Ballinger.

Comber, L., and J. Keeves. 1973. *Science Education in Nineteen Countries: An Empirical Study.* Stockholm: Almqvist and Wicksell.

Conroy, W. G., Jr. 1979. "Some Historical Effects of Vocational Education at the Secondary Level." *Phi Delta Kappa,* vol. 61, no. 4, pp. 267–71.

Corazzini, A. J. 1968. "The Decision to Invest in Vocational Education: An Analysis of Costs and Benefits." *Journal of Human Resources,* vol. 3, Supplement.

Court, D. 1972. *Village Polytechnic Leavers: The Maseno Story.* Working Paper no. 70. Nairobi: University of Nairobi, Institute of Development Studies.

―――. 1976. "The Educational System as a Response to Inequality in Tanzania and Kenya." *Journal of Modern African Studies,* vol. 14, no. 4, pp. 661–90.

Crossley, M. 1984a. "Strategies for Curriculum Change and the Question of International Transfer." *Journal of Curriculum Studies,* vol. 16, no. 1, pp. 75–88.

―――. 1984b. "Relevance Education, Strategies for Curriculum Change and Pilot

Projects: A Cautionary Note." *International Journal of Educational Development*, vol. 4, no. 3, pp. 245–50.

Cumming, D. E. 1984. "An Evaluation of Industrial Education in Kenya: The Contribution of Cost Studies." Edinburgh: Moray House College of Education. Processed.

DANE (Departamento Administrativo Nacional de Estadística). 1976. *XIV Censo Nacional de Población y III de Vivienda. Resultados Provisionales*. Bogotá, Colombia.

Davis, G., and R. Lewis. 1975. *Education and Employment: A Future Perspective of Needs, Policies and Programs*. Lexington, Mass.: D. C. Heath.

Diyasena, W. 1976. *Pre-vocational Education in Sri Lanka*. Paris: Unesco.

Dodd, William A. 1969. *Education for Self-Reliance in Tanzania: A Study of Its Vocational Aspects*. New York: Teachers College Press.

Dore, R. 1975. *The Diploma Disease*. London: Allen and Unwin.

Dumont, R. 1974. *Is Cuba Socialist?* London: Andre Deutsch.

Eggleston, J., ed. 1983. *Work Experience in Secondary Schools*. London and Boston: Routledge and Kegan Paul.

Evans, D. R., and G. L. Schimmel. 1970. *The Impact of a Diversified Educational Program on Career Goals at Tororo Girls High School in the Context of Girls Education in Uganda*. Amherst, Mass.: University of Massachusetts, Center for International Education.

Fields, G., and P. Schultz. 1980. "Regional Inequality and Other Sources of Income Variation in Colombia." *Economic Development and Cultural Change*, vol. 28, no. 3 (April).

Figueroa, M., R. Prieto, and F. Gutierrez. 1974. "The Basic Secondary School in the Country: An Educational Innovation in Cuba." Prepared for the International Bureau of Education. Paris.

Ford, J. 1969. *Social Class and the Comprehensive School*. London: Routledge and Kegan Paul.

Foster, Philip J. 1965. "The Vocational School Fallacy in Development Planning." In C. A. Anderson, and Mary J. Bowman, eds., *Education and Economic Development*. Chicago: Aldine.

———. 1966. *Education and Social Change in Ghana*. Chicago: University of Chicago Press.

———. 1983. "Essays on Curriculum Diversification." Washington, D.C.: World Bank, Education Department. Processed.

Freeman, Richard. 1974. "Occupational Training in Proprietary Schools and Technical Institutes." *Review of Economics and Statistics*, vol. 56 (August) pp. 310–18.

Fuller, William. 1976. "More Evidence Supporting the Demise of Pre-employment Vocational Trade Training: A Case Study of a Factory in India." *Comparative Education Review*, vol. 20, no. 1.

Furley, O. W., and T. A. Watson. 1977. *A History of Education in East Africa*. New York: NOK Publishers.

Godfrey, M. 1977. "Education, Productivity and Income: A Kenyan Case Study." *Comparative Education Review*, vol. 21, no. 1.

Gouveia, A. 1972. "Economic Development and Changes in the Composition of the Teaching Staff of Secondary Schools in Brazil." In Thomas J. La Belle, ed., *Education and Development: Latin America and the Caribbean*. Los Angeles: University of California, Latin America Center.

Grant, N. 1964. *Soviet Education*. London: University of London Press.

Gray, J. 1976. "Stalin, Mao and the Future of China." *New Society*, vol. 36, no. 704, pp. 9–11.

Grubb, W. Norton. 1979. "The Phoenix of Vocational Education: Implications for Evaluation." In *The Planning Papers for the Vocational Education Study*. Washington, D. C.: National Institute of Education.

Haddad, W. 1979. "Diversified Secondary Curriculum Study: A Review of World Bank Experience." Washington, D.C.: World Bank, Education Department. Processed.

Hanushek, E., and J. Jackson. 1977. *Statistical Methods for Social Scientists*. New York: Academic Press.

Heyneman, Stephen. 1984. "Diversifying Secondary School Curricula in Developing Countries: An Implementation History." Washington, D.C.: World Bank, Economic Development Institute. Processed.

Hinchliffe, K. 1983. "Cost Structures of Secondary Schooling in Tanzania and Colombia." Washington D.C.: World Bank, Education Department. Processed.

Holsinger, D. 1973. "The Elementary School as Modernizer: A Brazilian Study." *International Journal of Comparative Sociology*, vol. 14, nos. 3, 4.

Hu, T., M. L. Lee, E. W. Stromsdorfer, and J. J. Kaufman. 1971. "Economic Returns to Vocational and Comprehensive High School Graduates." *Journal of Human Resources*, vol. 6, pp. 25–50.

Husen, T. 1975. *Social Influences on Educational Career*. Paris: Organisation for Economic Co-operation and Development.

ICFES (Instituto Colombiano Para el Fomento de la Educación Superior). 1979. *Historia Estadística de la Educación Superior Colombiana, 1960–1977*. Bogotá.

———. 1980. *Estadísticas de la Educación Superior*. Bogotá.

Inkeles, Alex. 1983. *Exploring Individual Modernity*. New York: Columbia University Press.

Inkeles, Alex, and D. Smith. 1974. *Becoming Modern*. Cambridge, Mass.: Harvard University Press.

Instituto Nacional de Educación Media (INEM). 1973. "Principios Fundamentales de la Educación Media Diversificada en Colombia." Medellín.

Ishumi, A. G. M. 1974. "The Educated Elite: A Survey of East African Students at a Higher Institution of Learning." *Rural Africana*, vol. 25, pp. 65–72.

Jamison, Dean T. and Lawrence J. Lau. 1982. *Farmer Education and Farm Efficiency*. Baltimore, Md.: Johns Hopkins University Press.

Jolly, R., ed. 1969. *Education in Africa: Research and Action.* Nairobi: East African Publishing House.

Jolly, R., E. de Kadt, H. Singer, and F. Wilson. 1973. *Third World Employment: Problems and Strategy.* London: Penguin.

Kahl, J. 1968. *The Measurement of Modernism: A Study of Values in Brazil and Mexico.* Austin: University of Texas Press.

Karweit, N., 1983. "Time on Task: A Research Review." Report no. 232. Baltimore, Md.: Johns Hopkins University, Center for Social Organization of Schools.

King, Kenneth. 1977. *The African Artisan: Education and the Informal Sector in Kenya.* London: Heinemann.

————. 1978. *Education and Self-Employment.* Paris: Unesco and International Institute for Educational Planning.

Kipkorir, B. 1975. "Kenya: Development and Co-ordination of the Non-formal Programs." In Manzoor Ahmed and Philip H. Coombs, eds., *Education for Rural Development: Case-Studies for Planners.* New York: Praeger.

Klingelhofer, E. 1967. "Occupational Preference of Tanzanian Secondary School Pupils." *Journal of Social Psychology,* vol. 72, no. 2, pp. 149–59.

Knight, J. B., and R. H. Sabot. 1981. "Correlates of Educational Attainment in Tanzania." Discussion Paper no. 81–33. Washington, D.C.: World Bank, Population, Health, and Nutrition Department.

Lauglo, J. 1983. "Concepts of 'General Education' and 'Vocational Education' Curricula for Post-Compulsory Schooling in Western Industrialised Countries: When Should the Twain Meet?" *Comparative Education,* vol. 19, no. 3.

Lecht, A. 1979. *Evaluating Vocational Education: Policies and Plans for the 1970s.* New York: Praeger.

Leiner, M. 1975. "Cuba: Combining Formal Schooling with Practical Experience." In Manzoor Ahmed and Philip H. Coombs, eds., *Education for Rural Development: Case-Studies for Planners.* New York: Praeger.

Lema, A. A. 1978. *Education for Self-Reliance: A Brief Survey of Self-Reliance Activities in Some Tanzanian Schools and Colleges.* Dar es Salaam: University of Dar es Salaam, Institute of Education.

Lewin-Epstein, N. 1981. "Vocational Education." In J. Coleman, V. Bartot, N. Lewin-Epstein, and L. Olson, eds., *"High School and Beyond: Policy Issues and Research Design."* Washington, D.C.: National Center for Educational Statistics.

Lewis, A. 1966. *Development Planning.* London: Allen and Unwin.

Lillis, K., and D. Hogan. 1983. "Attempts to Diversify Secondary School Curricula in Developing Countries: A Literature Review and Some Additional Hypotheses Concerning Cases of Failure." Brighton, Eng.: University of Sussex, Centre for Educational Technology. Processed.

Lofstedt, Jan-Ingvar. 1981. *Chinese Educational Policy: Changes and Contradictions, 1940–1979.* Stockholm: Almqvist and Wicksell.

Lourie, S. 1978. *Production Schools and Rural Employment in Panama*. Paris: Unesco.

Low-Maus, R. 1971. *Compendium of the Colombian Educational System*. Bogotá: Editorial Andes.

Loxley, William. 1983. "A Comparison of Achievement Outcomes by Curriculum Track in Selected OECD Countries: An Analysis of IEA Data." Washington, D.C.: World Bank, Education Department. Processed.

Mbilinyi, M. 1974a. "Education for Rural Life or Education for Socialist Transformation." Dar es Salaam: University of Dar es Salaam, Institute of Education.

————. 1974b. "The Decision to Educate in Rural Tanzania." Dar es Salaam: University of Dar es Salaam, Institute of Education.

McCarthy, F. D., J. A. Hanson, and S. Kwon. 1983. "Structural Change and Sources of Growth in Colombia." Washington, D.C.: World Bank, Economic Analysis and Projections Department. Processed.

McClelland, D. 1961. *The Achieving Society*. New York: Free Press.

McGinn, Noel F., and E. T. Balart. 1980. "Una Evaluación de la Educación Media Tecnica en El Salvador." *Revista Latinoamericana de Estudios Educativos*, vol. 10, no. 2.

McPherson, A., J. Gray, and D. Raffe. 1983. *Reconstruction of Secondary Education: Theory, Myth and Practice since the War*. London and Boston: Routledge and Kegan Paul.

Meyer, R. 1980. *An Economic Analysis of Vocational Education*. Columbus, Ohio: National Center for Research in Vocational Education.

Meyer, J. 1979. "National Economic Development, 1950–1970." In John W. Meyer and Michael T. Hannan, eds., *National Development and the World System*. Chicago: University of Chicago Press.

Mincer, Jacob. 1974. *Schooling, Experience and Earnings*. New York: National Bureau of Economic Research.

Ministerio de Educación Nacional, Instituto Colombiano de Pedagogía (ICOLPE). 1974. *La Evaluación Institucional Aplicada a la Educación*. Bogotá: Centro Nacional de Información Pedagógica (CENDIP).

Ministerio de Educación Nacional, Banco Mundial, and Instituto SER. 1982. *Evaluación del Rendimiento Externo del Bachillerato Colombiano: Cohorte 1978*. Bogotá.

Mmari, G. 1976a. *Implementation of the Musoma Resolutions*. Papers in Education and Development no. 3. Dar es Salaam: University of Dar es Salaam. December.

————. 1976b. *Directive on the Implementation of Education for Self-Reliance*, Dar es Salaam: Ministry of National Education. May.

Moock, Peter R., and Joanne Leslie. Forthcoming. "Childhood Malnutrition and Schooling in the Terai Region of Nepal." *Journal of Development Economics*.

Moris, J. R. 1972. *Agriculture in the Schools: The East African Experience*. Nairobi: East Africa Academy.

————. 1966. "The Impact of Secondary Education upon Students' Attitudes Towards Agriculture: Some Preliminary Considerations." *East African Journal of Rural Development*, vol. 1, no. 1.

Narman, A., C. Hildesson, H. Sjolund, and J. Soderstrom. 1984. "What Happens to Kenyan Secondary School Students with Industrial Education: A Tracer Study One Year after the KCE-Exam 1983." Göteborg, Sweden: University of Göteborg. Processed.

Ntuah, R. R. 1981. "Pros and Cons of the Diversification of Secondary Education in Tanzania." In I. M. Omari and H. J. Mosha, eds., *Decentralization of Educational Research and Evaluation Capacities in Tanzania*. The Hague: Centre for the Study of Education in Developing Countries.

Nyerere, J. K. 1967. *Education for Self-Reliance*. Dar es Salaam: Government Printer.

————. 1977. *The Arusha Declaration Ten Years After*. Dar es Salaam: Government Printer.

Olson, J. 1974. "Secondary Schools and Elites in Kenya." *Comparative Education Review*, vol. 16, no. 1.

Omari, I. M. 1984. "The Predicament of Diversification and Vocationalization of Secondary Education in Developing Countries: Experiences from Tanzania." Washington, D.C.: World Bank, Education Department. Processed.

Orata, Pedro T. 1972. *Self-Help Barrio High Schools: The Story of 250,000 Students, Earning their Education and Preparing Themselves for Life*. Singapore: Eastern Universities Press for Seameo Regional Center for Educational Technology.

Oxtoby, Robert. 1977. "Vocational Education and Development Planning: Emerging Issues in the Commonwealth Caribbean." *Comparative Education*, vol. 13, no. 3.

Passow, A., and others. 1976. *The National Case Study: An Empirical Study of Twenty-one Educational Systems*. New York: Wiley.

Perry, W. 1981. *Training for Self-Reliance Project: A Formative Evaluation Progress Report*. Maseru, Lesotho: Government of Lesotho/World Bank, Diversification of Secondary Schools Curriculum Project.

Plowden, B. 1967. *Children and Their Primary Schools: A Report of the Central Advisory Council of England*. London: Her Majesty's Stationary Office.

Price, R. F. 1973. "The Part-Work Principle in Chinese Education." *Current Scene*, vol. 11, no. 9 (September).

Psacharopoulos, George. 1984. "The Contribution of Education to Economic Growth: International Comparisons." In J. Kendrick, ed., *International Productivity Comparisons*. Cambridge, Mass.: Ballinger.

————. 1983. "Education and Private versus Public Sector Pay." *Labour and Society*, vol. 8, no. 2 (April–June).

————. 1981a. "Lifetime Profiles of Earnings and Employment: A Survey." *Social Science Information*, vol. 20, no. 4/5.

———. 1981b. "Returns to Education: An Updated International Comparison." *Comparative Education*, vol. 17, no. 3.

———. 1973. *Returns to Education: An International Comparison*. Amsterdam and New York: Elsevier and Jossey-Bass.

Psacharopoulos, George, and Keith Hinchliffe. 1983. "Tracer Study Guidelines." Washington, D.C.: World Bank, Education Department. Processed.

Psacharopoulos, George, and William Loxley. 1984. "Diversified Secondary Curriculum Study (DiSCuS)—Survey Instruments." Washington, D.C.: World Bank, Education Department. Processed.

Psacharopoulos, George, E. Velez, and A. Zabalza. 1985. *Una Evaluación de la Educación Media Diversificada en Colombia*. Bogotá: World Bank and Instituto SER de Investigación.

Psacharopoulos, George, and A. Zabalza. 1984a. *The Destination and Early Career Performance of Secondary School Graduates in Colombia: Findings from the 1978 Cohort*. World Bank Staff Working Paper no. 653. Washington, D.C.

———. 1984b. "The Effect of Diversified Schools in Employment Status and Earnings in Colombia." *Economics of Education Review*, vol. 3, no. 4, pp. 315–31.

Puryear, Jeffrey M. 1979. "Vocational Training and Earnings in Colombia: Does a SENA Effect Exist?" *Comparative Education Review*, vol. 23, no. 2.

Roca, S. 1977. "Cuban Economic Policy in the 1970s: The Trodden Paths." *Studies in Comparative International Development*, vol. 12.

Rosenbaum, J. B. 1976. *Making Inequality: The Hidden Curriculum of High School Tracking*. New York: Wiley.

Ruddell, D. 1979. "Vocationalising Ghana's Schools: Purpose and Product." Ph.D., dissertation. Birmingham, Eng.: University of Birmingham, Faculty of Commerce.

Rumberger, R. 1983. "Dropping Out of High School: The Influence of Race, Sex, and Family Background." *American Educational Research Journal*, vol. 20, no. 2.

Sanyal, B. C., and M. J. Kinunda. 1977. *Higher Education for Self-Reliance: The Tanzanian Experience*. Paris: Unesco and International Institute for Educational Planning.

Sato, Kuniu. 1974. *An Alternative Approach to Vocational Education*. Bangkok: International Labour Organisation, Asian Regional Team for Employment Promotion.

Schiefelbein, Ernesto. 1979. *Education and Employment in Latin America*. Report Studies. Paris: Unesco.

Schnaiberg, A. 1971. "The Modernizing Impact of Urbanization: A Causal Analysis." *Economic Development and Cultural Change*, vol. 20, no. 1, pp. 80–104.

Silberman, H. 1978. "The Relationship of Education and Work." *New Directions for Education and Work*. Spring.

Silvey, J. 1969. "Unwillingly to School: The Occupational Attitudes of Secondary School Leavers in Uganda." In R. Jolly, ed., *Education in Africa: Research and Action*. Nairobi: East African Publishing House.

Squire, Lyn. 1981. *Employment Policy in Developing Countries*. New York: Oxford University Press.

Sullivan, G. 1981. "Secondary School Leavers and the Labour Market in Swaziland." *International Journal of Educational Development*, vol. 1 (September).

Tanzania Ministry of National Education. 1979a. "Estimated Unit Cost per Student and Total Cost of Running Secondary Schools and Colleges for the Year 1978/79." Dar es Salaam.

———. 1979b. "Guide to Headmasters (Kiongozi cha Mkuu wa Shule ya Sekondari)." Dar es Salaam.

———. 1980. *Basic Facts about Education in Tanzania*. Dar es Salaam.

———. 1984. *Educational System in Tanzania Towards the Year 2000*. Dar es Salaam.

Taussig, M. K. 1968. "An Economic Analysis of Vocational Education in the New York City High Schools." *Journal of Human Resources*, vol. 3 (Supplement).

Tchen, Y. 1977. "Education and Productive Work in China." *Prospects*, vol. 7, no. 3.

Thailand Ministry of Education and Faculty of Education of the University of Alberta. 1980. "Final Report of the Thai-Alberta Cooperative Assessment Project Concerning Thirty-two Rural Secondary Schools." Bangkok and Edmonton. Processed.

Unger, J. 1980. "Bending the School Ladder: The Failure of Chinese Education Reform in the 1960's." *Comparative Education Review*, vol. 24, no. 2 (June).

Urevbu, A. O. 1984. "Vocational Education in Nigeria: A Preliminary Appraisal." *International Journal of Educational Development*, vol. 4, no. 3, pp. 223–29.

Van Rensburg, P. 1974. *Report from Swaneng Hill: Education and Employment in an African Country*. Stockholm: Dag Hammarskjold Foundation.

Varner G. 1965. *Educación Secundaria en Colombia*. Informe a la Agencia para Desarrollo Internacional de los Estados Unidos, la Asociación Nacional de Educación de los Estados Unidos y al Ministro de Educación Nacional de la Republica de Colombia. Bogotá.

Velez, E., and C. Rojas. 1983. "Evaluación del Rendimiento Externo del Bachillerato Colombiano Que Saben y Cuales son Las Expectativas Educacionales y Ocupacionales del Bachiller Colombiano." Bogotá: Instituto SER de Investigación.

Vulliamy, G. 1980. *SSCEP and High School Outstations: A Case Study*. Education Research Unit Research Report no. 33. Port Moresby: University of Papua New Guinea.

Walters, P., and R. Rubinson. 1981. "Educational Expansion and Economic Growth in the U.S., 1870–1970." Paper presented at the Annual Meeting of the American Sociological Association, Toronto. August.

Wanasinghe, J. 1982. "A Critical Examination of the Failure of the Junior Secondary School Curriculum and Pre-Vocational Studies in Sri Lanka." *International Journal of Educational Development*, vol. 2, no. 1, pp. 61–72.

Watson, J. O. 1977. "Estimated Rates of Return to Investment in Public and Proprietary Post-Secondary Vocational Education and the Desirability of Subsidizing Proprietary Institutions." Paper presented to the 1977 Western Economic Association Conference, Anaheim, Calif.

Weeks, S. 1978. *The Foster Fallacy in Educational Planning*. Education Research Unit Research Report no. 32. Port Moresby: University of Papua New Guinea.

Weisberg, A. 1983. "What Research Has to Say about Vocational Education in the High Schools." *Phi Delta Kappa*, vol. 33, pp. 335–59.

Wijemanna, E. L., and G. H. F. Welkala. 1975. "Sri Lanka: Non-formal Education for Rural Youth." In Manzoor Ahmed and Philip H. Coombs, eds., *Education for Rural Development: Case-Studies for Planners*. New York: Praeger.

Wiley, D., and A. Harnischfeger. 1980. *High School Learning, Vocational Tracking and What Then?* Final Report prepared for National Center for Educational Statistics, Contract no. 300-78-0546. Evanston, Ill.: Central Midwest Regional Educational Laboratory.

Williamson, Bill. 1979. *Education, Social Structure and Development*. New York: Holmes and Meier.

Woods, E. M., and W. Haney. 1981. *Does Vocational Education Make a Difference?* Final report prepared for the National Institute of Education. Contract no. 400-79-0026. Cambridge, Mass.: Huron Institute.

Zachariah, M., and A. Hoffman. 1984. "Gandhi and Mao on Manual Labor in the School: A Retrospective Analysis." Paper presented at the Fifth World Congress of Comparative Education, Paris, July 2–6, 1984. University of Calgary, Department of Educational Policy and Administrative Studies. Processed.

Zymelman, Manuel. 1976. *The Economic Evaluation of Vocational Training Programs*. Baltimore, Md.: Johns Hopkins University Press.

Index

(Page numbers in italics indicate figures or tables.)

The most recent World Bank publications are described in the annual spring and fall lists. The latest edition is available free of charge from Publications Sales Unit, Department B, The World Bank, Washington, D.C. 20433, U.S.A.

George Psacharopoulos is chief of the Research Division in the Education and Training Department of the World Bank. William Loxley, a former consultant to the World Bank, is now with the Ford Foundation in Indonesia.